BURT RUTAN
Reinventing the Airplane

By
Vera Foster Rollo, Ph.D.

MARYLAND HISTORICAL PRESS
9205 Tuckerman Street
Lanham, Maryland 20706

Library of Congress Catalog Number 91-52844

ISBN 0-917882-33-4

Printed in the United States of America

First Printing 1991

Library of Congress Cataloging-in-Publication Data

Rollo, Vera A. Foster.
    Burt Rutan: reinventing the airplane/by Vera Foster Rollo. p.   cm.
    Includes bibliographical references and index.
    ISBN 0-917882-33-4
    1. Rutan, Burt. 2. Aeronautical engineers—United States—Biography. I. Title.
    TL540.R875R65   1991
    629. 13'0092—dc20
    [B]
                                                                                    91-10041
                                                                                    CIP

AUTHOR'S NOTE

This is a biography of considerable complexity. The reader can readily appreciate the difficulties it presented to the writer. The author has made every effort to ascertain the facts and to present events in a truthful and balanced way.

TABLE OF CONTENTS

ACKNOWLEDGEMENTS

When I set out to record Burt Rutan's 46 years of life, his designs for over 30 aircraft, a space vehicle and a racing yacht — to tell about his impact on aviation — obviously it was not to be an easy task.

Thanks to considerable application and to the assistance of many people, this book was written. I extend my appreciation to them and acknowledge that they have made contributions to the book. The responsibility for any errors, however, is mine.

Burt Rutan himself, in spite of a pressure-cooker schedule, gave me interviews that were enormously helpful. This is not an authorized biography, but his help has definitely contributed to it. In a most generous gesture he instructed his secretary, Kaye LeFebvre, to give me all past issues of the Rutan Aircraft Factory newsletter and a listing of articles that have appeared on his work.

At EAA's Boeing Aeronautical Library in Oshkosh, Wisconsin, Dennis Parks, Director of Archives and Library, and his staff, made available videos, periodicals and many photographs. This made a substantial contribution to the book.

At Mojave Airport, California, I met and talked with several key figures: Bruce Evans, Patricia Storch, Sally Melvill, Kaye LeFebvre, Lee Herron, Dan Sabovich and others. Down the flight line in the Voyager hangar, I interviewed Burt's brother, Dick Rutan, military pilot, Voyager pilot and currently both a pilot and a popular speaker. Contacted by telephone, Jeana Yeager made information and photographs available.

The story evolved into one of a remarkable American family as I learned the family history of Burt's father, Dr. George Rutan, Jr., and that of Burt's mother, Irene Rutan. Dr. Rutan has done considerable work on Rutan genealogy. The story of Irene Goforth Rutan's ancestry is equally fascinating. The two generously gave me many hours of visiting, interviews, and made available pictures of the family.

I also talked with Burt's sister, Nell Rutan. She told me about the early years of the three Rutan children and about her own life with American Airlines and her other interests.

EAA Chapter Four, Washington, D.C. members were helpful in introducing me to Rutan lore. Scott Wilson, Jim Eggleston and others shared their memories of meetings with the Rutans. Bob Woodall, engineer, airplane builder and pilot, introduced me to George and Irene. Bob also helped me scan the manuscript for technical accuracy. Further, the Chapter Four library made available to me all back issues of the EAA journal, *Sport Aviation*.

The Burt Rutan story has been documented by aviation's top writers, among them Jack Cox of EAA; J. Mac McClellan of *Flying* magazine; Peter Garrison, writer, pilot and friend of Burt's; Marc E. Cook and Mark R. Twombly of AOPA and others. Reading their articles furnished me with a great deal of data.

Also of value in writing this biography were overview books: *A Complete Guide to Rutan Aircraft* by Don and Julia Downie; *Canard: A Revolution in Flight* by Andy Lennon; and *Voyager* by Jeana Yeager and Dick Rutan with Phil Patton. Many other books were helpful and are listed in the bibliography.

Thanks are due to Linda Blachly for her great assistance in final editing of the manuscript. Thanks are also tendered to my friend Sue Isaacs and her talented staff at Graphica, Lanham, MD.

The story is really more than that of one man. It is a tale of an American family, of their friends, of the Experimental Aircraft Association and its fascinating leaders and members, a story of general aviation itself. In the time period on which this book focuses, 1970-1990, aviation has taken a turn, experienced a change.

Burt Rutan has played a leading role in this change.

CHAPTER 1

AS THE WORLD WATCHED

"It looked so small," Irene Rutan said reflectively. "It looked so very small." We were sitting in the Washington, D.C. Hyatt Hotel, having breakfast in the Hyatt's towering atrium area. Around the table were Irene Rutan, her husband, George, her daughter, Nell, and myself. [The Rutan children affectionately call their parents "Mom" and "Pop."] We were talking about the *Voyager* aircraft. It was almost a year to the day after the flight.

Irene remembers the day the flight was to begin. There it sat, the *Voyager*, focus of years of dreams and back-breaking work. It was the embodiment of an improbable aim. Her tall son, Dick Rutan, and his petite friend and fellow pilot, Jeana Yeager, planned to fly this fragile aircraft, designed by her younger son Burt Rutan, around the world, through sunlight and night.

It was a pusher-puller design. Both engines would be used for takeoff. Only one engine would be used for most of the flight to save fuel. The cabin for the pilots was located between the two engines. It was made of novel substances for aircraft construction, little metal, two layers of graphite fiber over a core of honeycomb paper-like composite. The wingspan was 111 feet, yet the design was a graceful one with two long booms and a forward wing (a canard).

The plane had no lightning protection, so for over a week, if the takeoff was successful, they would have to thread their way through scores of weather systems, avoiding storms. Also, *Voyager* did not tolerate turbulence well. Unless flown just right, the undulations caused by turbulence could tear the plane apart. It was also "a bear of an airplane to fly" and the 20-inch high crew cabin was "a torture chamber," Dick Rutan said.

The problem that Sunday early in the morning of December 14, 1986, was to get the plane into the air. The Mojave Desert air was fairly cool, a helpful factor. The California sun had not yet heated the area. Yet the plane had never been flown so heavily loaded. The fuel aboard the slender aircraft was stowed in the wings, in the booms, everywhere. It totaled over 1,200 gallons, more than 7,000 pounds of 100-octane gasoline. [Full capacity was almost 1,500 gallons.]

The takeoff was so uncertain a proposition, in fact, that just before the flight, Dick and Jeana made a videotape to be shown in the event they did not survive. They had the camera set up by a friend, who then walked out of earshot. They told the camera that they knew the flight would be hazardous and they might die in this takeoff. If that happened, they said, they wanted the people left behind to know that the risk was worth it, everyone had done their best, and even if the attempt failed, it had still been worth doing.

Then the pilots climbed into the airplane.

Dick and Jeana had flown *Voyager* on the afternoon of Saturday, December 13, 1986, over to Edwards Air Force Base, not far from Mojave Airport where the aircraft had been built.

Now at last, with family and friends watching, cameras running, they were ready.

1

"Mom and Pop" Rutan were there. Dick and Burt's sister, Nell Rutan, was down beside the runway. Burt walked over to Dick and went over the numbers for a possible abort of the takeoff with Dick a last time. Dick, intent on the task ahead, nodded and told him that he had the numbers well in hand—how far to go and what speeds were needed.

The parents stood quietly, their gray hair blowing in the light breeze—Irene, small, and slight; George tall and strongly built. Dick looked a lot like his father, Irene thought, as she watched her two sons talking. Dick was tall, at six feet one inch, but not quite as tall as his brother, who stood at six feet four inches. Burt's dark hair flopped over his forehead. Whenever Irene saw them she felt pride in her two boys welling up—Burt a famous aircraft designer, though barely forty years old, and the older son a veteran of years of Air Force service and combat flying.

The engines were started. Dick looked out at the ungainly droop of the wings, heavy with fuel and wondered if the device would fly at all. Would oscillations develop on takeoff?

Burt was ready in a chase plane, along with Mike and Sally Melvill, his long-time friends and employees.

Irene Rutan said later that she had great faith in Burt's *Voyager* design and in Dick and Jeana as pilots. "I just felt that if anyone could do it, they could." But that day at Edwards, at eight o'clock in the morning, "Mom" saw the plane began to roll and she knew her son must fly as he had never flown before to make this takeoff.

The plane rolled a little faster. The men helping to support the heavily drooping wing-tips fell back. "It went so slowly," she said quietly. "For so long a time and so far down the runway."

George Rutan added, "Yessir, it ran midway down Edwards' runway. The *Voyager* was so small out there that it just ran right out of sight."

The *Voyager* pilots couldn't see that the wingtips were touching the pavement. Burt, watching from the chase plane, could.

As the 7,500-foot mark passed, the plane was still on the ground, but Dick felt it accelerating and the engines strongly pulling/pushing. Beside the runway, Nell Rutan was watching, jumping up and down. "Take off *Voyager*, take off!"

Crew Chief Bruce Evans' voice came through, "We're low"—meaning low on airspeed. Bruce felt his knees weaken and knew death and disaster were only seconds away.

Evans had flown over to the Mojave Airport years before, just to see what was going on with the *Voyager* project and had stayed to work for the past four years. Evans had become the project's indispensable man, building, checking, smoothing out conflicts between Burt and Dick, acting as crew chief, putting his life on hold for the project.

Other pilots watching held their breath, too. They couldn't help thinking that they would soon see a smoke plume rising, hear the oily, greedy crackle of flames, overridden by the sound of sirens screaming. They thought they would soon see family members and friends standing there dumb with horror in the cool morning air.

"He's not going to make it," Mike Melvill said quietly, holding the chase airplane just off *Voyager's* wingtip.

2

The Voyager.
Photo courtesy the Experimental Aircraft Association.

"Pull the stick back, Dick," Burt radioed.

"Pull the stick back, Dick!" Burt repeated. Dick heard him but decided that this might make the plane porpoise. It would be a lethal oscillation. The pilots were unaware of the fact that both wingtips were dragging on the runway. Jeana, prone in the plane, steadily called off the air speed readings, "87 knots," she called, and only then—gently, gently, Dick with his "velvet arm" eased the stick back.

The nose came up, the wings started to fly. *Voyager* left the ground perilously close to the end of the runway.

Once they could see the plane was in the air, the crowd cheered with relief. Burt, in the chase plane, swallowed and unclenched his fists.

The *Voyager* pilots were elated as the situation stabilized. Everyone watching felt greatly relieved that this giant step had been accomplished. But with so little room to spare! This was the longest takeoff ever made at Edwards. In that long two minutes, *Voyager* used up 14,000 feet of the 15,000-foot runway. Only 1,000 feet from the end did the plane fly.

"They've damaged the right winglet," said George "Pop" Rutan as the *Voyager* flew back over the runway. At first no one believed him, but then the chase plane affirmed it. Would this rupture a wing tank? Melvill brought the chase plane close and Burt peered up at the wingtip. No, no fuel leak, okay to fly. Dick turned the *Voyager*, gained altitude, steadied the compass on course, and set out on a ten-day, around-the-world flight. Jeana began her flight log.

Returning to Mojave Airport, Burt now hovered over the ground consoles. There, weather and engine experts and other technicians were recruited to help *Voyager*. While Dick and Jeana battled darkness, fuel computations, fatigue, engine operation, turbulence and storms, Burt constantly followed the flight on the charts. Even though called away to Wichita, working at the Scaled Company in Mojave, the *Voyager* was never far from his thoughts.

Had his brother embarked on an impossible-to-do flight? The plane was so fragile, built just for this one task, would all those complex fuel lines hold? Would everything work? Could the pilots stand the ten-day ordeal?

Burt knew he had done everything he could to make the flight possible. He had made the plane strong yet light. He was always fighting that strength vs. weight battle. He and Dick had also fought many a battle over the past few years. An estrangement had taken place. Each felt the other was too demanding, not appreciative enough. Now Burt worried. He might not see his brother again and it was too late to tell him that the disagreements didn't matter.

After the hazardous, all-but-impossible takeoff from Edwards, Dick and Jeana, now more at ease in *Voyager*, exulted as the beautiful aircraft, minus both wing ends turned west. The whole width of the Pacific Ocean lay ahead.

All the world watched for the hourly reports of *Voyager* progress. Even President Reagan watched for them daily. Half a million American pilots hung over their receivers as *Voyager* flew.

This fame and furor all seemed a long way from the small California town of Dinuba, where the brothers had grown up. Where they had lain awake in the darkness talking, dreaming, talking, with airplane models swaying overhead. So much had intervened—Dick flying jets, Burt working on the F-4 *Phantom* for the Air Force and on the Beech *Starship*, romances, marriages, children, separations, the cheering crowds at Oshkosh, Wisconsin.

In a few short years they had come a long way from Dinuba.

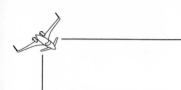

CHAPTER 2

GROWING UP

When Burt's father, Dr. George Rutan, Jr., moved his family to Dinuba, California, it was moving back into Rutan country. His family had owned property and lived near there for a hundred years. Dinuba lies inland, between Fresno and Bakersfield, not far from Clovis AFB and west of the foothills of the Sierra Nevada Mountains.

His children found the change from Los Angeles to the rural Dinuba a good one. Dick says in his book, *Voyager*, that old photos show the family looking like something out of *Ozzie and Harriet*.

And it really was an All-American family. Both George and Irene Goforth Rutan share American pioneer family backgrounds. Their grandparents and great-grandparents had traveled westward toward the Pacific in the mid-1800s. Like George Rutan's maternal family, they became members of the Seventh Day Adventist Church.

While in High School, George used to get up at dawn to earn a few dollars by tending 16 farm horses. They had to be groomed and harnessed for work on the farm. This was done to earn *extra* pay. Then he went on to work at 6 a.m. on the farm!! Not afraid of hard work, it appears that he has passed this joy in achievement on to his children.

George lived for 20 years in Whittier, California. He told me went to school with former President Richard Nixon. "Nixon," he remembers, "was a quiet kind of fellow. He would stand off by himself as the rest of us sort of tumbled and rough housed around. He was studious, always reading, rather a loner rather than a 'mixer'."

Irene and George met in Riverside, a town near Los Angeles. The tall, craggy young man was strongly attracted to this petite, and very pretty, young woman. They were married on June 1, 1937. The birth of their first child, Dick, soon followed in 1938, in Loma Linda. This was not an easy time, however, to marry and get started in life.

Those were Depression years. Jobs were scarce and money was short everywhere across the country. George and Irene talked the situation over and decided it was time to move. Taking every cent they had, they changed the money into half-dollars, plunked it into a condensed milk can and set off for Oregon.

They moved to a farm owned by Irene's father, located southeast of Portland, not far from a town called Estacada. It was here that a daughter was born, Nellie Ann, in March 1942 and a second son, Burt (Elbert Leander) in June 1943. George Rutan remembers "six years there on a rather primitive Oregon farm when the three children were small."

The Rutans witnessed the hysteria that swept the West Coast as World War II began, following the Japanese attack on Pearl Harbor in 1941.

George left to serve in the Navy as a Pharmacist Mate, 3rd class. He doesn't talk much about those years. When he finally returned to his wife and children, he decided to take advantage of his GI Bill educational rights and enrolled in college. He attended the School of Dentistry at the University of Southern California.

"When Pop was in Dental School," Nell Rutan says, "we lived at first in a converted barracks on the U.S.C. campus. We had one large room that Mother divided into two with hanging bed spreads. The folks' bed and our three bunk beds were stacked up on one end and the living room was on the other end of the room.

"It was there that Dick and I started school. With Mother working, Dick had to walk me home from school, but he didn't want his buddies to know about it. So, he worked out a plan. He would tell me to look for him at a certain time and place, then follow him home— some paces behind." All this so that his friends wouldn't be bothered by a little tag-along sister.

"We were enterprising kids, even then. When people would come to see the Freedom Train in the park, we'd sell cold lemonade!

"While Pop finished Dental School, we lived in a big apartment complex in Los Angeles. The three of us still shared a bedroom. There were lots of kids and pals around and we had our own separate friends. This may have led to us being so independent of one another. Dick, Burt and I have always been quite independent of each other and protective at the same time. Our friends took us in different directions.

"I remember lots of family get togethers, lots of cousins and other relatives and holidays.

"Then we moved to Dinuba, a small town in California's Central Valley. It was a small town environment and a very safe one, too." This move, in 1950, had a lasting effect on Burt, Nell and Dick. As Nell recalls, "We were given lots of freedom there to 'do our own things' and we did!" This freedom built self-reliance while their family training built responsibility.

According to George, after graduation he decided to set up a practice in Dinuba. He saw it as a business opportunity, a pleasant place to live, a place familiar to the extended Rutan family for many years and a good place to raise their three children.

"Yes," Irene comments, "we raised the boys in Dinuba. It's a small town, of about 5,000 population in a valley devoted to raising fruit crops, near the mountains."

The family was, and still is, close and loving. Nell Rutan says that they are exceptionally lucky to have this relationship between the five of them. Occasionally they have disagreements, but overall there is deep respect and affection between them.

When the Rutan kids were enrolled in the small-town school, they were each separated by two grades: Dick was in sixth grade, Nell in fourth and Burt in second grade.

Nell remembers: "When we were watching cartoons and something wild happened, Burt would say, 'Impossible!!' Even that young, Burt wanted reality, facts."

Dr. Rutan became interested in aviation. He had established his practice and was now financially able to learn to fly and buy a partnership in a plane. He owned his own aircraft and was a pilot for many years. He soloed in a Piper J-3 Cub, which he rented. He also flew a borrowed Piper TriPacer. Later on he bought a Cessna 140.

Irene often flew with him, as did the children. She commented that she did not want to actually fly a plane herself. She felt quite nervous when Dr. Rutan would ask her to hold the controls while he looked at a map or worked the radios.

Dr. Rutan, with partners, bought a Beechcraft Bonanza, A Model, which was the second model to be built after the 35 models.

Nell says that she never took flying lessons; she just didn't have the desire to fly except as a passenger. "Pop would fly us on family vacations," Nell comments. "We got to see all the western states on those trips. Not that we always wanted to leave the swimming pool and our friends, but later we were glad we had seen all these places."

Not all the trips were by plane. The family also did considerable traveling by automobile and camped in tents at night. George says musingly, "I used to love February 22. After that holiday, it would get warmer and I'd take the kids up into the mountains where it was turning green." Listening, I expected him to say that they would then enjoy the flowers, but no, he said, "...so we could hunt rattlesnakes."

After practicing dentistry for a considerable time, Dr. Rutan went to work for the state. California, like other states, supervises medical professionals and facilities. He called this "dry-finger dentistry." He examined dental health plans and facilities and checked on other dental facilities for the State of California.

In the late 1940s and early 1950s, Dinuba grew as did the rest of the Central Valley of California. Oil rigs loomed over some fields. Other fields were green with produce and trees thanks to water pumped up from deep wells.

Burt and Dick were given their own quarters—a room in back of the garage, formerly an open woodshed that George had finished off. It was small but comfortably heated. The boys slept with their beds arranged head to head. Before drifting off to sleep they would talk about cars, motorcycles and airplanes.

Dick built model airplanes. As is often the case the fragile little machines crashed. Burt, from the age of 10, would pick up the pieces, take them home and from them create new models, redesigning the original concepts.

Irene noticed Burt's interest in models and offered to take him to the shops to buy a model airplane kit. Burt chuckled and thanked her, but confessed that he would rather build his own airplanes from his own ideas.

It wasn't long before the boys' room was full of model airplanes, parts from engines, glue, balsa and tools. Burt was engrossed with the idea of building machines that would fly. Model airplanes with small engines and radio controls, these represented triumphs of skill over gravity.

Such single-mindedness and talent made its mark. In his teens, Burt began carrying off so many model airplane competition prizes that the associations changed some of their rules. One design that won attention was of a carrier-based Navy airplane that he almost succeeded in getting to hover in place. So even in his teens, Burt was given a heady taste of publicity and was sought out by reporters, his picture often in the papers. He liked it, as most people do.

There was one unfortunate incident at school. Burt brought a model plane in. It got away and crashed into the wall of the chemistry room. Even then his flying had its risks.

Irene often agreed to take Burt off toward the Sierra Nevada Mountains where he could

Nell Rutan, 1954 in Dinuba, California, and later in her American Airlines uniform.
Photos courtesy Irene and George Rutan.

fly his radio-controlled models. She used the family station wagon as his chase vehicle. Burt, in the back seat, would direct his aircraft.

Dr. Rutan, on the other hand, while interested in the models to some extent, worried that Burt would be a withdrawn scientist and told him, "Burt, get out of that room and get some exercise, take up a sport. Don't you want to get together with some friends?"

Maybe in response to this parental push, Burt told them that he was entering a foot race at school. The scientist was at work, however, since he counted on a large handicap—having the reputation as a non-athlete. This turned out to be the case. He had no proper running shoes so ran in some old wool socks. These didn't last the race but he ignored his bleeding feet and finished the race. Thanks to having correctly figured out the handicap, he won. This didn't make him a track team member, however. Having proved his point, he went on with his model plane building and flying.

"I never got into drinking or taking dope," Burt told me in Mojave in February 1990. "I had more interesting things to do."

Later on in Dinuba, Burt met an important person, one who would have a definite impact on his life. Martin Ghoering, a science teacher at Dinuba High School, instilled in Burt a curiosity about science and a love for technology. Ghoering was popular and for good reason: He inspired his students.

There were the typical teenage entertainments—cruising around in cars and experimenting with racing other teenagers with them. In 1956 Dick was engrossed in tinkering with motorcycles and riding them. He generally kept off the highways when he raced with others, using dirt tracks. Dick took to heart the results of a fatal accident in which a rider was struck by a truck, and decided that he was better off away from the highways. This adventurous spirit, tempered with common sense, remained with him in his adult years.

Because he was older, Dick was the first of the brothers to take to the air in a real airplane. He was fascinated with wings. His father was now a pilot and a part-owner of an airplane. Dick, working in the fields, raised enough money to take a flying lesson when he was only 15. Later, Irene drove him to the Reedley Airport so that he could solo on the first day he was legally able to do so—on his 16th birthday. Then she drove him downtown to get his driver's license!

Dick went on to get future licenses, right up through a flight instructor's rating, the same way—as soon as he could. He worked for the money, devoted himself to lessons and built up flight time. His enthusiasm was contagious.

When Burt was 16, the earliest legal age to do so, he flew an Aeronca 7AC Champion solo. He showed a deep understanding of the flying machines and became a very good pilot. He knew the planes he flew and savored the independence flying gave him. The clouds and expanses of sky were in a way, home for him.

All the Rutan children (Nell to a lesser extent) were engrossed in flying, as they grew up in California. Since the parents were also interested in flying, the family would seek out places with airplanes to see. There were air bases not far away, Castle AFB was the nearest, and there were bases at Merced, and Fresno.

Just about every Armed Forces Day found the family on the flight line at Castle AFB,

Burt Rutan and some of his model airplanes.
Photo courtesy Burt Rutan.

admiring the F-100s and other military planes, and the jump-suited pilots displayed in the sunshine, flags flying.

Dr. Rutan is a strong, craggy, practical man. He is honest, hard-working and interested in a wide variety of things: Travel, maps, mechanical things, aircraft and meeting people. He is still a pilot, albeit not as active in flying as he once was. He has confidence and is a ready, expressive speaker. He obviously has served as a role model for his children.

Irene has also served as a role model of everything a woman should be to her children. She is attractive, active, and not afraid to travel. She took great interest in her children's activities and helped them by driving them here and there, helping with her support. She understood the technicalities of aircraft. True to her early training, she is modest and does not step into the limelight, yet she is strong and efficient. It was Irene who got Burt quickly to a doctor when Burt, as a youngster, fell playing Tarzan and broke his ribs. She is a "can do" lady.

The three children no doubt took their parents' role in subconsciously—the dominant, outspoken strength of the male; the quiet strength of the female.

"Our kids 'flew the coop' *literally*! The boys discovered aviation and never looked back!" Irene says.

A friend answered, "Irene, you and George raised your kids, only you raised them higher than most! All three are involved in aviation!" Burt is a designer, engineer, pilot; Dick is a military jet pilot, a record-breaking pilot, one of the *Voyager* pilots; and Nell is an airline attendant with possibly more hours than any of the family.

In his office, Burt Rutan has a photograph of himself as a teenager. He is kneeling on concrete with a variety of his flying models around him. In a way, nothing has changed, he still is a "hands-on" builder, still innovating designs, still kneeling on the concrete surrounded by aircraft. His planes are bigger now. They carry people, fly fast and—far!

CHAPTER 3

THE RUTAN ANCESTRY

The Rutans

Burt Rutan's rich family heritage has helped to mold this young genius' personality. His two grandfathers, both pioneers in their own right, have passed onto him both a canny business sense and a mathematical bent and mechanical aptitude.

In 1675 Burt's ancestor, Abraham Rutan, arrived in America from the province of Lorraine which is located in northern France. One of his descendants, Samuel Rutan [Burt's great-great grandfather] was born in Pennsylvania in 1809. Samuel lived in Ohio until 1852.

Then, Samuel heard a man talk about the land and opportunities in California and Oregon. One hundred men grew enthusiastic and agreed to go West. But only Samuel actually went home, sold off his property and came West.

He made the 2,000-mile trip by ox-wagon, accompanied by his wife and children. Samuel Rutan's oldest son was 17 and the youngest, Samuel Rutan, Jr.,(Burt's great grandfather) was only a year old. "A pioneer," laughs Burt's father today, "is a guy with an arrow sticking out of his rear end!"

Family legend recalls that the younger Samuel was only a baby when the Rutan family came West by wagon train. He learned to walk on the way. "A long walk!" says Dr. George Rutan, Jr., today.

The family reached California and settled in the delta area of the Mokelumne River. The younger Samuel's eldest child, born 1874, was George A. Rutan, Sr. (Burt's grandfather). This boy grew up in Los Angeles where the family had moved because of his father's failing health. Samuel Rutan, Jr., died at age 32 from tuberculosis. His son, George Rutan, Sr., worked as a pumper in the developing oil fields of the San Joaquin Valley but dreamed of owning a farm one day. This dream came true following much hard work. After he married at age 38, he and his wife were able to move onto a small fruit farm in 1919 in the eastern part of Fresno County.

This is the area that George Rutan, Jr. now remembers. He recalls the rural school he attended, the coal-oil lamps that everyone used, the many farm animals and the excitement of the spelling bees. Rich and varied memories include those of plucking chickens, eating oatmeal mush, outhouses plus the closeness and security of his family.

The Goforths Migrate

Irene Goforth Rutan's ancestors came to America from Yorkshire, England. They are thought to have made the move in the late 1600s. One of these migrants from England was a minister with the Society of Friends. He crossed the Atlantic in company with William Penn in 1682, aboard the ship *Welcome*.

From Pennsylvania descendants of the Goforths gradually moved westward. By the early 1800s, some of the family were located in the Ozark Mountains near the Arkansas-Missouri border.

Political troubles and strife were not left behind in England, however, as political factions in the United States arose. During the Civil War, the Goforths suffered the tragedy of having some sons in Union forces and others fighting with the Confederacy.

Around 1913, moving westward, Irene's grandparents, together with three sons (one of these was Irene's father) homesteaded several sections of raw land in Quay County, eastern New Mexico.

Irene's father was 27 and his wife only 17 when Irene was born. She arrived in a sod shanty on her father's claim. Her mother barely survived Irene's birth. This land, except for the section held by the grandparents, was sold soon after title was gained. Irene's parents had tried to raise cattle on the claim. Irene remembers they lost cattle to the freezing cold. These animals were dragged off to a ravine for the buzzards to eat. When an elderly neighbor died, Irene asked her mother when the neighbor would be taken to the ravine! There were more bad times to follow, including no rain for the pasture. This forced them to move on. This was not unusual in those days, as opportunity beckoned settlers on, over the next horizon.

Irene was a bonny two-year-old when her family moved north in 1918, to settle just across the state line in Colorado. There in Jaroso, a thriving little farm community, her father worked as a blacksmith. Irene's sister and brother were born there.

Interesting stories of California, its beauty, its gold, and its promise, were told. Irene's father was a capable man, able to earn a living almost anywhere, a good businessman. He liked what he heard about California and arranged to trade his Colorado property for three acres of California land with a small house, in LaSierra (now Arlington), Riverside County.

Anxious to see what they had acquired, the family prepared to make the trip in spring 1926. Another family, the Jamesons, travelled out at the same time in a new 1926 touring car.

The Goforth transport was to be a nearly-new 1925 Ford Model T. With a wife and three children, there would not be much room to take household goods. An auction date was set, Irene writes: "All our worldly belongings we just couldn't hang on that Ford car." So even the children's toys had to be sold, little wagons, a tricycle, and Irene's doll.

"But Mama, my dolly!" the nine-year-old Irene protested.

"Well dear, if you sell your dolly here, we'll get you a new one in California."

Irene thought this over and handed over her dolly to be sold with the family's other goods in February or March 1926.

The auction poster for the two family's possessions has been preserved by Irene and George. It is mounted on a wooden base in excellent condition in March 1989, some 63 years later.

It must have been hard to give up these items. The poster reads:

2 oak dressers	Several small rugs	Vegetable, apples
1 chiffonnier	1 Wardoleum rug	potatoes and beans
1 bookcase	2 small tables	1 Vacuum washer and wringer
1 library table	3 gas lamps	1 Silvertone phonograph
3 coal oil lamps	1 Auto-cycle washer and wringer	2 full-size beds
1 8-day clock	1 iron bed & springs	3 sewing machines
2 little wagons	1 sanitary couch	4 window shades
1 tricycle	2 mattresses	window curtains
other articles,too	1 davenport	2 kitchen cabinets
numerous to mention	1 baby bed	2 dining tables
1 feather bed	2 heating stoves	kitchen chairs
2 small rockers	4 rocking chairs	2 high chairs
1 cupboard	1 Wilton rug	1 ice cream freezer
1 rag rug	canned fruit	3 tons of alfalfa hay
21,500 lbs seed peas		
MACHINERY:	1 Ford truck	1 1919 Dodge car
	1 wood saw with engine	1 5-tooth garden plow
	small tools	
LIVESTOCK:	1 Black Horse	1 Jersey cow
	1 milk cow	2 Holstein heifers
	1 sow with pigs	4 brood sows
	1 doz. Plymouth Rock hens	1 rooster
	2 doz. chickens	

"I remember," Irene writes, "the backseat cushion of our Ford was filled with pinto beans, 'just in case,' my folks said. It made the seat hard to sit on, but we three kids, ages 9, 7 and 2, didn't know the difference. (Smile!) There was a chuck box on one running board for the simple food we had and the cooking pans. We had an iron skillet for frying potatoes and another one for chipped beef gravy. This must have been my favorite dish for it's the only one I remember.

"I recall this being cooked on a wood fire stove in an auto court cabin. We stayed in a big cabin that combined two families. The six kids slept on the floor.

"The other family that came with us [the Jamesons] had three children." These were, like the Goforths, two girls and a boy. They drove a 1926 touring car. The trip in March 1926 was not an easy one. The roads were not always paved and there were few service stations or even tourist cabins along the way.

"We had ten flat tires on our car," Irene remembers. Luckily her father was an excellent and handy mechanic. The two families kept in sight during the trip so that they could help each other when necessary.

"My friend, Daisy Jameson, and I have kept in close friendship all these years since. She is my best friend. I was one of her bride's maids. She was my maid of honor at my wedding. She is like a sister to me. Daisy was a great backer of the *Voyager* flight, too."

Going Back Home

Recently, in the late 1980s, Irene and George, with her friend Daisy and others, went back to her old hometown in Colorado. They took pictures and found much still there in the "ghost town." After the Goforth family had moved away the railroad line was relocated away from Jaroso. Gradually the residents drifted away.

But still remaining, there was the post office, her father's "Goforth Blacksmith Shop," "Jameson's Garage," the bank and the hotel. These were "sky scrapers" of two floors and maybe ten rooms.

Both sides of the street had a dozen businesses and extended a good block long.

"It is sad to go back now after 63 years and see what is left." Irene writes. "After our trailer-RV trip down there this last summer, Daisy and I looked at the video we took. She was a lot of help remembering what and where it all was. They had stayed in the hotel for a few weeks at one time, years ago. The house she lived in was nearly all gone with just one adobe wall or two still there.

"My old home had stood the test of time better. The roof was on and the walls were up, only because they were stuccoed on the outside when we were there and they still are.

"I saw that a bathroom lean-to had been added to the back, otherwise it was the same—two rooms in the main part and an added on kitchen and a back porch. I remember the snow being so deep at the back of the house that dad went out of a window to shovel it away. It got to 20 degrees below zero, I remember my folks saying.

On the 1926 trip to California from Colorado, the families had to carry enough supplies to be self-sufficient. Generally at night they found shelter in a primitive auto court.

As Dr. Rutan comments today, "A measure of how transportation has improved is the fact that, between bad roads, flat tires and other impediments, ten days were required to complete the journey." Irene comments that, "Sitting on those hard pinto beans for ten days made an impression!"

One uncle stayed on in New Mexico. His descendants now live in Grants, New Mexico.

Irene's father had planned to raise chickens on his three acres to support his family. This was not to be, for as Dr. Rutan writes, "... a midnight fire singed his hopes." So the capable Mr. Goforth secured employment with a small domestic water company and worked there until 1944.

Others of the Goforth family came to California during the 1920s, Irene recalls, the grandparents and four sons.

What has Burt Rutan's ancestry given him? Talking with his parents, I could see that they were both full of intelligence, energy and good health. They have passed these attributes on to their three children.

16

Irene remembers her father as being a canny businessman. He had only a fourth or fifth-grade education as was usual in those days at the beginning of the century. Yet, "He was so good with figures," Irene said, "able to calculate in his head, that he was hard to cheat. Only one time was he bested," Irene remembers. "It was when selling out to move to California. A man took a truck, promising to return with the price $200, in the morning after the auction, but he never returned."

Mr. Goforth seldom bought property, rather he traded, always "trading up," exchanging one property for a better one. He enjoyed this trading and traded cars and properties for years.

The Goforths, Dr. George Rutan says, were inveterate tinkerers, they could make all sorts of mechanical things to do work around the house and the farm.

This canny business sense, mathematical bent and mechanical aptitude, may well have devolved to Burt Rutan from his grandfather Goforth. His father is also an excellent business manager and a man who understands building a house, putting in a block wall (as he was in spring 1990 by his Palmdale home), or fixing an engine. So, from both sides of his family, Burt Rutan has a rich heritage.

FAMILY TREE

SAMUEL RUTAN crossed America in 1852 from Ohio/Illinois to San Joaquin County.

SAMUEL RUTAN, JR. his son, 1851-1883 b. Will Co., IL

GEORGE ALBERT RUTAN, SR., Samuel Sr's grandson, 1874-1943, b. San Joaquin County, CA

DR. GEORGE ALBERT RUTAN, JR. b 7 Apr 1916 at Coalinga, CA
    Married June 1, 1937, to:
        IRENE GOFORTH (RUTAN) b. 1917, Quay County, New Mexico.

DICK (RICHARD GLENN RUTAN) b. July 1, 1938 at Loma Linda, CA.
    Married Geraldine Tompkins (Rutan) "Geri" 1959
        dau. Holly Lynn 1965
        dau. Jill Lynn 1970
        Sep. 1980, div. 1988

NELLIE ANN "Nell" RUTAN b. Portland, Oregon, 1942
    Schooling—High School Dinuba, CA

BURT (Elbert Leander) RUTAN, b. 1943, June 17, Portland, OR.
    Married Judith C. Prather, 1962, div. 1970
        B. 1962 Jeffery Albert Rutan (m.Jessica Killingsworth)
        B. 1965 Dawn Annette (m.Eric Davis)
            dau. b. Dec. 17, 1986 Whitney Dawn Davis,
            (born during the *Voyager* flight)
            and August 22, 1988 Lindy Leann Davis.
            Third child, Eli Paul Davis, June 16 1990.
    M. Carolyn Brown (Weaver) 1971, div. 1979
    M. Margaret Rembleske 1984, div. 1986.

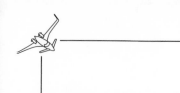

CHAPTER 4

LOVE AND MARRIAGE

She was a slender, yet rounded girl with a shining mane of hair. Her name was Judy C. Prather. They were both in their teens, and for the first time Burt was deeply attracted. He was happy with Judy around.

What could be more romantic than California nights when you are young and in love? Judy, in turn, was swept away by Burt. She was fascinated by his energy—those dark good looks, his interesting lifestyle so caught up in airplanes and his original ideas about them.

Girls had always swirled about Burt. In high school he had found them interesting but not as interesting as airplanes. The way they sought him out was puzzling to him. He thought about sounding out his brother, Dick, on the matter, but he might laugh. He considered talking with his sister, Nell, about girls and possibly dating; after all, she was a girl. But she was busy with her friends.

Tentative comments to "Pop" had brought out some gruff recommendations about remembering to respect womanhood. It was his mother that yielded the most useful information: "Don't ever hurt their feelings, Burt." Yet, she told him he shouldn't date a girl unless he was really interested in her. Just going out to please the group was not required, she said. So during his high school days, though girls sought him out, Burt hadn't gone out much.

It was when he met Judy that he began to understand the delight to be found in the company of the fair sex. "Judy." Burt said in a 1990 interview, "She was my childhood girlfriend. We married really young." This was early in 1962, and in spite of the fact they had practically no money, they were happy.

Soon a lot was going on with the young couple. Burt was going to California Polytechnic in San Luis Obispo, studying aeronautical engineering. They lived in a mobile home for a time then found a small apartment. In a way, their first months of marriage were similar to those of Burt's parents back in the 1930s: Not a lot of money, inadequate housing, glad to be together and a lot of work to do.

In 1962, their young son, Jeffery Albert Rutan, was born. It wasn't easy for Judy to make a home and care for a baby with scant funds. It was better when they managed to rent a small house in Lancaster, California. Judy often felt restless. She was very young to carry the role of wife and mother. She threw herself into her tasks headlong, however, even taking time to help Burt with building his first airplane. There may not have been a lot of money, but their parents helped them out and there certainly was a great deal of interesting activity going on.

Burt's brother, Dick, by the way, had married Geraldine "Geri" Tompkins four years before, in 1959. Dick and Geri were married in the chapel on Edwards Air Force Base. Dick and Geri became parents with the birth of their daughter, Holly, in 1965.

Burt's first homebuilt aircraft, the *VariViggen*, was a design he began working out in 1963. It took into consideration two designs that he had seen and liked. They "looked right" and he thought they would fly well. One was the North American XB70 and the other the Saab Viggen Fighter. His *VariViggen* was rather like a giant model airplane and was made mostly of plywood. Plywood was a material that a struggling student like Burt could get at the local lumber store.

While Burt was still in college, Judy found she couldn't bear the marriage at times and left him for a while. On one of these occasions, Burt's parents, unaware of any crisis, called to arrange a visit to Burt and his family. "Sure," he said, cheerfully enough. "Come on over, we'll have some supper at the house."

When they got there, the house was bare. The only things left in the house were a table and chairs, a spoon, a fork, and a bed. Judy and the baby were gone. Burt was there with a big container of fast-food chicken. "You know," Irene murmured later, "he hadn't said a word!" After a while Judy came back and tried again to make a go of her marriage.

At the university, Burt's abilities were recognized. His thesis for his bachelor's degree in Aeronautical Engineering won the national award from the American Institute of Aeronautics and Astronautics. He had built a radio-controlled aircraft model in order to study differential aileron yaw. He instrumented the model with on-board graph computers. The paper was entitled, "*An Investigation of the Effect of Aileron Differential on Roll-Yaw Coupling During an Abrupt Aileron Roll.*" At the same symposium, space scientist, Dr. Werner von Braun was honored.

In 1965, Burt graduated, third in his class, from California Polytechnic in San Luis Obispo. His wife, child, parents and friends all watched him receive his diploma.

Now he had to make a choice. Would he look for a career in space engineering? This was the time when orbital flight had been achieved and the moon landing lay ahead. Still, Burt was interested in airplanes. He shied away from the manufacturing behemoths such as Boeing, Douglas or Lockheed companies. He could easily become just a cog in their engineering departments, working on one facet of one part of an airplane.

So, Burt sent applications to Cessna and Beech Aircraft. Finally he saw that perhaps the most exciting design work would be near at hand in the flight test department at the Edwards Air Force Base. So he became a civil servant and went to work for the Air Force at the Flight Test Center, Edwards Air Force Base, as a civilian test engineer. The young couple's money situation took a turn for the better.

In 1965 a daughter, Dawn Annette, was born. She was a gorgeous baby. We have the word of her grandparents on this. Now Judy was such a busy young wife and mother that she looked ahead to the time when the children would be a little older and she would have a moment to herself, or a moment to be with Burt. She was unhappy at times and longed to be back in her girlhood home.

Burt looks back to that time. "Dawn was born just after I got to Edwards [Air Force Base], a couple of months after I got there in August 1965." He, his wife and the two

While working for the U.S. Air Force as a civilian engineer Burt built a prototype *VariViggen* in his garage.
Photo courtesy Burt Rutan.

children are shown in dozens of photographs stored in Irene Rutan's album.

For seven years, Burt stayed with the Air Force at Edwards. He worked on aircraft ranging in size from fighters to large cargo planes. They lived not far away at Lancaster, California. Burt had discovered the Experimental Aircraft Association (EAA) by now and was a member of EAA Chapter 49 in Lancaster, #26033.

Judy sometimes watched and lent a hand to balance a piece of the equipment, as Burt fitted a rig atop a 1966 Dodge Dart station wagon. He had no wind tunnel, so he would place a wing, a model, a wing, on top of the station wagon, and add test instruments to get measurements. Then, driving at night on the emptiest roads he could find, he would test the surfaces. He is said to have driven the test-bed car for 10 or 20 miles at a time on desert highways at up to 80 miles per hour.

Actual construction of the *VariViggen* began in the garage of his Lancaster home in 1968. It filled the two-car garage with its 19-foot wingspan, 8-foot canard, and 19-foot length. Just to be with him, Judy would hold a light, and hand Burt tools as he worked.

Judy went flying with him when she could. Unfortunately, she didn't really care for flying. The more she was around airplanes, the less she liked them. She found it strenuous but fun when she went to the EAA conventions at Oshkosh, Wisconsin. There were miles of parked aircraft of every description, tents murmuring with forum speakers constantly in use and orderly crowds. There were also, blessedly, refreshment tents, plenty of places to sit, and other comforts. EAA is notably a family-oriented group. Children carried to Oshkosh as babies have returned each summer with their family. They say they have grown up with homebuilt aircraft and EAA.

There were many times when Judy felt envious of the attention that Burt's beloved aircraft received. His narrowly focused attention and his obsession with his created aeronautical beauties made him an absent-minded husband. [In fact, Burt was to tell a reporter later, unwisely and probably facetiously, that when it came to choosing between Judy and his *VariViggen*, "There was no question in my mind which I wanted to keep."]

Somehow Burt found it hard to understand her situation. She was alone with the children not only during the day, but often at night when he was working on problems of aircraft design, building a plane and following his own interests. She was confined to their home in the Mojave Desert, with its constant dry winds, sand and heat. After the intensity of their early romance, she missed him and his attention. By 1970, their differences led to divorce after seven years of marriage.

Judy and the children lived alone now. The parents of both Burt and Judy were supportive and helped as much as they could. It was a difficult period for Judy. Yet soon she found herself being sought out by eligible men. She was in her twenties and a very attractive woman.

Burt remembers the period: "I raised a family for seven years. Judy was never really interested in airplanes. She was religious and kept the kids in church school. When she left she remarried immediately and took the kids out of state, so I didn't see them. They went to Texas, Ohio, and then to Idaho and only later closer to home, California, so I didn't get to see them during those years."

21

Irene was sorry to see them divorced. She longed to see her grandchildren, but for a time could not. Later, Judy agreed to let Irene and George visit the grandchildren and accept the letters and presents they sent. It was only much later that Burt was able to be closer to his children.

"I was single for a couple of years," Burt recalls and then I found someone who I fell in love with. She worked at McDonnell Douglas and I was working with the company on the F-4. She was a computer programmer at the flight test facility. Burt married again in 1971 to Carolyn Brown Weaver. They settled down together with Burt absorbed in his exciting and demanding work at Edwards Air Force Base.

"Carolyn liked airplanes. We got the Rutan Aircraft Factory founded. She learned to fly and went everywhere with me in the airplanes. She had two girls, Jetta (the eldest) and Kye M. (Weaver), from a previous marriage when she married me. They were five and seven years old."

Meanwhile, Burt's children, Jeff and Dawn, used their stepfather's name. It was simpler as they grew up. Years later, Jeff reclaimed his Rutan name. The matter didn't arise for Dawn, for she married and took her husband's surname.

CHAPTER 5

THE MAN WHO SAVED THE *PHANTOM*

While working at Edwards Air Force Base, Burt told his parents of his goals in life.

He told them that he really wanted to make something of himself in aviation. He was lucky, he said, to have had the intense aircraft modeling experience. He was speaking in reference to the late 1960s when student unrest had been boiling everywhere, particularly in California. Young people, he said, would be happier and better off with an interest such as the one he had in models—something interesting, active and concrete to do.

It wasn't long before Burt Rutan got his wish to do something notable in aviation.

Just after he graduated from California Polytechnic in 1965, he was employed at Edwards Air Force doing flight-testing work. The task at hand was attempting to tame the spin characteristics of the F-4 *Phantom*, a workhorse fighter-bomber used in Vietnam.

A spin is a maneuver in which one wing is stalled and the other wing is not. This results in a tight descending corkscrew path. It differs from the term "spiral" in that the word spiral in aviation means that *both* wings are flying. The flight path of both the spin and the spiral is, of course, a spiral, but the two maneuvers are quite different. In a spiral the speed builds up; in a spin it remains constant and rather low! A spiral can overstress a structure, the spin does not.

In a spin, the plane rotates, the nose of the plane is down, one wing is stalled and recovery is usually possible. Some aircraft in a spin tend to "flatten out" so that the plane is not descending in a nose-down spiral but in a flat configuration. Recovery from flat spins are difficult and sometimes impossible. In testing an aircraft, then, it is vital to know what spin characteristics it will have.

Stalls are aeronautical terms not well understood by the public. Non-aeronautical people often think, quite logically from what they know about automobile engines, that it is the engine that stalls and stops. Actually, pilots mean that it is the wing that stalls. That is, air breaks away from the lifting surface of the wing (the top of the wing in normal flight) and that wing "stalls," or loses its lift. It is obviously very important indeed to know the stall characteristics of aircraft before they are put into service, whether military or civil. No user wants the aircraft that is apt to stall too easily. And, as we have noted, if only one wing stalls, the plane can veer over into a spin with its sharp loss of altitude.

Pilots are trained early in their flight training to avoid stalls and spins. They know how to avoid them and also how to recover from them if they should inadvertently stall or spin.

Stalls and spins can result from a couple of flight situations. One might be when the aircraft is slowed down to the point that the air over the wing cannot adhere, breaks away and lets the wing lose its lift. Another situation that can result in a stall is at any speed when the wing is suddenly presented to the relative wind (that air opposite to its path of flight) and the air breaks away from the lifting surfaces. A heavily loaded aircraft is easier to stall then one less heavily loaded. Also, a plane can be loaded down by a steep turn or pull up.

There is a third situation which combines these above in which stalls and inadvertent spins may occur, that is when a plane is slowed to speeds normally safely above stall speeds and flown through very turbulent, gusty air. Again, a sharp gust can stall the wing. That is why experienced pilots maintain extra speed on approaches in rough air.

Even military aircraft, though very "hot" by civil standards, must have a certain margin of safety lest they be unusable in combat and training. A dangerous design can cost too much in lives, in use restriction and in dollars.

So it was that Burt joined a team of engineers and pilots to find out how to tame the F-4's spin characteristics. Not much was expected of this young, green engineer just out of college. Yet Burt's engineering training, his flying experience in civil aircraft, and his extensive model building did lead to results. That "Rolls Royce" brain of his examined the problem intently.

The workhorse fighter-bomber Phantom F-4 was strongly built but also quite heavy. Planes that are heavy in relation to their wing area are said to have a "high wing load" factor. (High weight per square foot of wing area.) The higher the wingloading, generally the easier it is to stall and spin these planes. The F-4 was no exception.

In fact, pilots grew wary of the F-4, especially in later models loaded down with more and more equipment, or when extra fuel tanks and bombs were attached. The plane, it seemed, would flip into a spin unexpectedly. Pilots and planes were lost.

Many factors entered into solving this problem. Was it just the weight in relation to wing area? Was it a center of gravity problem? Should the controls be changed?

The only way to discover spin characteristics and ways to recover from spins was to— yes, to take the aircraft up and spin it. Not an attractive plan to many. To make survival more likely, a parachute to be deployed by a mortar was attached to the tail of the aircraft. This would yank the tail up and put the plane in a nose-down position. Then recovery could be made by releasing the chute, building up speed.

Young Burt Rutan, a just-hatched engineer, was assigned to the back seat of the test F-4, flown by Jerry Gentry. On one of these tests, the plane was spun seventeen and one-half turns, then the mortar was fired, and the chute came out. The plane nosed down and was safely flown to a landing.

The next day, after this harrowing but successful test flight, the plane went back up. This time, however, the parachute failed and the plane would not recover from the spin. As it bored down toward the ground below, the two occupants ejected and parachuted down. The plane piled into the desert below, creating a crater full of mangled metal.

It was vital that the Air Force find out how to use the F-4 more safely. Burt, using the experience from the test spins, wrote a pilots' manual with clear recommendations on both spin prevention and ways of getting the plane out of spins. On the basis of this work, in 1969 and 1970, Burt was called "the man who saved the F-4 program." He was awarded the Air Medal, an unusual honor for a civilian.

Burt could have chosen to stay with the Air Force and to have gone on to more studies and problem solving. One wonders what effect this would have had on Air Force aircraft design. Would anyone have listened to the young engineer with his daring, yet often simplified and practical design ideas?

Burt Rutan at EAA Convention.
Photo courtesy of the Experimental Aircraft Association.

We'll never know. For Burt, after several years at Edwards AFB, left the security of his Air Force job, the exciting test engineering work, and decided to go to work, designing aircraft for homebuilders to build.

Burt's next step up at Edwards would have taken him into supervisory work, desk work, meetings. He chose to step aside from this for a time and to enjoy getting paid for working on homebuilt aircraft.

On February 27, 1972, Burt "rolled out" his almost completed *VariViggen*. It was written up by Art Stockel in the May *Sport Aviation* (EAA) magazine. At that writing Burt was off to Kansas to work for Bede Aircraft. Jim Bede had called him, invited him to come out to Kansas and work for him. Burt was asked to focus on the BD5J Aircraft.

His sister, Nell, says that all his life Burt has wanted to follow his own bent, do what he enjoys, work on his designs. With this move to Kansas into the homebuilt field, he no doubt saw a way in which he could combine work and inclination. He could enjoy designing and yet make a living.

He would work for Jim Bede who was designing aircraft for homebuilders to make. He could also start his own company and work on a part-time basis.

So, Burt loaded his household effects and his *VariViggen* into a moving van and, with Carolyn, Jetta and Kaye, set out for Newton, Kansas.

Chapter 6

WORKING FOR BEDE

Burt's new job was to direct the development and flight testing of new airplanes for Bede Aircraft, Inc., at the Bede Flight Test Center in Newton, Kansas. Burt and his family planned to live in Wichita.

Jim Bede has been called "the mysterious Jim Bede, aviation's bad-boy genius, a pixie genius," and "a dark celebrity to thousands." Hundreds bought into his project, the ill-fated BD-5 Micro Jet homebuilt, an aviation writer reports in a December 1989 flying magazine article. This plane now flies under the sponsorship of Coors at airshows. "If only Jim Bede had been able to follow through with his plans," spectators sigh.

Jim Bede first operated out of a farm airstrip near Newton, Kansas. The farmer, a pilot, was one of the first people to fly Bede's BD-5. Actually, it lifted off the ground as he was making test taxi runs. Bede moved to a bigger hangar at Newton.

It was there that Burt worked on the financially ill-fated BD-5 design. But due to factors that he is unwilling to discuss even today, by the summer of 1974 Burt Rutan and Bede parted company. His two years there had been fascinating ones.

Bede is aviation's talented inventor and free-wheeling business operator. He reels off ideas by the score. Many years ago, Bede talked about going around the world without refueling.

Bede is reported in the Dec. 88, *Sport Aviation* as currently working on a "Supersonic Homebuilt" the BD-10J. His new company is Advanced Aircraft, Inc., E. Kansas City Airport, Grain Valley, MO with T. J. Brown and Buzz Lynch.

The BD-10J may use the CJ610 turbojet engine, have tandem seating, be 1,500 pounds gross weight, have a Mach .91 cruise, with a possible Mach 1.4 capability if problems in control and safety can be worked out. (Supersonic is illegal over land in U.S.)

"Many absolutely fascinating things happened when I worked for Bede. That's a book in itself. The problem is, for me to give you a reasonable shot at that picture would take hours and hours."

"Even Jack Cox doesn't know the inside story of that time."

You just can't brush Jim Bede off, reporters admit, he is a brilliant designer of exciting concepts. His BD-4, a hot and nimble little airplane, has been built by homebuilders and several are flying today.

Bede's seminar tent at the EAA's Oshkosh '89 Convention was filled. Bede, a short and active barrel-shaped man with a grizzled beard, held the crowd spellbound. He spoke of reviving the BD-4 design and answered technical questions. The BD-5 program is now totally dormant, even though Bede says hundreds of people bought into his planned BD-5. Most people, he reported, wrote saying they wished he had been able to make it, and "I got 68 really nasty letters."

Bede laughs sometimes at himself, as his words flow out and pick up speed. "I normally speak 80 words per minute, with gusts up to 110."

His latest enthusiasm in 1989 was the BD-10J, a supersonic jet trainer that looks like a baby F-15.

The original (now the Grumman *American Yankee*) *Yankee* was the BD-1. It was designed by Bede and supposed to sell as a homebuilder's kit for around $2,500. The customer was to supply the engine. This could be from 65 to 90 horsepower. The wings would be folded for travel to and from an airport. With bonded skin, ridding the plane of rivet drag on the airframe, it was supposed to cruise at around 100 mph, a respectable speed for 90 horsepower.

Writer Mark Phelps says that, "If great men stand on the shoulders of those who have gone before them, then Jim Bede must have a lot of scuff marks on his epaulets."

The design was taken over by Russ Meyer (now CEO at Cessna) and certified and financed by the American Aviation Corporation in Ohio. Meyer abandoned the folding-wing concept, installed a Lycoming 108 horsepower engine. Two years later, the AA-1 was taken over by the Grumman Corporation and became the AA1-A. This went out of production in 1979.

Sisters of the *Yankee* were named the *Cheetah*, the *Tiger*, and were refined by talented designer Roy LoPresti.

Yankees are now sometimes called "little orphan AA1s." Production rights and tooling have been purchased by a new company, American General Aircraft, with plans to have *Tigers* ready to sell in 1990. Jim Bede's design lives.

Eighty *Yankees* turned up at Oshkosh '89, their owners members of the American Yankee Association.

In February 1990, Burt was full of excitement and anticipation. He was planning another "Bede Reunion." Bede and people that have worked with him were coming out to the Mojave Airport for a party which would extend into the weekend. The press was not invited. Writers can only longingly imagine the fascinating stories that were told there.

Rutan was not willing to work for Bede long but he still admires and likes the wild and woolly inventor. But, getting back to the 1970s...

VariViggen Tests Begin

Burt completed the *VariViggen* and began his taxi tests in 1972 while working for Bede Aircraft. For his first flight, he says he got the wife and kids out to the airport, set up a movie camera and began. Flight testing proceeded with only minor hitches.

Just nine weeks after the first flight, Burt had logged 75 hours in the airplane! Then he flew it to the 1972 EAA Convention in Oshkosh, Wisconsin. There his years of planning and working paid off. Builders and pilots crowded around the strange-looking new aircraft. Burt won the Stan Dzik trophy for design contribution.

During the winter of 1972-73, he made all the fly-ins he could. It was a winter of widening horizons.

He even checked out his wife, Carolyn, in the aircraft. She was a student pilot at the

Burt and Carolyn Rutan show off the *VariViggen*.
Photo courtesy the Experimental Aircraft Association.

29

time with about 35 hours of flying. They took the plane off to California for a five-day vacation in April 1973.

He wrote in the August 1973 issue of *Sport Aviation* (EAA) that he was in the process of preparing "a complete definition of the *VariViggen* for public sale." But, he warned, due to his demanding job, he would not be able to lend much time to builder assistance.

Emergency Landing in Town

It was in the fall of 1973 that Burt ran into winter flying trouble. The Californian had been to New Orleans demonstrating his *VariViggen* at the Air Carnival there. He had to be in Idaho shortly, so rushed his preparations and took off with only a short check of the weather forecasts.

"I thought to myself as I approached the Rockies over Laramie [Wyoming], that few things could approach the satisfaction that results from soaring over the seemingly lifeless ground traffic in an aircraft fabricated with one's own hands."

Driving the plane through low visibility, rain, turbulence and with the threat of snow, he arrived at Burley, Idaho. He found his aircraft unharmed by the rough trip. The faithful Lycoming engine had performed for 1,600 hours. Burt was unable to get a hangar, so had to tie the plane down outside in freezing rain. He did not refuel but hurried to the warmth of the indoors.

When he came back to the airport three days later, he was glad that the long rainy spell had ended. Now, however, he found his fingers numb in the minus 10-degree Fahrenheit cold. He had made a careful study of the forecasts and now brushed the ice off his plane, loaded it up and broke the wheels free of frozen puddles.

He called the Flight Service Station and filed a VFR (visual flight rules) flight plan for Boise, Idaho. He took off, climbing out over the town and, at just 600 feet, lost power. In spite of doing everything he could, the power still dropped. He had to land. He had time to call the flight station and advise them that he was landing.

Burt planned to land with the landing gear up to lessen the damage to the plane, but just as he flared the flight path to land, he saw that the ground was frozen hard. He fought to hold the plane off for the eight seconds it took for the gear to come down—and made it! Amazingly, when the plane rocked to a stop on the rough ground, he found there was no damage.

The sheriff arrived, along with the highway police and a passing pilot. Carefully they tugged at the plane (with the engine now running again to assist) and dragged it from the rutted field. With the aid of the sheriff, Burt was soon taxiing the aircraft through the center of town, waving at startled motorists.

He called Flight Service, told them he was at First and Main Streets and to please close his flight plan out. This must have made an unusual entry into the FAA Flight Service station log.

Back at the airport, he explained the situation, checked over the engine carefully, and decided it was ice in the fuel lines, which was now melted, that had caused the power loss.

The engine ran smoothly for the rest of his trip—west to Oregon, and south to San Francisco—where he joined his sister, Nell, for Thanksgiving dinner. He was thankful to be unharmed and that his beloved one-of-a-kind aircraft was safe, too.

CHAPTER 7

THE *VARIVIGGEN* DESIGN AND THE RUTAN AIRCRAFT FACTORY

Even before Burt Rutan broke away from Jim Bede and launched out entirely on his own, he had begun his own business. Formed in 1969, he called it the Rutan Aircraft Factory (RAF), a play on "Royal Air Force."

His father and mother offered to finance Burt's incorporation of the RAF. With encouragement and a $10,000 loan from his parents, Burt made the break and left his job with Bede.

Originally a part-time business, RAF was set up to sell plans to people building Rutan-designed aircraft. In spite of the name, his RAF did not make aircraft for sale. It sold plans for aircraft. The only planes actually made were the prototypes built to prove out concepts, work out problems and test the designs for strength and safety.

Burt was to sell the plans and directions for building the *VariViggen*. This was his first plane, begun in 1961 when he was an undergraduate in aeronautical engineering at California Polytechnic Institute. The design was loosely based on the Saab *Viggen*, a sleek, Swedish canard-configured military fighter. Burt had been intrigued by the Swedish "Viggen" jet fighter which came out in 1962. It had remarkable short takeoff and short landing capabilities. One reason for this was the use of a canard, a forward small wing.

The *VariViggen* embodied Burt's developing concepts for a cross-country sport aircraft with safe, low-speed handling. Central to all of Burt's designs is a high-aspect-ratio, cambered, high-lift canard. By obviating the need for a down-loading empennage to balance the up-loading of the main wing, the Rutan canard contributes to lower mass, weight and wetted area. More importantly, it provides stall and spin resistance.

Builders could expect to spend about four to eight years of their leisure hours to build the *VariViggen*.

As early as 1964, Burt had placed a canard on one of his model aircraft. In building a full-sized aircraft, the *VariViggen*, Burt wanted a small plane that would handle like a fighter. He painted his plane in the colors of the Air Force *Thunderbird* Aerobatic Team aircraft. The painted *VariViggen* was then nicknamed the "Thunderchicken!"

Much later, in November 1974, the *VariViggen* was invited to take part in the open house display at Edwards Air Force Base. The futuristic little airplane blended in well with Air Force aircraft.

The *VariViggen* had fully retractable landing gear, lights for night flying, and a pusher engine.

1974 - 1975

At first, Burt was going to develop a new airplane and sell plans for its construction. It all seemed simple and straightforward. Just a set of plans, however, soon proved to be less than what was needed. He wanted to advise those inquiring about the availability of the plans, and then, advise builders about how to build the best, the safest aircraft from the plans. He was pioneering in both design and materials. Then too, he was learning a lot himself.

He did not want to go into manufacturing, however, nor into the business of supplying materials. Since quality materials were essential for building a safe aircraft, he got around this by recommending certain suppliers and carefully specifying the materials needed. Even so, whenever possible, Burt used off-the-shelf parts, even model airplane parts. His motto was, and is, "Keep it Simple."

Many such a venture has failed, even ventures financed with millions of dollars. There in the desert, Burt planned to design, build and market plans for radical new designs. Not only that, but he planned to build the prototypes, often using a material new to homebuilt, hand-crafted aircraft, of composites. Was this to be just another irrational dreamer, another impractical dream?

He had been working simultaneously in his spare time (spare time?) with NASA on stall/spin research. This research made him even more interested in his canard designs. He was to submit to NASA an entirely unsolicited design, the skew wing. It was one that they were intrigued with, and one that would eventually be built by Rutan.

He next found himself editor of a most necessary and quite demanding newsletter to builders. Then he found that he needed to provide builders of his plane with certain machined parts and fiberglass parts. He sold these to his customers to save them time and to offer safe parts.

In addition to this a need for an owners manual had surfaced, so Burt was working on that.

The RAF Newsletter

Practical Burt Rutan sat down at his very old typewriter to write the *VariViggen News*, Issue Number 1, in May 1974.

He made the newsletter a mandatory part of the plans purchase. In this way he could be sure builders had all the warnings, tips, and improvements made in the plans and in the building directions. This is important in understanding Burt. It shows that he cares about people and is a responsible man.

Into the new newsletter went a potpourri of RAF news, builder comments and experiences, technical drawings, and advice on building and flying the *VariViggen*.

When the first newsletter came out, Burt was still in Kansas with Jim Bede's company. He named himself Editor-in-Chief; his wife, Carolyn, was official proof reader. It was mailed to all who had purchased plans and also to those who had written to say they anticipated building a *VariViggen*.

Even though the typewriter blotted the letters a, e, and w, the newsletter was still carefully done. Changes made in the plans were carefully explained and illustrated with crude but clearly drawn illustrations. The photocopied pages showed blurry photographs, but ones that illustrated his points. Builder input was requested and the newsletter was open to serve as an exchange of information to help both builders and Burt himself.

The Rutan *VariViggen*.
Photo courtesy the Experimental Aircraft Association.

In this first newsletter, which reads much like a letter to a friend, Burt reported that he and Carolyn had spent a busy fall and winter preparing the *VariViggen* plans and getting them mailed out. "My apologies to those who waited several months," he wrote.

The prototype *VariViggen* had passed her 300th flight hour and the low maintenance requirements had been most satisfactory. By May 1974 the plane had given two airshow performances and eight more were scheduled for the year.

Even at this early stage, homebuilders, inveterate tinkerers that they are, were asking Burt about installing more equipment in the *VariViggen*—metal propellers, more powerful engines. Burt cautioned them that these changes were not recommended. He was amazed and appalled at some of the ideas proposed. He shuddered to think what these would do to the center of gravity and the flying characteristics of the *VariViggen*.

The Rutan Aircraft Factory and a New Design

Peter Garrison, a long-time friend and pilot, reported in *Flying* that the second time he ran across Burt Rutan was in 1974. He found him on a ladder in Mojave, California, nailing wall material to studs in the old barracks building that was to be RAF's first office.

Stored in a room nearby, Garrison notes, was "the missing link between Newton and Mojave [Newton, Kansas was where Rutan worked for Jim Bede]: It was a stretched BD-5 fuselage equipped with a metal canard. Rutan's mind was full of plans for new and irresistible aircraft. His business card offered: "Proud Birds For Your Pleasure."

One of Burt's important strengths is his "can do" attitude. It didn't matter to him, out there in the Mojave Desert, with no money to speak of, a relatively unknown designer at the time, that he planned to do what aircraft manufacturers spend millions of dollars, with hundreds of engineers and craftsmen, do—design, build and land test a new aircraft design with materials not widely used at all in aviation.

He showed Garrison a strange-looking model aircraft one day and asked what the pilot thought of it. Burt had the words "VariEze" on a blackboard.

At the time he was testing out his unique designs with models of about four-foot wingspan attached to a rig on the roof of a decidedly shabby old car. Surely such a threadbare setup could not result in a viable, a unique aircraft. But it did.

In Burt Rutan's own words at an Oshkosh seminar, he tells about branching out on his own: "By 1974, I got into the plans business, selling plans for builders to use. "I quit my job and went along to the desert to do this," Burt told a 1988 Oshkosh Convention crowd.

RAF was a full-time occupation. Burt was working on what he called a *speed wing* adaptation for the *VariViggen*.

And, after one false start with an all-metal design, Burt began work on the plane that was to bring him fame, the *VariEze*. The goal was to achieve better speed and fuel efficiency than the *VariViggen* could provide, without sacrificing the safety and easy handling of the *VariViggen*.

When the second issue of *VariViggen News* came out in Oct. 1974, RAF sported a new address—"Building 13, Mojave Airport, Mojave, California."

With very little money, Burt had rented an abandoned barracks building on the almost deserted Mojave Airport near the cross-roads town of Mojave, California. Yes, right in the Mojave Desert! He was attracted by the excellent flying weather that prevailed and the low rent of the building available.

Not far away loomed Edwards AFB, where he had once worked and the huge "Plant 42" airport, with its massive hangars, at Palmdale. There, aviation history had been made for years and still continues to be made.

The Mojave Airport belongs to Kern County. The federal government built the airport for the Marine Corps on the Hat Farm. Marine pilots were trained there. Not far away is the Test Center, Edwards Air Force Base and Plant 42 Airport. The area around these airports is barren and mostly uninhabited desert, perfect for test flying.

"Yes," *VariViggen News* issue Number 2 stated, "we are now conducting a full-time business primarily to support *VariViggen* builders. Our facility on the Mojave Airport (100 yards S.E. of tower building) consists of an office and shop sufficient to allow us to provide *VariViggen* components, related engineering support for *VariViggen* builders, technical and educational material (the car-top wind tunnel project is aimed primarily at high schools and colleges) and engineering analysis/test consulting."

Burt told his readers that he and his wife, Carolyn, had left Kansas in June 1974. "We spent July touring southern California, looking for a home for the RAF." He goes on to report a schedule of flying that only two young people could undertake! "We took N27VV (the prototype *VariViggen*) on a 4,500-mile trip which included the Oshkosh, Wisconsin EAA Convention [1974]." N27VV participated in the evening airshow and won the Outstanding New Design Trophy for 1974.

At the EAA Convention in August, they had met outstanding aircraft designer Fred Weick, editors of prestigious magazines, and many of the *VariViggen* builders. Jack Cox, EAA writer, did a flight evaluation of the plane along with other well known aviation writers.

After Oshkosh they visited *VariViggen* builders on the island of Manitoulin in Ontario, Canada. They went on to airshow appearances in Ontario, Indiana, Missouri and Kansas.

Then, having found this new location, they tackled the big move to California, arriving in Mojave the first week in September 1974, airplane and all.

Before the boxes were unpacked, Burt and Carolyn flew off to the EAA Western Fly-In at Porterville, California. There "the star of the show was Burt Rutan with his *VariViggen!*" Burt won two trophies, a first-place cash prize and a spot-landing contest. He noted in his RAF newsletter #2 that the plane had won every spot-landing contest it had entered.

In the second issue, Burt went on to explain how the newsletter would aid builders and how to subscribe to it. *VariViggen* builders now totaled 128. In among all the serious advice

Burt holding the EAA's Outstanding New Design, 1974, trophy, awarded him for designing the *VariViggen*.
Photo courtesy the Experimental Aircraft Association.

and engineering information Burt found room on a margin to relay a joke: "Stewardess to passengers: 'Come on now! Some clown doesn't have his seat belt fastened, and the captain can't start his engines.'"

An October 1974 news note, in the RAF newsletter, added that Peter Garrison, aviation writer, had flown the *VariViggen* and planned to write an article on it in an upcoming issue of *Flying* magazine, the largest general aviation magazine.

Burt again warned builders to be careful about making changes to his *VariViggen* plans. Things that look good, may not be structurally desirable, nor "fly good!" Before building in changes, Burt asked that he be contacted and that a $6 consulting fee be paid.

He had to explain the rather unfamiliar canard design to builders. Builders wanted to change this and that, wing length, nose length, wanted to add equipment. Burt cautioned, "Remember, this aircraft was not developed by 'guess work' but by a very careful design-test program. Small changes can be full of surprises!"

CHAPTER 8

PIONEERING IN COMPOSITE MATERIALS

New fabrication techniques Burt pioneered for homebuilding sent shock waves through the homebuilt world, according to aviation writer and editor Jack Cox. There were cautions, however, about doing it right and being careful of the chemicals involved. Burt planned a book to give homebuilders information on the new process.

Cox was also enthusiastic about Burt's idea of drawing plans for his car top test rig to become the homebuilders' own "wind tunnel." [Burt expected to offer plans for this car-top rig but later decided against it.]

Sailplane Structures Inspire

In 1974, the structures of European sailplanes had come to Burt's attention. There was a shop on the Mojave Airport where Fred Jiran ran a repair facility for sailplanes. Burt looked at the sleek, flowing lines of the glass composite materials. "I spent hours drooling over the smooth, contoured, efficient glass composite European sailplanes," he said. If sailplanes could use composite materials, why not light aircraft? After all, stresses imposed on sailplanes are quite high at times.

The smooth, light-in-weight structures had better resistance to corrosion than metal and a longer resistance to fatigue failure. But could these materials be used by amateurs? To date homebuilders had used tube, fabric, wood and aluminum materials.

The European sailplanes were made with complex mold lay-ups. These would not be available to the homebuilder. Burt decided to find a way of fabricating aircraft components of this light, strong material, that was simple enough for homebuilders to use. This was to be an enormously important decision, one to greatly affect the homebuilding movement, and, in fact, future planes of all kinds.

In a way, Burt's affiliation with the Experimental Aircraft Association and its members shaped his thinking. Had he still been with the Air Force, he might have thought in terms of giant factories with huge molds and teams of composite-using experts. As it was, his ingenious mind attacked the problem in a unique way—how could homebuilders use composites? (Yet, he had access to nearby Air Force laboratories.)

Burt tested some of his fabrication samples of composite materials on the material testing machines at Edwards Air Force Base. He came up with a concept. He planned to use an all-composite-fiberglass-foam sandwich. Fiberglass was to be laid up over a shaped foam core.

But that was not all. With typical focus and energy, Burt was tinkering with the design of his *VariViggen*. This would lead to most important developments, not only in design, but into a new way of using composites for aircraft.

New Composite Design Rumored

Rumors of Rutan's work filtered through to the interested EAA membership. In March 1975, the association magazine, *Sport Aviation,* told its readers that Burt was using a daring new fabrication technique—one that could be used to build even primary structures, such as wing spars, by laying up layers of unidirectional glass fiber over both sides of cut-into-shape urethane foam. The result was a remarkably strong and light fabrication with only simple hand tools needed.

The needed tools were a pair of scissors, a paint brush and a carving knife. Materials cost about the same as metal, but the building time could be incredibly short—a wing built in two days. Most of the hours were spent in drying time.

Burt first used the new fabrication techniques to improve the *VariViggen* design. These changes would give the *VariViggen* added fuel capacity, new wing panels, and NASA-developed "winglets," to improve performance. Burt reported that 150 *VariViggens* were in the process of being built and plans for more had been bought.

Other designers began to explore the safety features of the canard designs, inspired by Burt's success with the *VariViggen*. They were later to be even more influenced by the new materials, composites, that he was now beginning to explore.

1975—First Use of Composites

It happened this way. In his third newsletter, January 1975, Burt wrote he was developing a Special Performance Wing for the *VariViggen*. "We have started construction on an entirely new outboard [originally aluminum] wing panel design for testing N27VV.

"First a little background: we have done extensive testing on a new construction method using urethane foam and hand lay up unidirectional fiberglass." With this modest statement, Rutan went on to revolutionize aircraft design—*all* aircraft design.

In his modest, nine-page, photocopied and typed RAF newsletter, he went on to explain: "We actually make a tapered spar very easily by laying up layers of unidirectional 'glass, carve a wing using only three rib/templates, and cover with two crossed layers of thin unidirectional [fiberglass] cloth.

"This method is light, strong, requires no particular skills or tools, and best of all, can be done in about 1/4 of the man-hours required to build the metal wing. If this system meets text expectations, we will supply plans for outboard wings and rudders, *thus taking the aluminum construction totally out of the design.* [Author's italics.] A small cost savings is also possible.

"Since unidirectional glass with the epoxy surface treatment is somewhat difficult to obtain in partial rolls, we are importing a large quantity from Europe and will make available kits for the outboard wings and rudders. No aircraft-quality wood is required.

Rutan estimated a substantial increase in climb and a few miles per hour increase in speed, and with an auxiliary fuel tank, an increase in range. All of this, he concluded in the newsletter, "... is an if, so please don't bother us a lot with further questions now ... ." He promised to have test data and a decision as to whether the plans for a new wing would

Burt Rutan and his brother Dick.
Photo courtesy Burt Rutan.

be made soon. Even so, he suggested that builders might want to postpone building the outboard wing of their *VariViggen* for a while.

In this direct, amazing, practical way, Burt Rutan brought composite construction within the reach of amateur builders. The use of composites that huge companies had not had the courage to try, Burt did!

The aviation world began to know that out in the desert this young engineer was breaking traditions. He was definitely a man to watch. Just how much he was to affect aeronautical design was not yet apparent. More was to come.

And, as they say in novels, "In the meantime ... "

"Death Race 2000"

In spring 1975, a film producer wanted to use the *VariViggen* in a movie, *"Death Race 2000,"* the plot set in the future, to "strafe and bomb" an equally futuristic-looking automobile, Burt reported in his January 1975 newsletter [*Variviggen News* 3]. Burt flew his plane in the action-packed chase and bomb scenes. He flew the *VariViggen* down a canyon while movie crews filmed, "strafing" a "Monster Car" driven by David Carradine.

The next scene was to show the plane crashing. The crash to be done, of course, with a model! In fact, Burt built the model for them. The newsletter shows pictures of the *VariViggen* in close formation with the car in the desert. Then it shows Burt setting up the model for filming the "crash" scene.

Zest, youth, enthusiasm, daring and skill—all of these words can be used to describe the fun Burt had doing this flying. It describes the attraction of the man. A man of action, enjoying his work and life, it's no wonder he attracts attention and admiration—and envy.

In the April 1975 newsletter, Carolyn is shown smiling by a fanged and scaly automobile, her pretty hair tumbling down over her shoulders. She is noted by movie writers in many articles as "Burt's charming wife," as indeed she was. One windy day a reporter commented that the *VariViggen* "came steadily in," landed without any problem with the high winds, taxied in. Burt, Carolyn and the two children, Jetta and Kaye, climbed calmly out.

"We had a lot of fun doing the film," Burt writes in his April 1975 newsletter. "It involved many hours of flying, doing close-in passes on race cars. On many of the passes, explosions were set off around the car just as I pulled up. The model built for the crash scene was built from our radio controlled model plans. The movie is rated "R," so be ready for a little crude language and nudity." The film opened April 30 in the Los Angeles area.

Burt's beautiful little plane, N27VV, had so far won trophies, fame and even a part in a major motion picture.

Demonstrations

On a quieter, yet still adventurous note, the young Rutans flew to airshows and fly-ins from Canada to Nevada and points west in spring 1975.

Writers who flew with Burt on demonstration flights found it hard to believe what they experienced. The plane leapt into the air, and could be safely turned very soon after takeoff and still climb. Its maneuverability was amazing, particularly in the hands of its experienced designer-builder-pilot. All this with a relatively small engine (150 horsepower)!

This pleased and surprised the aviation world, yet this was to be only the beginning.

An Abandoned Design—"Mini-Viggen"

Some of Burt's designs did not work out. He could recognize this. For example, in 1974 Burt started to design and build the "Mini-Viggen" to make available a low-cost design for homebuilders. This was to have been an all-metal, two-place (tandem seating), aircraft with a high wing and a low canard.

The drawings showed a beautiful aircraft. Yet, Burt decided after working on it for a time, that the design *using metal* was *too heavy and too complex* for homebuilders. Also, his tests revealed that the plane had undesirable stability characteristics at low speeds.

The partly-done prototype was scrapped.

This occurrence offers an important insight into Rutan's design attitude. He can admit when a design is not going right. It also shows that he was thinking about some way to get a simpler-to-build, lighter structure. Metal was no longer really satisfactory.

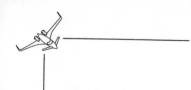

CHAPTER 9

THE "MIND BOGGLER" DESIGN

A March 1975 *Sport Aviation* article, called it "the *real mind boggler*, a completely new design." One using the new foam and glass fiber method. The new design was called the *VariEze*. Burt's sister, Nell, is credited with coming up with the name.

In September 1974, Burt begun work at his RAF on the *VariEze*. Why? He wanted to offer a faster, more fuel efficient aircraft than the *VariViggen* and one that could be fabricated quickly and easily by amateur builders; hence the name *VariEze*.

"The name *VariEze* refers to the aircraft's ease of construction. The prototype," Burt reported in his July 1975 newsletter, "was built entirely from fiberglass in composite form using rigid foam as core material, and simplicity was the key in structural/system design."

The *VariEze* was the first aircraft to use the NASA winglets not only to improve performance but as control surfaces as well.

The prototype *VariEze* was made of fiberglass and plastic foam and powered by a 620-horsepower converted Volkswagen engine.

In June 1975, photos show Burt and his wife, Carolyn, with the nearly-complete new plane, the *VariEze*.

Aviation writer Jack Cox told EAA members that the new *VariEze* was full of new and ingenious ideas. For one thing, the nose gear can be manually retracted to allow the plane to "kneel." This lets passengers get in and out more easily. It makes preflight and handstarting the engine easier. Once the engine is started, the pilot cranks the nose gear down and taxis out.

When parking the plane, the kneeling feature also helps prevent the plane from being blown about by the wind.

Newsletter Announces the VariEze

Burt announced in the April *VariViggen News* that plans and kits for the *VariEze* might be offered if it proves to have good flying qualities and safety and when all flight testing is complete.

It is interesting to note that, again, the newsletter reads like a letter to a friend. Burt knew he was writing to people who would appreciate what he was doing. He took them into his confidence as he worked on his various projects.

Somehow the hampering effects of past precedents—of lack of confidence and "it can't be done,"—has been left out of Burt's mental attitudes. He works from a sound engineering knowledge, knows about past experiments and successes. He simply goes ahead and does the job. It's a unique combination of being a pilot, trained engineer, model builder, and hands-on aircraft builder.

He was excited with his new materials and configurations. He could *see* the possibilities.

Burt and Carolyn demonstrate cockpit seating and mode of exiting the, then wingless *VariEze* in the spring of 1975 at Mojave Airport, California.

Photos courtesy the Experimental Aircraft Association.

Burt and Carolyn Rutan hold a wing in place to show how the *VariEze* will look.
Photo courtesy the Experimental Aircraft Association.

Pictures in the newsletter show Carolyn, smiling, her hair blowing in the ever present Mojave wind, holding up a wind-tunnel model of the new plane. It was a clean, elegant design. In other photographs, Dr. Rutan was shown beside the *VariEze* prototype. Background shown in the photographs reveals that Burt is still working out of the old barracks building on Mojave Airport. He doesn't even have a hangar, yet was building a plane that would revolutionize aircraft design and materials.

Test Flights

On May 21, 1975, the *VariEze* made its first flights.

Burt was doing his own test flying. He made the first flights of the *VariEze*, and on July 16 flew the new all-glass special performance wings for the *VariViggen* for the first time.

After designing and building the planes, he conscientiously took them out and flew them to see if there was any control flutter. Flutter can contribute to loss of control, tear a control from an airplane, or even cause the plane to tear apart in flight. It is not to be taken lightly. Once detected, flutter must, of course, be corrected in the design before it is offered to the public.

First flights are also an unknown. Will the plane get off the ground? Will it be controllable? Does it have nasty characteristics to surprise the pilot? Stall and spin testing can be hazardous but exciting. Burt designed his planes so that it was almost impossible to stall them in normal flight situations. The elevator on the canard was limited, thus the main wing was never in a stall configuration. Even so, Burt had to find out the flight characteristics of his *VariViggen*'s new wing, and those of the new plane, the *VariEze*.

"This newsletter," Burt wrote in July 1975, "is being written in the last few days of hustling around, completing all the preparations for Oshkosh 1975. The last few months we have really been busy with our new airplane's first flight only eight weeks ago and the new SP wings for the *VariViggen* being flown only a week ago."

Even so, Rutan took the time to explain winglets. "Winglets are two vertical fins on each wing tip. They were designed by [active and eminent] Dr. Richard Whitcomb from NASA .... *VariEze*, N7EZ, was the first aircraft to fly with winglets although hundreds of hours of wind tunnel tests were previously conducted by NASA ... Winglets are optimized to unwind the wing tip vortex to the greatest extent possible. This reduces induced drag, resulting in a 6 percent fuel saving ...."

Today winglets are found on business jets and many other aircraft as designers follow Burt Rutan's lead.

The new wings for the *VariViggen* were to be "service tested" on the Oshkosh trip with work on construction drawings to begin upon their return. Interesting that the plane came first, the drawings last!

VariEze First Flight

The *VariEze* made its first flight on May 21, 1975, almost exactly three years after the

47

VariViggen prototype. By July 8, Burt had completed the initial test program and had "flown off" his area restrictions. [Experimental aircraft must stay within a few miles of the home airport until a certain amount of time—50 hours—is flown.]

With the new plane just out of its test flights, Burt felt confident enough to promise an assault on FAI (Federation Aeronautique Internationale) World Records for Speed and Distance, in the under 500-kg (1102-pound) weight class.

The way Rutan tweaked his aircraft would make a designer for a large aircraft company's head spin. He temporarily corrected an undesirable pitching moment by taping metal tabs to the trailing edge of the wing. When one canard airfoil was unsatisfactory, he simply researched others and built new ones until he was satisfied with performance.

Burt relayed news of plans to tool up for components to be furnished by RAF. He advised that he still would not supply materials but that he would recommend good suppliers. Drawings ready to sell would be ready early in 1976.

VariEze Construction

Originally the *VariEze* was to be an aluminum aircraft. After studying composite construction methods being used by some European sailplane manufacturers, Burt decided that fiberglass offered greater flexibility than aluminum with ease in achieving complex shapes, yet conceding no compromise in structural strength or weight.

The aircraft's wing consisted of a fiberglass center-section spar with fiberglass outer wing panel spars which are buried in foam blocks. (No ribs, formers or stringers.) The primary structure of the aircraft consists of fiberglass plies, bonded with epoxy.

Builders were told to cut paper airfoil templates from plans from RAF, tack these to blocks of wood and then shape the wood to the patterns. A wooden template was placed at each end of a length of foam and then a metal wire heated by a small electric transformer is stretched between the blocks and pulled over the wooden templates to easily cut the foam.

With fiberglass cloth draped over the foam, epoxy is then applied and the "lay up" is left to "cure" at room temperature. The fuselage is made up of thin foam panels covered with fiberglass.

RAF recommended that the aircraft be finished in white to avoid high temperatures in hot sun which could weaken the structure. Also, a special primer was recommended to protect from ultraviolet rays which can deteriorate epoxied fiberglass foam.

The *VariEze* prototype has two 12-gallon wing fuel tanks, and a 2-gallon fuselage reserve tank. Some *VariEzes* carry more fuel.

Winglets The *VariEze* was the first aircraft to incorporate winglets developed by Dr. Richard Whitcomb of NASA. These large winglets provide yaw stability and control, and reduce induced drag by blacking span-wise flow of air from the underside to the top of the wing. Each winglet has a one-way, deflecting-outward rudder.

Elevons on the first *VariEzes* were not as satisfactory as Burt wanted, so he simply redesigned the plane. He required his builders to follow suit to solve low-speed control problems. RAF mandated changing elevons to a slotted elevator and the installation of conventional ailerons on the main wings. Also, leading edge droops were required to fix a wing-rocking characteristic in stalls and near-stalls.

The *VariEze* was found to be so aerodynamically efficient (slippery) that RAF added a belly flap to, "dirty it up," and increase the descent rate.

After many flights, Burt found that the plane was quite stable and easy to fly. It landed at a slightly high speed of 74 mph. The range was around 700 miles. All this work and care was to pay off.

Handpropping was used to start the engine because builders wished to save the weight of the starter. If a starter and battery were added, Burt warned builders that an aft center of gravity situation might result.

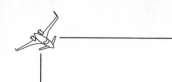

Chapter 10

A "SENSATION" AT OSHKOSH

The prototype *VariEze* was flown to the EAA Convention in August 1975. Its debut was a sensation. Home builders loved its rakish looks and its promise of performance.

Burt's brother, Lt. Col. Dick Rutan, flew the *VariEze* to Oshkosh. He wanted to make the 1800-mile trip non-stop, but 300 miles short of Oshkosh, he made a landing to check out rising oil temperature in the Volkswagen engine. Even so, he had flown 1500 miles with a ground speed of 170 mph.

Burt and Carolyn flew the *VariViggen* to Oshkosh, Wisconsin, joining thousands of EAA members and hundreds of aircraft there. It was to be a memorable visit. The RAF had a booth this year to display plans and components for the *VariViggen* and to answer questions about the *VariEze*.

"We were extremely pleased to be presented the Outstanding New Design Trophy for the *VariEze*. This is the same award garnered by the *VariViggen* in 1974."

Record Flight

When Dick Rutan flew the *VariEze* to Oshkosh, Wisconsin, he was still in the Air Force. His title was Lt. Colonel and Field Maintenance Squadron Commander of the 355th Tactical Fighter Wing at Davis-Monthan AFB near Tucson, Arizona.

It is interesting to note that Burt had great confidence in his brother, handing over the one-of-a-kind prototype aircraft to him to fly to Wisconsin.

While at the convention, with Dick at the controls of the *VariEze* and Burt flying chase in the *VariViggen*, an attempt was made to break the World's Closed Course Distance Record of 1554.297 miles, set by Ed Lesher in 1970. An oil leak forced Dick back to the airport.

The Rutan brothers found that the Volkswagen engine was beyond quick repair, and was just not as satisfactory as Burt wanted. No other place on earth offered more engines, parts and people to lend a helping hand. Fellow EAA member John Monnet generously offered Burt an engine. Other EAAers helped to replace the *VariEze* engine in an all-night session.

A second attempt was made to break the record. Thirteen hours and 1,638 miles later, after a victorious high-speed pass over the runway at Wittman Field in Oshkosh, Dick landed, breaking the world record. As he neared the flight line, he was greeted by thousands of EAA members waving greetings and applauding.

As it happened, plans for this original *VariEze* were never sold, since Rutan later decided that the Volkswagen engine was not reliable enough. Also, the prototype airplane exhibited certain poor low-speed roll control, and had a higher stall and landing speed than he wanted.

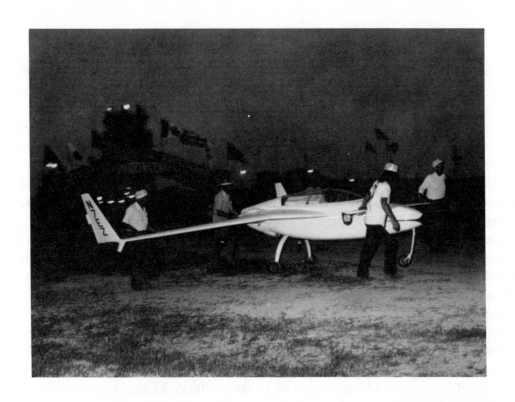

After a pre-dawn roll out the *VariEze* returns to a jubilant group. Left to right: Paul and Audrey Poberezny, Dick and Burt Rutan, Harold Best-Devereaux and Bill Turner.

Photos courtesy the Experimental Aircraft Association.

Aviation History Made

The sleek, futuristic *VariEze* aircraft made of fiberglass composite swept the EAAers away. Orders for the plan sets poured in. [Over 800 aircraft were built in the next few years.]

Almost single-handedly, Rutan created a pivotal point in aviation history. Since then, the canard design has caught on, and has been incorporated in ultralights, gliders, transports and fighter aircraft.

Andy Lennon, in his book *Canard: A Revolution in Flight*, said that once Rutan introduced his composite-built, canard design at Oshkosh in 1975, a breakthrough had arrived.

Oddly enough, quite a few canard designs had been flown. The Wright brothers' *Wright Flyer* had a canard, but somehow this had not, before Rutan's designs, caught on, according to Lennon's book on canard aircraft. Perhaps the timing was just not right. Some had safety problems. Perhaps the materials that would make them effective were not available. At any rate, Burt Rutan had the right combination.

Burt went back to Mojave after the Oshkosh Convention and made many changes in his first *VariEze*. He made changes that made the landing speed lower, added instrumentation, comfort, and a rollover safety structure. He also made the control better and changed the engine from Volkswagen to a Continental A-75 engine.

Another change, the newsletter was renamed the *Canard Pusher*, beginning with the October 1975 issue. A better typewriter was now available but the newsletter remained a homely, helpful publication.

Second Prototype

A second prototype of the *VariEze*—which had a 100 horsepower, 0-200 Continental engine and a new canard—was built. It first flew in March 1976. [At Oshkosh in the late summer of 1976, RAF would begin selling *VariEze* plans. *Fast* development!] Once plans were released, over 2,000 sets were sold in the first 90 days of their availability.

In general Burt scaled the entire airplane up. This entailed building another prototype. This proved to be a necessary step, in any case, since the first plane had been built without tooling. Even the simple *VariEze* needed some tooling for homebuilders to use for certain parts of the aircraft.

Burt was able to report to his builders in October 1975 that he had solved the problems inherent in the first prototype. A reliable aircraft engine, the Continental 100-horsepower (the 0-200B) could be used. This would make the empty weight of the plane 480 pounds, still much less than the light Piper *Cub*! He planned complete spin and stall testing before releasing more information.

New record flights were planned for the distance record, over 2,600 miles from San Francisco to Miami, including extensive night flying.

Unprecedented Development and Building Speed!

While most airplane designers and builders were using teams of engineers, assistants and test engineers and pilots, Burt Rutan worked in his Mojave desert ex-barracks, assisted part-time by Carolyn and one or two other people. The desert wind blew, the sun broiled the airport and the buildings. He was happy.

Burt revealed that, even under these conditions, he built his second *VariEze* in an amazingly short time. "RAF activity since the October [1975] newsletter has been primarily the construction of the *VariEze* homebuilt prototype. [The second *VariEze* prototype.] This aircraft (N4EZ) is the Continental-powered aircraft that we are basing the plans on....

"Construction of N4EZ was started on 15 October 1975. It is now (14 January 1976) being primered and finished.

"Yet to be completed are the cowling, instrument installation and hooking up the engine controls. It should be flying by the first week in February."

This would have been an amazing achievement under ideal conditions with plenty of assistance. As it was, it was almost unbelievable. This was and is the surprise of Burt Rutan, the man who "can do" and does!

He promised if the flight tests (including dive tests to 240 knots and spin tests) went well, then plans would be available to buyers by April or May.

The first pilots to check out for solo flight in the new design, the *VariEze*, were: Peter Garrison, aviation writer; Tom Jewett, aircraft designer and builder; Tom Poberezny, EAA officer; and Burt's brother, Dick Rutan. Every Saturday from noon to 2 p.m., the two unique designs the *VariViggen* and the *VariEze* were rolled out of the hanger for discussions, flight demonstrations and rides.

RAF was still housed in its ex-barracks building. Seminars were held there on Saturdays. Again and again in his newsletters, Burt pleaded with interested pilots and builders not to expect him to show planes or stop work to talk. This eats up time and delays the program, he commented. "After the *VariEze* is on the market," he said, "come by any time!"

The airplanes at RAF were designed to follow strict criteria. They had to carry a pilot and passenger and very little baggage, swiftly and safely through the sky. There was no room for excess weight (for example, pilots could not exceed 210 pounds). Also, dual controls, starters, batteries, and inverted fuel systems were all put "on hold" until the basic airplane was completed and flown. The design was set for a "no frills" mode to get good balance, range and cruising speeds.

Builders' wives were invited to add their skills to those of their husbands by cutting the fiberglass cloth accurately. First-time aircraft builders were reassured as to how hard it would be to build an airplane of the new materials. "If you can chew gum and walk a straight line simultaneously, you won't have any trouble at all." Skills required, he promised, were less than those needed to work with wood, sheet metal, or welding tube structure.

1975, the *VariEze* design won Burt his second EAA Outstanding New Design trophy.
Photo   courtesy the Experimental Aircraft Association.

"The *VariEze* plans are much more than just drawings—they are a very detailed 'education' and step-by-step construction procedure description." Very few tools, none of them very expensive, were required.

Carolyn's name is missing from the masthead of the *Canard Pusher* newsletter for April 1976.

Rutan reported in the April news that the second *VariEze* prototype had made its first flight on March 15. The plane flew 35 hours in the next month as Burt test flew it for ease of control and for safe flying characteristics. He wanted it to be stable, able to fly "hands off" for a time, and able to trim it easily for all flight conditions.

Gleefully Rutan reported: "Stalls in the *VariEze* can best be described as 'boring.'" He had to solve an engine overheating problem by designing a new airscoop. He improved on the retractable nose gear, and provided ways of combating sunlight damage. Typically, he simply did the work and passed on the information.

Air Traffic Control centers reported that even though his planes consisted largely of fiberglass, they were picked up on the radar scopes.

As *VariEzes* were built and problems arose, Burt worked closely with builders to solve them.. The nose gear retraction system was redesigned. Cuffs were added to the wings to make the flying characteristics more reliable, safer.

In 1975, aviation writer Jack Cox predicted that Burt Rutan's designs would send shock waves throughout the aviation world. Cox noted that Burt dared to be different in the design of this aircraft and dared to ask a lot of it by going for a record with it in its first year.

It is interesting to note that, in the years that followed, Dick Rutan and Jeana Yeager were to make many successful record distance flights at the controls of Burt Rutan designed aircraft. Burt seems to have stepped back from this long-distance flying to devote his time to design work. Time! He always seemed to be hard pressed to find enough of it to do all he wanted.

"Jiran Prefab Wing"

For the *VariEze*, a new prefabricated wing was static tested early in 1979. This was the "Jiran Prefab Wing." Fred Jiran, a sailplane maker, had worked out a way to make prefabricated wings and center sections that he believed would be not only light, but very strong indeed.

NASA turned up to see for themselves. Burt, Dick and Mike Melvill were present as Fred Jiran static loaded his *VariEze* prefab wings and centersection.

NASA had installed 24 strain gauges all over the wings and centersection spar. With no trouble, the wings withstood their design limit of 7.5 "Gs" (forces of gravity). In fact they did better than that. By mistake the wing had been loaded to 8.25 "Gs" and to almost twice the expected torsional loads.

Pleased, Burt planned to begin flight testing of the Jiran wing and centersection the following month (May 1979).

But Owners Have Troubles, Too

Even though many *VariEze* builders and flyers reported sheer happiness with their airplanes, others ran into troubles. The airplane itself shielded one of these from harm.

One pilot (reported in an early 1979 newsletter) hit the runway hard and cartwheeled while bouncing about 30 feet into the air, coming to rest inverted in a snow bank. The pilot was used to larger airports and had been trying to land on a short strip with a 10-knot crosswind.

The plane was substantially damaged, but the pilot came out of the landing with a scraped knee.

A second accident reported in the April 1979 newsletter had a more serious outcome for the occupants of a *VariEze*. The aircraft was seen to go out of control after climbing out to an altitude of only a few hundred feet. Investigation showed no malfunction of the aircraft. The canopy lock was on the safety catch.

It was thought that the pilot, only marginally qualified in the plane he'd bought, was distracted by roaring of the airstream as the canopy opened up against the latch and perhaps by his passenger (the passenger was on his first airplane ride).

Burt published accounts of the accidents in his newsletters in order to warn builders and flyers of possible hazards. He wrote up the accidents and described the subsequent investigations. Many an aircraft designer or manufacturer would not have published this information.

Builders certainly could never accuse Burt of withholding information. Faithfully he relayed suggestions and notes about the building and flying of the designs. The newsletter was a mix of intricate technical information clearly related and homely gossip of builders' activities. Certainly it was an amazing demonstration of a very close relationship being maintained between the designer and the builders.

CHAPTER 11

"HOMEBUILDERS" AND THE EAA

For years in the United States, ordinary men had begun to build planes that embodied their own ideas and dreams. Ordinary women, if they wanted to remain married to these dreamers, often did a lot of the building, too, and later flew in the planes. These "homebuilders," led by Paul Poberezny, banded together in the 1950s into an organization called the Experimental Aircraft Association (EAA).

Driving out to see Rutan one day in 1989, I said to a friend travelling with me, "Burt Rutan is the guru of homebuilders who build with composite materials."

"You mean to say they build homes with that stuff?" A logical response, but in aviation a "homebuilder" is a person building an aircraft at home, or at least near home!

EAA Background

Pilot Paul Poberezny began flying in high school by rebuilding a damaged Waco Primary Glider. His high school teacher sold it to him for $67 in 1936. He got hold of a book on how to fly and taught himself to fly the thing and made over 2,000 successful flights. He was pulled into the air behind an old Willis-Overland car. (Before that, he had built model aircraft.) His first official solo was in 1938 in a 1935 *Porterfield* aircraft.

In his teens Paul met former members of the Milwaukee Lightplane Club who had built and flown their own aircraft. He delighted in the companionship and interest shared by these early homebuilders. This may well have been the seed that later was to grow in his mind and mature into his concept for the Experimental Aircraft Association.

In 1941 he entered glider pilot training in the Army Air Corps. Later, in 1943, he became a civilian flight instructor in Helena, Arkansas.

In 1944, he accepted a commission in the Air Transport Command and flew for them for a year-and-a-half. Out of the service, he took any jobs that he could find. In 1947, he joined the Wisconsin Air National Guard and was back to aircraft. In 1948 he transferred to the Wisconsin Army National Guard. This was his only paycheck, until his retirement in 1969 as a lieutenant colonel.

It was back in 1947 that he bought a tattered little *Taylorcraft* which had been manufactured in 1937. Paul rebuilt the plane and modified it so that it could be flown in air shows. From 1948 to 1951 he kept remembering the idea of an organization of people who liked to build airplanes, get together for airshows and who loved flying.

After World War II, while in Wisconsin, Paul, flying a *Navion*, would sometimes run across Duane Cole, a famous air show pilot. As early as 1950, while weathered in together, Paul talked with Duane about some of his ideas about pilots, airshows and airplanes. They talked about the pleasures of flying, the joy in restoring aircraft, building planes themselves and modifying aircraft. They talked about the interesting and really wonderful people engaged in grassroots aviation.

Paul H. Poberezny, founder and longtime President of the Experimental Aircraft Association.
He is now Chairman of the Board of EAA.
Photo courtesy the Experimental Aircraft Association.

Paul wanted to initiate an organization to foster air shows, small air races, fly-in breakfasts and gatherings where pilots and aircraft enthusiasts could show off their latest original aircraft or a shining restoration project.

In 1951 Poberezny began such a group in Milwaukee, Wisconsin. It started out with a few friends meeting in the basement of his home.

After a slow start, the little organization began to grow. Paul, his wife, Audrey, and some friends handled the mail and business on a volunteer basis.

Paul was called away, however, to fly in Korea in 1952. Audrey carried on the work and kept in touch with the members of the group. When he came home two years later, the little organization originally formed to sell sport aviation, had only gained three or four more members. Paul decided to expand the group and make it more effective. He enlisted Bob Nolinske and Carl Schultz to help him do this. The new workers settled down to help him write letters to every homebuilder in Milwaukee and nearby areas.

Reorganization and Growth

By January 26, 1953, reorganization was complete. Thirty-six members started the reorganized group. They named it the Experimental Aircraft Association.

One of the early members was Steve Wittman who had been building and racing aircraft since 1926. [The airfield at Oshkosh, Wisconsin, now the location of the EAA headquarters, is named for Wittman.]

At first EAA held an annual fly-in/camp-in at an airport near Milwaukee, Wisconsin. The first on was held in 1953. There were 40 airplanes there, and 141 members and guests. The event included new designs and modifications of old designs, as well as the restoration of antique airplanes.

A magazine was initiated in 1953. Paul Poberezny continued to fly with the National Guard. While visiting air bases across the country, he found time to meet with aircraft builders and restorers.

The 1954 Fly-In attracted 24 airplanes in the experimental and restricted categories.

In 1956, Paul and Audrey moved to a new home in Hales Corners, Wisconsin. This gave them more room for EAA office space. August 1956 saw the EAA Fly-In moved to Oshkosh, Wisconsin. Attendance at the fly-ins continued to grow. In 1957 there were 34 airplanes registered, 24 homebuilts and 10 antiques. In 1958, 58 planes attended.

The city of Rockford, Illinois offered its airport to EAA for the 1959 annual fly-in. Eighty aircraft showed up. Thirty families camped out in the nearby campsite.

By 1960 EAA had grown to 7,000 members. Paul was talking about beginning a museum. An office building was needed.

By 1963 the EAA headquarters located at Rockford had taken shape. Volunteers had graded tie-down areas and camp sites. Paul had $18,000 collected for his museum project.

By 1964, there were over 6,000 factory-built aircraft attending the EAA annual fly-in at Rockford. The 175,000 attendees included 152 homebuilts and people attending various events. By 1967 a small museum building was in place. Nearly 40,000 memberships had been issued!

Paul retired from the military in 1969. At that time he was entitled to wear seven different military wings! Among those were the wings of an Air Force senior and command pilot. Only then did he accept full-time employment with EAA.

A New Home in Oshkosh

After 11 years at Rockford, Illinois, the EAA had outgrown the site. These had been good years for the organization and its members. A larger, more welcoming, environment was needed, however, so a search began.

In 1970, EAA selected Wittman Field, Oshkosh, Wisconsin as its new headquarters and convention site. Ample land was available, an excellent airport, and most important of all, the city and citizens of Oshkosh promised to support EAA. Oshkosheans have kept their promise. The people of the town help EAA members all year and in particular during the summer fly-ins. The University of Wisconsin at Oshkosh makes vacant dorm rooms available to EAA members and their families.

The 1970 Fly-In at Oshkosh was a memorable one. EAA members from all the states and from abroad attended in droves. There were 43 "Warbirds," 39 competition planes and a few other exhibition aircraft on hand. Over 2,500 manufactured aircraft flew in.

EAA is a family affair. Second generation pilots have been to the annual conventions every summer of their lives. Tom and Bonnie Poberezny are among these. Tom is now head of EAA. In 1989, Paul announced that he was retiring from the position of president, but would remain in the organization. He was 67 years old and had logged nearly 30,000 hours of flight time.

The EAA Today

Today EAA has 700 local chapters throughout the world and over 121,000 active members. Begun as a homebuilders' organization, the EAA now also fosters competition in aerobatic contests, races, between antique and classic aircraft restorers, "warbirds," rotorcraft and also fosters ultralight flying.

Each year Wittman Field in Oshkosh, Wisconsin, becomes the world's busiest airport. In 1988 over 12,000 aircraft flew in and were parked at Wittman for the early August event. Aircraft movements, takeoffs and landings, numbered much more each day. Despite temperatures of just below 100 degrees, thousands of EAA members and interested people, hovered over the hundreds of homebuilt, classic, ultralight, antique and warbird aircraft gathered there.

The daily airshows were, as always, exhibitions of almost inhuman flying skills. The B-1 bomber was on display and the beautiful *Concorde* flew in. Aircraft restored from the World War I era, like ghosts of the past, flew slowly by. Seminars hummed in tents as knowledgeable people shared their adventures and skills with EAA people.

Each year General "Chuck" Yeager, the current FAA Administrator, Duane Cole, Bob Hoover and scores of other fabulous flyers come to Oshkosh. New planes are shown off by manufacturers and homebuilders.

EAA people admit,"inveterate tinkerers tinker!"

Aviation writer Gordon Baxter, says that EAA is doing what Wright, Bleriot, Curtiss, Cessna, Piper and Beech were doing in their little shops, all alone, during the first few years of flying. EAA, he said in April 1989, "is the cutting edge of general aviation today!"

When asked, "What is the future of general aviation, concerning design and manufacturing?" Baxter replied, "Go see a Mr. Burt Rutan!"

The 51 Percent Rule for Homebuilders & Other FAA Regulations

In 1950, FAA agreed that if a person (or persons) did over half the building of an aircraft for educational and recreational purposes, then the resultant aircraft could be called a "homebuilt." If over half the plane was built by a commercial outfit and sold, it was not a homebuilt aircraft and had to comply with FAA's complex and thorough type certificate testing process.

This federal rule has worked well. There are legal reasons for the 51 percent rule. Manufacturers are under siege since there is a endless and very strict liability assumed if you manufacture a product. Homebuilders take on this liability as they "manufacture" their aircraft.

Hang Gliding has been another phenomena in recent years. People wanted to experience the glorious feeling of flying, of almost literally having wings. In the 1960s, hang-gliding became a popular sport in California and wherever people could launch themselves off hills or cliffs with a fabric-covered wing. It was not very safe. An FAA inspector in Maryland told me that even the experts had problems and that one should only fly as high as you were prepared to fall!

The Ultralights In the 1970s, small engines were attached to wings and hang-gliders. The ultralight "vehicle" movement was born. FAA doesn't regulate these hang-gliders or ultralight "vehicles" or their pilots. Sportspeople now had a freedom to fly and experiment as long as they stayed out of the way of other flying machines.

Today, several thousands of the ultralights have been made. The enthusiasm for this mode of flight has waned to some extent, but still thousands of people enjoy their ultralights today.

Then Rutan! He came along with his new materials, new designs, innovative ideas, and perhaps most importantly his "can-do" philosophy. He has rejuvenated light aircraft design and has created a new and needed interest in general aviation.

When he established his Rutan Aircraft Factory, he sold plans to homebuilders. He revolutionized homebuilding with his directions on ways to build his designs with composite materials. He used the materials in new ways. The result is a very strong, very light and very efficient aircraft.

61

His first appearances at the EAA Conventions, with his *VariViggen* and the *VariEze* won awards and instant recognition. Each year he gives seminars that are swamped with fascinated listeners at the EAA Conventions in August.

Tom Poberezny.
Photo courtesy the Experimental Aircraft Association.

CHAPTER 12

DESIGN PIONEER

When Burt Rutan came along in the 1960s, aircraft design was on a plateau of development, particularly in light aircraft design. With all the progress in transport and military aircraft, electronics, and all-weather navigation and flying, the light aircraft scene was rather stagnant.

FAA demands such strict trials that aircraft design remained static rather than introduce new designs that must go through expensive trials.

The new planes manufactured after World War II changed very little in the next 30 years. Engines became more reliable and instruments were much improved. Omnirange navigation and other electronic navigational aids provided much better chances of getting where you wanted to go "weather or not." The older four-leg, low-frequency radio ranges had been difficult to use and blurred by static just when you needed them most. Yet, save for the changeover to nose gear, made possible by having more paved airports, rather than tail-wheel aircraft, the design of the light aircraft was quite "set."

After World War II one of the few new designs was the *Ercoupe*. This is still a remarkable, all-metal aircraft of almost fool-proof design. The wing is virtually unstallable due to control restrictions and the wing design itself. It was one of the first of the nose-wheel airplanes.

Pilots rejected this innovative little aircraft, however, primarily because the ailerons and rudder were interconnected and controlled via the control wheel. There were no familiar rudder pedals on the floor. Had pilots worked out the cross-wind landing situation (that ailerons stall out first when you slow down to land and that leaves you with still-functioning rudder control) plus the fact that the landing gear was designed to castor straight, even if landed at an angle, it would have had more appeal.

Fred E. Weick—Pioneer

Aircraft designer Fred E. Weick was a pioneer in 1930s with his experimental personal airplane the W-1. He used pusher-prop, tricycle-gear aircraft when these were rare.

Over 55 years ago, Weick, who also did some of the test flying, built a research airplane, the W-1A, with tricycle landing gear, a term he coined. Most planes at that time had a tail wheel aft and two main wheels forward. This tail wheel configuration was so common that it is even today known as "conventional."

Weick was an early innovator in variable pitch propeller design, cowling design and tricycle landing gear . He helped design the Piper *Cherokee* in the early 1960s.

Later Weick designed the *Ercoupe* for Engineering and Research Corp. with its interconnected controls. It was almost impossible to stall, impossible to spin.

After World War II the sleek Beechcraft Bonanza and Bellanca low-wing fourplacers emerged to give fast, luxurious transport to lightplane owners and pilots. These were joined by Mooney, another fast, low-wing aircraft with retractable landing gear and controllable pitch propeller.

Executive aircraft went into pressurization and jet engines. Bill Lear brought out his Learjet.

But for all the designs that came out after 1945, there ensued a period of virtually no innovation. Light aircraft may have a single high wing, or a single low wing. They have nose gear configuration, some have retractable gear. A few have controllable pitch propellers, too. The instrumentation and radios are much improved over pre-1945, yet they all look remarkable the same as they did in the 1940s.

The one design that was truly innovative, the *Ercoupe*, did not do too well commercially. It was a low wing plane, with tricycle gear (nose gear steerable), no-stall, no-spin, easy-to-fly. Pilots rejected it because they were used to rudder pedals on the floor and thought they would not have the exact control they were used to in the three-control aircraft. Actually, the plane was quite controllable and a really advanced design, yet this pilot prejudice reduced sales.

Aircraft manufacture, afflicted by these ills, entered a slump in the 1980s. The primary reason was and is the liability problems associated with building aircraft for sale to the public. There is no time limit on the liability carried by manufacturers. A plane can be 40 years old and the manufacturer still can face liabilities. Also, the manufacturer is supposed to continue to advise customers of any problems developing with the aircraft. This is reasonable up to a point, of course, but it seems to be carried to extremes.

Into this period of little change came Burt Rutan. His planes were sleek and fast—sporting strange new canards and winglets. They were made of a material not common to aircraft construction at the time.

Aircraft design needed an impetus—and it got it in Burt Rutan, early in the 1970s.

CHAPTER 13

PROBLEMS AND SOLUTIONS

1976

Like a frontiersman, when Rutan needed something, he invented it. With the Mojave Desert sun beating down "366 days a year," he designed a solar hot water heater.

When baggage was a problem in his slim, carefully-balanced aircraft, he designed light, triangular, luggage which would fit in the baggage compartment of the *VariEze*.

Working six or seven days a week, from 10 to 16 hours a day, the *VariEze* manufacturing manual was completed — a massive task. The manual described in detail just how to build the airplane! Burt was also completing the installation of a Continental engine, with a two-bladed wooden propeller, in the *VariEze*, to get it ready for the giant 1976 Oshkosh Convention in Wisconsin late in July.

Burt was always deep into his creative processes and his time was poured into his many projects. Carolyn was left to her own devices much of the time. She had generously taken part in the work and the trips, yet now she needed more than the constant work at the airport and at home, the Mojave's constant heat and wind. In a word, Carolyn and her daughters felt neglected.

The Saturday demonstrations took more time. They did show Burt just how remarkable his new airplane was. It flew every demonstration, canceled only twice—once for heavy rain, and once for being elsewhere at an airshow. It was never down with a problem. Nor did the gusty winds at the Mojave Airport ground it, even when other light aircraft could not safely be flown.

The new materials were working. Even though composites were new to aviation and homebuilder's use, they have "found them to be so durable in service that no failures or degradation was found that required redesign."

Many homebuilt aircraft were not spin tested, since this was required only for aircraft manufactured under a type certificate. Even so, Burt wanted the *VariEze* to be spin tested.

He selected Peter Lert, aviation writer and experienced pilot, who at 135 pounds, was light enough to allow for certain loading conditions to be tested. The chase plane was the *VariViggen*. As Rutan expected, the *VariEze* was essentially unspinnable, even under strange and large control inputs and power settings. It also was not really "stallable" but would instead, bob, sink, and not really drop away into a full stall. Recovery from all unusual attitudes was easy and predictable.

Static load tests showed how strong the structure was. "Drop tests" demonstrated the strength of the landing gear.

Landing tests showed that the plane could land in crosswinds as high as 20 knots. It was also successfully flown in gusty winds of up to 45 knots. Heavy air turbulence did not damage the aircraft or cause loss of control. High speed dives showed that the plane was as strong, or stronger, than its design predictions. Red Line Speed, that is the "never exceed" speed, was moved up to 220 true airspeed in the pilot's handbook.

The more the second prototype flew with its sound Continental engine, the more remarkable it was found to be. Soon Burt would be able to sell plans and retrieve the $100,000 spent on developing the design. This is a great deal of money for an individual, but to develop a new design it is very little indeed. Burt could hardly wait to get to Oshkosh.

Wouldn't homebuilders be intrigued by the unique shape and extraordinary performance of this airplane? He could picture them watching as the *VariEze* pilot lifted the airplane's nose up from the nose-down parked position, locked the retractable nose gear down, then entered the airplane by climbing over the side to taxi away.

Builders would love the idea that the wings and canard could be removed so the aircraft can be brought home on a trailer. This in spite of the fact that most homebuilders park their planes in an airport. They like to think that they needn't.

The practical utility of the airplane was going to be equally interesting, with Burt predicting a range of 1,000 miles, speeds of up to 200 mph and a low landing speed of around 47 knots. One could have this airplane by investing in a set of plans (for less than one hundred dollars) and recommended materials plus, Burt estimated, about 500 man hours of work. Builders for the most part took more time to build.

The *VariViggen* prototype flew to Oshkosh for the fifth time. Burt had very little trouble with the airplane. He gave rides to those builders who were working away at building their *VariViggens*. He was still selling plans for this aircraft, commenting that it "will not stall or 'mush' in," received the Omni Aviation Safety Trophy at Oshkosh in 1973 and the Outstanding New Design Award in 1974. "Comfortable tandem cockpits, three-suitcase baggage area...adequate cruise speed...and it's road towable!" Plans were only $59.

Oshkosh 1976 proved to be much more than Burt had envisioned. The second prototype *VariEze* simply "knocked the socks" off the homebuilders. The RAF booth was swamped with interested pilots and builders. His three seminars were jammed.

Stamina was needed at the EAA Convention. Both the *VariEze* and the *VariViggen* were flown to Oshkosh. Both planes performed in the airshows during the nine-day fly-in. Also, two-hour construction seminars were conducted each day. "Builders-only" discussions took place around the two prototype aircraft. Burt hoped that in 1977 some of the people now building planes would have them completed and would fly them to Oshkosh to "take a little of the heat off of the prototypes!"

When Burt got back to Mojave Airport, orders for the building plans poured in. "Demand for the plans far exceeded our expectations," Burt wrote in his October 1976 newsletter, "And at times our ability to keep up with orders."

So many orders came in that when plans were sent and the happy builders ordered materials, the suppliers began to run out of supplies and had to scramble to catch up.

Suppliers turned out to be a stumbling block. Burt and his builders found out that the quality of the supplies of fiberglass, foam, and epoxies, varied a great deal. Too much time was needed to test every supplier's wares, so Burt wrestled with the problem. Thanks to fiberglass expert, Fred Jiran who built sailplanes, a solution was found. It was a specially designed weave of fiberglass, but it was available only from Europe and in rather large quantities. So, though reluctant to get into the supply field, Burt ordered enough to be able to sell it to his customers.

The next problem was with available epoxies. These were not easy to work with, and were toxic to the point that skin and lung protection were needed. As Burt mysteriously writes in his newsletter: "About that time we met with several composite engineers working in the advanced composite development department of a large aerospace corporation."

Burt explained to them his problems with the available epoxies. With their help, he worked out a system that was less toxic and also had better fatigue and peel-strength characteristics. Burt worried, too, about adding $200 to the builder's cost of the airplane. But finally he was able to find a combination that worked, got suppliers to stock it, and even got the price down.

The epoxies can be very dangerous indeed. Some builders developed an intolerance to the chemicals and had to abandon their projects. There was always the danger of eye injury as well. In Burt's and many homebuilder's shops, containers of water stood ready to immediately flush away epoxies to prevent blindness or damage to the eyes.

Aside from a suitable epoxy, another essential ingredient needed to build the airplane was the foam used as a core for the composite structure. A certain strength and stiffness was needed. This problem, too, was solved by designating certain suppliers and making sure that they understood the kind of foam needed.

The cost of a homebuilt *VariEze*, as of October 1976, was estimated at between $1,400 to $2,700 for materials, plus the cost of the engine and avionics. Burt noted that engines with plenty of flying time left in them might be obtained for $1,000 to $1,500. "So the $3,000 airplane is not impossible, just improbable! We have about $5,800 in N4EZ ..." including the engine and the radio. The cost of the plans and newsletters amounted to less than $150 to RAF! Builders reported that, depending on the engine and avionics used, the typical cost was from $9,000 to $12,000.

"In general, builder's acceptance of the construction methods has been excellent. We have received very little feed-back from anyone who felt that the building skill requirements were too high."

Work piled up. There were some tests to be flown on tweaking the fuel system design into better shape, there were more instructions to be written. Burt was trying to design a spoiler of some sort to "dirty up" his sleek *VariEze*, because it was so aerodynamically efficient, it was a bit hard to slow it down for a short landing. Also, there were distractions as people tried to find out more about Rutan's designs and Rutan himself. In Rutan's words it "kept us at a gallop" to keep up with the hectic summer of work.

Not all was success and smooth going, however, for the first prototype of his *VariEze* design was involved in a landing accident. Burt doesn't say who was flying. The airplane landed upslope, in soft dirt, about 400 feet short of the runway. The main gear failed (it had not been improved as had the second prototype), and the right wingtip dug into the soft

67

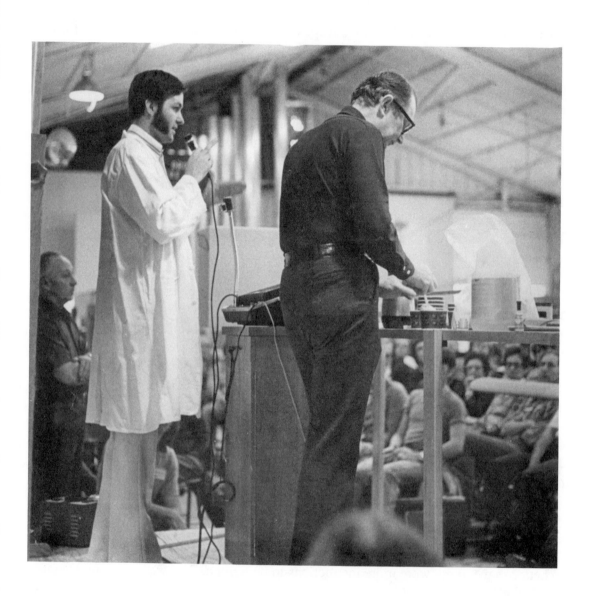

At Oshkosh Burt talked to homebuilders about epoxies.
Photo courtesy the Experimental Aircraft Association.

68

dirt. The plane bounced up in a turn and nose-high attitude. The next contact was on the nose at the end of the concrete runway in a steep bank and moderately nose-down position.

Even with this bad luck, Burt salvaged good from it. He pointed out that such an accident would have destroyed a wooden or metal airplane. As it was, the structure of the plane absorbed much of the impact. The sandwich of glass/foam/glass provided energy absorption, limited the damage and protected the pilot.

All of this activity left little time and attention for Carolyn. She resented his almost total involvement with his work. She had long joined him in his airplane interests but long, hot days in the little desert town, tending children, doing housework, helping in the spartan office quarters or shop on the airport — was beginning to pall. Still, she kept her smile in place and obligingly handed over the first set of *VariEze* plans to the proud buyer for the camera in a photo published in late June 1976.

CHAPTER **14**

THE FAMOUS AD-1, "SKEW WING" AIRPLANE

NASA Skew Wing Aircraft 1975-76

Financially, Burt was making it, but only just so in his first few years. He was famous but still poor. Yet, his fame began to pay off. The National Aeronautics and Space Administration (NASA) examined his unsolicited design for a "skew wing" aircraft, submitted in December 1975. Was he serious? NASA officials wondered.

There was great doubt at NASA, and in fact in the aircraft industry, that a manned, adjustable skew-wing, jet-powered research aircraft could be designed and built for less than many millions of dollars. It sounds unbelievable, but Burt Rutan's RAF AD-1 design work was done, in an amazingly short time [May 1976 to February 1977] and the cost to NASA was only $15,000.

Ames Industrial Corporation (AIC) of Long Island, N.Y., won the construction contract. AIC then, did the paperwork (plans and documentation), consulting, static load tests and delivery of a complete aircraft, ready for flight, to NASA. The price tag? About a quarter of a million dollars ($239,000)! This was an unbelievably low price for the delivery of a prototype aircraft to the military.

Burt dryly remarked in his April 1979 newsletter, that the work by AIC and RAF was done at a profit to both companies and yet cost much less than the NASA tasks of wind-tunnel testing, simulation and *contractor monitoring*.

The first mention Burt makes of the skew-wing in his newsletter is in October 1976. Only a brief mention: "[This summer] we also completed the detail design of a research airplane for NASA utilizing *VariEze* technology. The NASA airplane is a small, one-pilot test vehicle that is intended to test the handling characteristics of a future (1990s) yawed-wing airliner."

"The AD-1, designed at RAF and being built by Ames Industrial Corp., New York, is 70 percent finished and should be delivered to NASA late this year," Burt reported in the July 1978 newsletter. Burt noted that the plane's structure is quite similar to that of the *VariEze*.

The AD-1 aircraft was an all-composite structure. The technique Burt had used in the *VariEze* was used by Ames, working from his designs. All of the basic aircraft structure used the glass-foam sandwich techniques and materials. Two TRS-18 microturbo turbojet engines were used. The wing can be skewed up to 60 degrees and is skewed by electric motors.

More information on the skew-wing aircraft was given in the January 1977 *Canard Pusher* newsletter. "Some of our time," Burt reported, "has also been spent on further design work of the NASA AD-1, a small, all composite (foam and glass) research aircraft, using the skewed-wing concept. The AD-1 is a 15 percent-size manned, flying model of a *Boeing-designed transonic airliner*."

70

The skew-wing plane was completed, its static load tests done by January 1979. It was delivered to Edwards AFB in February.

Government test officials installed instrumentation and began to test their astonishing new test vehicle. It was flown to the 1979 EAA Convention later, where homebuilders admired it, and marveled at the design.

"While we expect the AD-1 to provide the basic subsonic skew-wing stability data it was built to provide, we expect its major impact will be that it *is* possible for the government research agencies to procure a truly low-cost aircraft, working with a small contractor and employing the moldless composite construction similar to [that used] in the *VariEze*."

Because of the low cost of the prototype, some at NASA couldn't believe that it was any good! Subsequent tests, however, showed that it was a most effective research aircraft. Burt's design, used to test ways of reducing drag as aircraft go from subsonic to sonic flight speeds, attracted a great deal of attention for him. The AD-1 is on display at Edwards Air Force Base at present.

When shown at the Oshkosh Convention, builders surrounded it. They loved the innovative idea of it. It wasn't something they wanted to build but rather, it was another demonstration of the Rutan talent they liked.

CHAPTER 15

THE MOJAVE DESERT—AIR FRONTIER

Huge old airliners loom across the runway, in storage, in limbo, awaiting their fate now retired from the airlines. One sign over a hangar reads: "Voyager."

This is the Mojave Airport, where Dick Rutan has offices and carries on business. Not far away is the famous "Hangar 78" where Burt Rutan's Scaled Composites Company designs and builds prototypes for aircraft, space vehicles, and even sails for a racing yacht. The hangar is so well known in aviation circles that not even a sign is needed to identify it as Burt Rutan's Scaled Composites.

Visiting the airport in March 1989, on the ramp in front of the hangar I saw a forlorn, beautiful little aircraft, the 85 percent scale flying prototype of the Beechcraft *Starship*.

Inside, the lobby of Hangar 78 has one wall covered with magazine covers featuring Burt Rutan and his designs.

Inside the hangar I saw planes with wonderful, smooth and complex shapes, parts of new designs, a nearly-completed 2000-horsepower air racer, the flying surfaces of a space vehicle, and offices for engineers and other workers. Burt's office is here also.

Not far away, beside the big hangars on the flight line, is Building 13, a converted barracks building, where Burt's company, the Rutan Aircraft Factory (RAF), began in June 1974. RAF continues support activities for those who have ordered plans for his aircraft and have built them.

Mojave Airport

The Mojave Airport was built as a Marine training installation during World War II. Today it hosts firms with far-reaching consequences, people working on the frontiers of aircraft design and construction. It is a remarkable civilian flight test center.

But how did this airport survive? Why wasn't it abandoned, out here in the "middle of nowhere," to a fate of crumbling runways and rusting buildings? The answer is largely Dan Sabovich. A former Bakersfield alfalfa and cotton farmer, Dan liked to fly his Cessna and had friends at Edwards AFB. Sabovich campaigned to save the airport when he saw it crumbling from misuse. In 1972 he was named general manager of the newly formed East Kern Airport District.

He started by leasing a taxiway to a farmer who needed space to dry 700 tons of grapes into raisins. Gradually he lured large companies to the airport—General Electric, Tracor Flight Systems, Airbus Industries, Northrop and others.

From the abandoned Marine air base he has built today's Mojave Airport into a world renowned civilian flight center with an annual budget of about seven million dollars. He has managed the airport for 20 years now. He is, thanks to his interest in aviation and good business abilities, widely known for his work at Mojave Airport.

More than a hundred tenants, including Burt Rutan, at Scaled and RAF, and Dick Rutan

Mojave Airport, California, 1991.
Author photo.

at the Voyager hangar, work at Mojave Airport. A large employer is Aerotest, Inc., which refurbishes older jet airliners—a growing business as our airline fleet ages. Hangars large enough to house Boeing 747s are being built today at Mojave Airport. This is forecast to bring the airport's total work force up to 2,000.

There's an old FAA control tower in operation, with a new one soon to come, overseeing the operation of all manner of new and strange, as well as tried and tested aircraft.

Manufacturers of golf clubs, aircraft devices and others use the refurbished small buildings back of the flight line.

There's a test pilot school. A variety of civil and military aircraft can be seen parked on the tarmac. Dan Sabovich looks after his tenants, making sure they are satisfied with their spaces and that safety is maintained. He has to understand the unique desert environment of wind and sun to do this.

"Are those bushes and trees out there planted as windbreaks?" I asked him. "You'll never stop that wind. They are a part of the budget to enhance the looks of the airport and help the ecology of the place."

Winds roar into the desert by way of the Tehachapi Mountains, setting the blades of 4,000 windmills going, in the nearby windmill "farms" that generate electrical power. The mountain pass there is known as one of the windiest places in the world. When the wind roars over the airport, planes that are not secured can fly away or tumble.

Edwards AFB

First settlers in the area in 1910 were Clifford and Ralph Corum. They tried to attract people to their land by opening a store and a post office, which they named Muroc.

Not far from the Mojave Airport is the huge Edwards Air Force Base, described by former astronaut Frank Borman as looking like a giant concrete Band-Aid on the tan hide of the desolate, windswept Mojave Desert. Burt worked there as a young test engineer on the F-4 *Phantom* before going to Kansas to work for Jim Bede.

The base is located 150 miles northeast of Los Angeles . It is made up of about 30,000 acres of wind-swept, sun-baked sand, clay and scrub vegetation. Borman commented that being stationed on the moon would be only a little less comfortable than living in the Mojave. This view has held by most people until very recently.

It started back in 1933, when the Army Air Corps set up a practice bombing range at the Muroc Dry Lake, sometimes also called Rogers Dry Lake. The Army Air Corps found the flat lake beds could be used as enormously long runways. The AFB occupies 470 miles of desert land. Also, the weather is good enough to fly most of the time all year. For years the lake bed (Muroc) served as a runway. Its hard, dry surface twenty-five miles long was long enough for the most stubborn take-off and the most untamed rollouts on landings.

Men and workers stationed at Edwards in the early days took a train to the little town of Mojave, then rode a bus 40 miles over to the bleak wasteland that was the airfield. There they found a few rough office shacks and some hangars.

By 1946 Muroc was considered both a training base and a full-fledged flight test base. Captain Glen W. Edwards, a test pilot, was killed on June 5, 1948, while flying the experimental YB-49, a flying wing. On January 27, 1950, the base was named for Captain Edwards.

It was at Edwards that Captain Charles B. Yeager broke the sound barrier in the X-1 in October 1947. And from then on the test crews continued to push the flight envelope.

Everything at Edwards is on a huge scale. One hangar covers four and one-half acres of ground. The AFB has a working population of around 10,000 people. There are recreation centers, clubs and, of course, guards watching the restricted areas of the base.

NASA has a test center at Edwards.

By 1960, Edwards AFB had become the site of the test pilot school, the USAF Experimental Flight Test Pilot School. It had grown to a military base with 10,000 people living and working there. The streets were named, somberly enough, after pilots killed in the line of duty there.

Paved ramps and runways now supplemented the dry lake bed test strips. There were now at Edwards a post exchange, modern hangars and clubs. Yet it was still a barren, bleak environment. Angular Joshua trees lent a note of dusty green.

The XB-70A, supersonic bomber, was tested at Edwards AFB. There, too, may be seen all manner of test aircraft. The X-15 rocket ship was one of these.

Mojave, California

As you approach the little town of Mojave from Palmdale today, a mountain looms off to the left side of the freeway. It is slowly, but surely, being dug away. In a fantastic scheme, the whole mountain is being mined. The earth is dug out, carried over to some plastic sheets, soaked with cyanide sprays (yes, *cyanide*) in order to recover gold.

This operation is not far from Burt Rutan's new house (on Rutan Road) and the mining is a concern for him. After all, leaks are bound to occur and the ground water can become contaminated. Further, it hardly seems safe for wildlife or people in the area. In environmentally-aware California, this mining seems something of an anomaly.

The town of Mojave began in 1876 when the railroad came through the Mojave Desert area. An earlier resident, Elias Dearborn had set up an eating house and stage station there in 1860, about two miles away. It was sometimes called Cactus Castle, and a dry place it was.

Civilization sought out the children of Mojave in 1884 when the first school opened.

A leading economic factor was the unloading of borax freighted in from Death Valley and Searles Lake to the railroad at Mojave. In 1894 Mojave had its own gold boom when W. W. Bowers found gold south of the town. Another economic rise was experienced when the aqueduct was built in 1905, making water easier to get.

Mojavians joke about their town—"How many people live in Mojave?" they ask. "About half of them," they chuckle. In fact, there are around 4,000 people in the small desert town today. It's a place that generates the adjective "dry" the moment you see it.

Desert and mountains form a vast backdrop for the town of Mojave, California, 1991.
Author photo.

Yet you find hospitality and cool iced drinks in the old Reno Restaurant and good food. True, giant moose and deer heads adorn the walls, but it is a modern, comfortable place as well as a unique one. Other restaurants and shops cater to your well being in Mojave.

The railroad, a division point of the Santa Fe/Southern Pacific, runs through town and up over the mountain pass to the west.

Growth at the airport is giving the town growing pains. Mojave is located at the crossroads of two highways, 14 and 58, and is a trucker's haven. Ranchers come into town to shop.

Palmdale, California

Palmdale is a town a few miles from Mojave and Edwards Air Force Base. Burt lived there for years. His parents live there now. Palmdale is located at the northern edge of the San Gabriel Mountains and at the Antelope Valley arm of the Mojave Desert. Running through the area from southeast to northwest is the San Andreas Fault.

American Indians knew the land for thousands of years. Wyatt Earp staked a gold claim in the southern hills about 1842.

Linking the towns of Palmdale, Lancaster, Rosamond and Mojave is Highway 14, and also the Southern Pacific Railroad. The railroad came to the area in 1876. The price of land shot up from 25 cents an acre to 50 cents an acre.

A few years later, German Lutherans and Swiss families came to an area near today's Palmdale, around 1884-86. Originally the place was named Palmenthal because the immigrants mistook the Joshua trees for palm trees. This certainly reveals the fact that they had never seen a palm! [Joshua trees are so called by Mormons in 1857 for the man who led the Israelites to the Promised Land!] A post office was opened in 1888. By August 1908, the name was changed to Palmdale and the little town had been moved over closer to the railroad.

Captain John Fremont, crossing the area in the 1880s with famous guide, Kit Carson, wrote that the Joshua trees were "the most repulsive in the vegetable kingdom!"

Agriculture became the area's main business when water became obtainable in 1924 with the completion of the Palmdale-Littlerock Dam. Desert land turned into fertile fields of green crops, alfalfa, wheat, fruits and nuts, vegetables and citrus.

It was in 1917 that Palmdale was introduced to the air age when two JN-4 "Jennys" landed on the local baseball field. But it was not until the mid 1900s that the economic base of the town shifted over to the aerospace industry.

During World War II, the Palmdale Airport was leased by the government for one dollar a year. A few years later it was taken over by the aircraft industry. Today Palmdale can call itself the "Aerospace Capital of the United States." Edwards AFB is near, and most major aerospace companies are located at the Air Force Plant 42. A local man, by the name of John likes to sit on his property off the end of the Plant 42 runway and look over the newest designs through powerful binoculars. Residents often stop by to talk and help him look.

Palmdale is one of the fastest-growing communities in the country. In 1986 Palmdale had 23,000 residents; in 1988 it had 53,000! The Chamber of Commerce says that the area, "has 300 smog-free days a year." It also has affordable houses within commuting distance via good roads into Los Angeles.

Lancaster, California

Lancaster is another small town near Edwards AFB. It is sometimes said to have been begun as a Scot's Colony around 1884 with about 150 people. Moses L. Wickes, an early landowner from Pennsylvania, is believed to have named the town after Lancaster, Pennsylvania.

Lancaster today serves Edwards AFB as a shopping center and has a fairly active farm economy as well.

Ames-Dryden Research Center

NASA's Hugh L. Dryden Flight Research Facility at Edwards is one of two installations associated with the Ames Research Center located at Moffett Naval Air Station, on the southern side of San Francisco Bay. It is called for that reason, the Ames-Dryden facility.

Hugh L. Dryden was a pioneer in aeronautical research. He worked in the research area of turbulence and high-speed aerodynamics. By 1949 Dr. Dryden became director of the National Advisory Committee for Aeronautics (NACA), forerunner to NASA.

As NACA's director he supervised the construction of the original Ames-Dryden facility. All through the 1950s he led programs of the famous "X" series of research aircraft. In 1959 he became deputy administrator of NASA.

The facility was so remote and its projects were so secret, that the public was unaware of the dramatic events taking place there for many years. It was the X-15 that broke this silence. In 199 missions the rocket-powered aircraft, between 1959 and 1968, set speed and altitude records. Many of these still stand today.

It was the space shuttle, however, that kept Dryden in the public eye. Not many people realize, however, that the research done at Dryden on lifting body projects tested the feasibility of the shuttle spacecraft—a spacecraft capable of returning to earth and landing like an airplane.

Engineers, pilots, technicians and support people work at Dryden today extending the boundary of human knowledge in aerodynamics. Among the projects now at Dryden are the Mission Adaptive Wing (which can change its shape in flight). Another is the Forward-Swept Wing (to test new ideas in airplane control and design) and the HIDEC F-15 being tested to improve performance with engine and flight control systems electronically linked. Another project is high angle of attack research in which Dryden engineers are using an F-18 fighter to enhance aircraft maneuverability and safety.

This part of the Mojave Desert proves that you can sell air. The air in the desert is clear 99 percent of the time with no smog and excellent visibility. Miles of desolate land offer areas over which test aircraft may be flown.

Here in this rather unlikely spot, this dry corner of California are located major military and civil flight research and development facilities. There are probably more talented aeronautical engineers here per square foot than anywhere in the world.

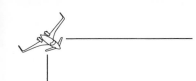

CHAPTER 16

HOMEBUILDERS MAKE PLANES

As 1977 opened, none of the Rutan designs built by the homebuilders had flown, but several were nearly finished. Burt hoped that both of his designs would be flown into Oshkosh by builders in August.

Over 2,000 people had attended Burt's *VariEze* construction seminars in the western and mid-western states. He continued to improve the aircraft, tinkering with better brakes, a better fuel system, a landing "flap" which Burt called a "drag device," to slow the sleek plane down for shorter landings. And the device did dramatically shorten landing distances.

The *VariViggen* was flown to a fly-in breakfast, but was rather "on the back burner" for the time being. Burt wanted to use it for record attempts since it had a considerable distance capability.

He was reaching out overseas from his minute operation in the Mojave Desert. Documentation on the *VariEze* was sent to aviation regulatory agencies in Australia, Canada, South Africa, West Germany, Belgium, Great Britain, Iceland and France.

Finances and the development of designs were promising. His personal life had undergone stormy seas, however, as he and Carolyn had their troubles. But his work life swept him on.

Practicality still reigned. When homebuilders asked for a heater in the plane, Burt replied that the canopy acted as a solar heat collector, so no heater was needed.

One customer asked, plaintively, "When are you going to freeze the design and stop making changes? I don't want to build an airplane that is still undergoing changes." Burt replied: "We are more interested in the research and development aspects of aircraft than in marketing/promotion.Trying different things to improve an airplane is where our expertise lies. We expect to continue to use the*VariEze* as a research test bed for a long time, experimenting with several interesting concepts and may be making changes 10 years from now."

At times Burt advised builders that certain changes were "mandatory." True, these were strongly recommended for safety, but FAA sees each builder as a manufacturer and does not mandate changes. So some builders ignored some warnings.

Good News and Bad News

The good news early in 1977 was that Rutan's RAF had moved to their new building on the Mojave Airport flightline. Airplanes were now on display there. Burt had flown the length and breadth of the United States, and had even gone to England to give seminars on building the *VariEze*.

The bad news was the *VariViggen* homebuilt program suffered a tragic beginning. An accident occurred on an initial test on February 21, 1977. Builder Jim Cavis was seriously injured as he attempted to taxi test his just-completed *VariViggen.*

When he had heard that the plane was completed, Burt, on his way home from a workshop in Denver, stopped by the Falcon Airport at Scottsdale, Arizona to assist Jim in preparing for tests. He was present at the time of the accident.

Burt did some of the high-speed taxi tests of the *VariViggen.* Minor problems were corrected as they cropped up. After some slower runs, the plane flew a few hundred feet down the 4,300-foot runway at one to three feet above the ground. The plane was slightly retrimmed before the next run. The plane had a 180-horsepower engine, with no rollover modification.

Two more successful runs with low flight down the runway were made and then Burt turned the airplane over to its builder, Jim Cavis, for its first real flight the following day.

Jim got in the aircraft to take it back to the hangar, but couldn't resist a couple more medium-speed taxi runs. He wanted to gain some feel for the aircraft since he felt that his flight proficiency was low. Burt cautioned him about a few techniques and then stepped back.

A wobbly lift off and flight then occurred. Jim seemed uncertain as to whether to get into the air or not. The plane nosed up, then it heeled over at about 10 feet up; power was down, increased, then went down again. The nose went up, the plane rolled to the right and stuck the right wing tip, then the right canard, then the nose and canopy, nearly inverted. Jim sustained a very serious head injury and broken wrist.

Burt speculated in the newsletter about the cause of the accident and advised pilots to prepare for first flights with some training flights in other aircraft, and to be sure to wear a shoulder harness and a helmet.

At press time, Jim called Burt and said that he was rebuilding his *VariViggen* and that he still had no clear recollection of the events preceding the crash.

VariEze Homebuilders Take to the Air

The *VariEze* homebuilt program was reported to be in better shape with four airplanes now flying and many more almost complete.

One *VariEze,* however, ran through a snowbank but was repaired and was back in the air. Another *VariEze,* flown by an experienced pilot, Tony Ebel, had a narrow escape on its first flight, when control problems occurred. It was found that the plane was built "crooked"—and Burt warned: Please measure your airplane and build it straight! Tony was able to correct the conditions and fly his plane without further incident.

With experience, Burt had to report to his newsletter readers that he had, "... observed an almost appalling lack of good judgment of many who have and are doing test work." He went into detail as to the many items they must be sure of before flying and while flying tests. Builders who followed his recommendations for text flights had little trouble.

Another problem was that quite a few builders developed an allergy to the epoxy being used to build the Rutan designs.

Still, a thousand *VariEze*'s were being built, and more and more *VariEze*'s were flying—even one in Germany. Pilots were delighted with them and with the attention the beautiful aircraft attracted. Builders Mike and Sally Melvill completed their *VariViggen*. Burt helped Mike with the first test flights and checked him out in the airplane.

As he completed the newsletter, Burt was busy getting ready for Oshkosh, finishing up some film sequences for Ferde Grofe Films. He was refining the *VariEze* with an electrical system, quieter mufflers, new ailerons.

"Hair-raising" First Flights

While congratulating RAF for the outstanding showing at the EAA Convention at Oshkosh in August 1977, Burt also reported some hairraising experiences homebuilders had with the *VariEze*. He suggested safety items to consider.

The hair-raising events occurred because in two instances the *VariEze* canopy came open in flight. Builder Peter Krauss reported that he took off without the canopy locked in place. It opened wide at 100 mph during the initial climb, about the worst place for anything to go wrong on a flight.

Peter somehow grabbed the canopy, dragged it closed against the 100 mph blast, and pulled it closed on his fingers. He managed to hold it closed, circled the field, and made a good landing using the other hand!

The other experience was a vicious and wild one. The normally tame and well-behaved *VariEze* turned into a raging maniac. This is what happened:

Builder Tony Ebel made an uneventful takeoff and climb. He was flying at 6,000 feet at 185 mph, enjoying the flight. His canopy latch was installed a bit loose so that the canopy would rise and fall noticeably during flight. Tony doesn't recall whether or not he bumped the latch, but suddenly the canopy opened. Tony said, "... It was as if someone threw a hand grenade."

The plane yawed, pitched down past a vertical dive, did a quarter of a turn of a spin, then pitched up. Tony grabbed the canopy but its slick surface tore out of his hands (he had no knob on the inside). Six terrifying times the plane repeated the violent gyrations, poor Tony was naturally terrified but fought valiantly to save his life.

Finally he got the canopy closed with his fingers on the outside. The plane resumed level flight at only 800 feet above the ground. Only then did he notice that in the course of the wild flip-flops his engine had stopped running.

"I had trouble thinking," Tony reported. He remembered thinking it was getting dark. He was only barely conscious and had only a couple of minutes to locate a field and make a landing. He glided toward a bean field. Fearing that the canopy might pop open and cause another loss of control, he did not land normally. He simply pushed the controls forward and hit the ground hard. He heard the nose gear breaking and then passed out.

Tony's airplane dug a large hole, cartwheeled once, tore off the right wing and ended up inverted. Tony came to, dug himself out, and found that he had only minor injuries—cuts and bruises!

When Burt heard of the accident, he flew over the following day. "It's surprising that the canopy didn't tear off when it came open at that high speed," He said.   Also, the gyrations and forces that they imposed on the airframe should have resulted in airframe failure, but the sturdy airplane had not failed.

From these experiences, amazingly non-fatal, important lessons were learned about securing the canopy, a better locking installation and a warning horn. All of these Burt lost no time in passing on to his customers in the newsletter.

Positive points reported to *Canard Pusher* readers, included first flights in ten *VariEzes* and two in *VariViggens*. Builders clubs for the airplanes were forming. Mike Melvill and his wife, Sally, finished their plane and wrote a glowing letter to Burt.

"Thank you so much for a fabulous flying machine! ... no problems .... I must say I really get a heck of a kick out of flying it. I painted it off-white with dark green trim.

"Sally sends her best regards. Thank you again for making it possible."

Later, however, even Mike's *VariViggen* gave him a harrowing experience. He had flown the little ship with no problem for about 50 hours when about a foot of one exhaust pipe fell off. The pipe hit the propeller and a part of one blade was sheared off. "The resulting severe vibration made the wing tips invisible and set off the ELT." [The ELT is the Emergency Locator Transmitter which goes off on impact and helps a crash site be located. All planes have them.]   Even with all this going on and parts of the plane gone, Mike managed to shut down the engine and land in a field.

With typical homebuilder aplomb, Mike congratulated himself on the strength of the airplane, replaced the exhaust with modifications to prevent further trouble — and flew it away!

Cost

Builders wrote to Rutan to report that there were two categories of getting a complete plane. Those who bought all available pre-built components spent about $4,900 plus the engine price; and spent about 900 hours building. Those who built most parts themselves, spent around $3,000 plus the engine cost; and it took them about 1,400 hours of work. Average time and money spent was more like 2,000 hours and $7,000, plus the engine cost.

"Galactic Western"

A feature movie, "*Centurion One*," solicited owners of Burt's *VariEzes* for flying scenes. Burt described the movie as a "Galactic Western where the setting is a hostile planet and instead of a horse the cowboys fly *VariEzes*.... Two *VariEzes* will be needed for filming in remote areas, including South America, Alaska, Africa and Southeast Asia."

Life around Rutan might be busy but it was certainly never dull.

CHAPTER **17**

BURT'S SINGLE-MINDEDNESS AND
HIS GREAT YEARS OF DESIGN

1976-1982

It was during these years that one can see Burt developing a defensive attitude to conserve his time and creative energies. Single-mindedness is needed if you are to create an idea and follow it through with its complexities and problems to a final viable flying machine. Idle talk and time-wasting chat with people who don't really know what you are doing has to be pruned back.

Not that Burt is not civil. He is. He has an innate courtesy. Yet he protects his time and energy. It began in those years at the Rutan Aircraft Factory when he perfected his sleek and successful designs. He wanted to help homebuilders but found that he had to, severely at times, protect his work hours.

He has been accused of being rude to strangers. It is true but understandable that he has a low tolerance for people who impinge on his time.

Interestingly, however, Burt wants very much to share his enthusiasms. He bounces into workshops and seminars at the EAA Conventions with a contagious energy and charm. That's the only word for it. He and his audience of pilot-homebuilders spark off an immediate rapport. They know that one of his goals is to make aircraft ownership possible for many people. These people understand what he is doing and ardently support his work.

Early on, his relationship with the press was apparent. Again, aviation writers were savvy people, well informed and knowledgeable. He didn't have to waste time explaining rudimentary aviation lore, but rather could communicate his latest work and enthusiasm directly to them.

In 1976, reporters becoming aware of this new man in aviation first approached him for inside information about his former boss, Jim Bede. Burt was, and is, the soul of discretion about his time with Bede. Writers, however, found him of great interest in himself, quotable and friendly. They were amazed at the wild and wonderful aircraft designs he rolled out of the Mojave Airport hangars where space was rented by RAF. They loved the easy atmosphere and cheerful energy at Rutan's "factory."

These years from 1976-82 at Mojave are looked back upon with nostalgia by the people who first knew and admired Burt Rutan. There were few employees. In fact the first two aircraft prototypes were built with the help of only one assistant.

After all, he not only had to think up aircraft, but he built prototypes with only a few dedicated workers, and he did much of the flight testing himself. This resulted in some scary moments in the new planes. No one had built certain configurations before, and no one knew how they would fly. Burt, in a typically direct fashion, built them with certain safety factors and then, trusting in his own designs, took them up and flew them.

The Defiant

The *Defiant* was Burt Rutan's "Model 40." It got its name in a contest. Curtis Barry, of Port Jervis, N.J., submitted the name, because the name infers that it "defies all common assumptions about current production twin-engined aircraft, in pilot skill required, safety, performance, construction and handling."

The concept was originated late in 1977. Just seven-and-one-half months later, the prototype would be designed and built! This was typical of Burt Rutan. There were few drawings and a minimum of paperwork involved in the process.

Piper Proposals

The light twin, Rutan noted in a January 1978 newsletter, was being developed for Howard "Pug" Piper. Piper planned to certify and manufacture the plane in the next four years.

When Bangor Punta took over the venerable Piper Aircraft Company, Howard "Pug" Piper, son of founder William Piper, Sr., found himself on the outside of the Piper company. "Pug" had headed Piper Aircraft until 1974. He then joined Beechcraft where he managed the group that developed the Beech Model 77 airplane.

"Pug" Piper suggested in 1977 and 1978 that he put the *Defiant* into production, but this project for the plane was never realized.

Instead, after talking with Burt Rutan, "Pug" hired George Mead, who was a talented designer and an associate of Burt's, to design and construct the "Pugmobile," design PAT-1.

It was meant to be a production airplane. It was to be made of composites and was to use a canard "foreplane." Before the first flight, its sponsor, "Pug" Piper died suddenly. Early flight test results were promising. However, later on the prototype aircraft crashed killing George Mead and two passengers.

The Defiant Design Continues

Burt continued his work on the *Defiant*, building a proof-of-concept prototype. He wanted the airplane to be a super safe, super efficient, twin-engined aircraft. Like the Cessna *Skymaster*, the *Defiant* has an engine mounted in the nose and one on the back of the fuselage. The plane can cruise at 216 mph at 75 percent power settings, yet lands at a fairly gentle speed of 80 mph.

Burt planned a plane that would be in a class by itself. It was to be a very basic airplane with few complex systems and much lighter than its competition. It was to feature ample cabin room, no flaps, fixed pitch propellers, retractable nose gear only. Two 160 horsepower Lycoming engines would power the plane.

Stall and spin resistance would be a major safety feature. Also, if one engine failed, there would be no dangerous yawing characteristics for the pilot to contend with.

Features of the *Defiant* made it much safer than conventional twin-engined aircraft. Andy Lennon, aviation writer and pilot, speaks of the *Defiant* as being "undoubtedly the most important single breakthrough in general aviation for many decades. It well deserves the name 'Defiant.' "

Burt planned the *Defiant* as a production aircraft, not as a homebuilder design. In the light of his recent successes with the homebuilt market, this new design would seem to have great appeal for the manufacturer of business aircraft. By April 1978, Burt was writing in his newsletter that the Model 40, "our light twin is now nearing completion." He gave some preliminary figures that promised remarkable climb capability, engine-out climb and *safety*.

With Burt at the controls, on June 30, 1978, the plane made its first flight safely. Within a week he and his brother, Dick, had "flown off the hours" (50 hours) required by FAA to remove its home airport area restriction.

Burt was delighted with his new plane. It was quieter than anticipated and quieter than its rival the Cessna *Skymaster*. It's handling and performance were superb.

By April 1979, Burt reported to his newsletter readers: "We have decided to proceed with a type certification program on a light twin based on the *Defiant* prototype." With this calm statement Burt took up the challenge of a process known to cost manufacturers millions of dollars, and thousands of man hours in the past. With only a handful of people and limited money—the young designer methodically set about his task. This was truly an astonishing display of confidence, capability and sheer nerve!

Describing the new *Defiant* design, Burt said the cabin was to be completely different from the prototype. It will provide roomy seating for five adults, room for baggage and have a clamshell door, he noted in April of 1979. Burt anticipated flight tests in late 1980 with "certification anticipated in late '81 or '82."

"Meanwhile," the designer went on, "we continue to gather operational data on the *Defiant* prototype. Last week it flew nonstop from Mojave to Wichita (1,265 miles) at 17,000 feet, at a speed of 175 knots , burning only 5.4 gallons per hour per engine and landing with an hour-and-a-half of fuel aboard.

"It is being evaluated in the IFR environment, including approaches at minimums, a zero-zero takeoff and light ice on four occasions." From these terse remarks, we can see that Burt Rutan and his flying associates were not leading a dull life. "It has seen 270 hours of very vigorous testing of all types including aerobatics and spin-attempts, and has yet to cut a flight short due to a precaution of any kind." This last refers, no doubt, to flutter and other design problems that might crop up with a new design.

"Defiant" Film

Ferde Grofe of Malibu, California, made a film called "Defiant" that gave those interested an advance look at the capabilities of the new design.

The film was completed in 1978. "Defiant" gave those interested an advance look at the capabilities of the new design. The plane was put through its paces plus loops, rolls, single engine takeoffs and comparisons with the Beech *Baron*. This same firm had made a film in 1977 "Flying is VariEze."

At the National Business Aircraft Association meeting in 1979 this ease of flying indeed seemed to be the case. Offers to make production possible came in. They all seemed, to Burt, to be ones that would (a) alter his simple, elegant design; and (b) curtail his personal freedom considerably.

He was living a life he loved. Why risk changing it?

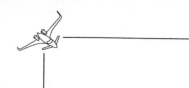

CHAPTER 18

1978—A POTPOURRI OF EVENTS

The Quickie

In 1976, Tom Jewett and his associate, Gene Sheehan, came to their old friend, Burt Rutan, for help in designing an airplane that would be very easy to build and cost very little.

Both Jewett and Sheehan were pilots. Tom was an engineering graduate of the Ohio State University, and a flight test engineer on the Rockwell B-1 Bomber Team. Tom had known Burt when they both worked for Bede. Gene had attended the University of Texas and had been in aviation for over 20 years. He was also involved with several homebuilt aircraft.

The two partners were as secretive as the Wright brothers. In fact, they called their shop on the Mojave Airport their "skunk works." This term is derived from Lockheed's designer, Kelly Johnson, and his secret skunk works which developed the "Cold War" U-2 Spy Plane, the P-38 of World War II and the Supersonic SR-71 *Blackbird*.

After a search that began in 1975, they finally found the engine they wanted—the Onan engine—a popular four-stroke industrial engine of 18 horsepower, with two horizontally-opposed cylinders, which weighed only 70 pounds, dry. Their plan was to develop a small but very efficient homebuilt. Construction began in August 1977, but the design was known to very few people until it flew late in 1977.

In his January 1978 newsletter, Burt noted that the *Quickie* was being developed as a joint venture by Tom Jewett, Gene Sheehan and himself. The plane was to be marketed and sold as a complete kit with engine in the summer of 1978 by Jewett and Sheehan. They named their company, "Quickie Enterprises."

The Quickie construction phase took only two months. It is a comment on how quickly the techniques of composite construction can be taught, for most of the construction was done by Sheehan, who had no previous composite construction experience!

All three men, Jewett, Sheehan and Rutan, flew the plane on its first day after completion in mid-November of 1977. And, all three men took part in the five-month flight test program and did the test flying. Peter Lert flew the last spin attempts, as he had done for the *VariEze*, two years before. Burt reported in his April 1978 newsletter that "The *Quickie* finished its very thorough flight test program on April 14, 1978," five months after first flight.

Once the plane was designed and a prototype built and tested, Rutan bowed out of the project. After the design freeze on the new plane in the spring, Burt and RAF dropped out of the design.

In the *Quickie* Burt had come up with a novel tractor, canard, tailless "biplane" design. It was nicknamed the "2/3 EZ" since it contained about two-thirds of the materials needed for the *VariEze* and would require only about two-thirds of the time to build.

Jewett and Sheehan set to work to market the tiny airplane as a kit. Quickie Enterprises was set up on the far end of the Mojave Airport from RAF.

The *Quickie* has a good (600 mile) range and cruises at over 100 mph. It is inherently resistant to stalls and incapable of spinning. Testing proved the new-to-aviation engine and the unusual configuration to be both safe and efficient.

Oshkosh 1978

The Rutan-designed *Quickie* was awarded the *Outstanding New Design Award* by the EAA at the 1978 Oshkosh Convention.

In fact, the little *Quickie* was the lightest plane and had the lowest horsepower of any flown to Oshkosh that year. The trip from Mojave to Oshkosh was flown leisurely by Jewett and Sheehan, in two-and-one-half days. They logged in 2,025 miles in about 19 hours of flying time even though they flew into a headwind most of the way. One of the most amazing statistics of the flight, however, was their fuel burn rate of over 65 miles per gallon.

Wherever they stopped for gas on their way to Oshkosh, crowds gathered and asked them questions. At one stop the line girl asked if they would wait while she went home to get her camera! This enthusiastic response was also the case at Oshkosh—non-stop questions.

Tom and Burt flew demonstrations in the new plane and gave forums to overflow crowds. Peter Lert, writer for *Popular Mechanics*, flew a photo session in the *Quickie*. Asked how he liked it, he told the crowd, "Flying a *Quickie* is the most fun a person can have in public during the daytime!"

Magazine writers gave the plane excellent marks for economy, ease of flying and safety. They praised its low cost and ease of building. True, it wasn't designed to fly into icing, or be loaded down with instrumentation, radios, or even an oversized pilot, but it fulfilled its intent—flying enjoyment at a reasonable price.

Rutan Designed Aircraft at Oshkosh 1978

It was quite a sight to see, as Burt reported to his builders, when in the "fly-bys," Mike Melvill's *VariViggen*, and 13 *VariEzes* were airborne in the pattern together. Thousands of EAA members and guests looked up at the parade of futuristic Rutan aircraft. There were 24 *VariEzes*, a *Quickie* and a *VariViggen* flown to Oshkosh that year.

One of the most beautiful of these aircraft was the *VariEze* flown in by builder Fred Keller from Anchorage, Alaska. It won Rutan's *VariEze* Trophy and also the EAA's "Best Workmanship" Award. This was the first time the trophy had gone to a composite aircraft. Keller reported that he had kept the cost of his beautiful aircraft down to under $6,000 by building most of the parts himself.

Dick Rutan won second place in the Lowers-Baker-Falck Efficiency Contest during Oshkosh '78. The old master of homebuilding and air racing, Steve Wittman, took first place.

"EZE Street," at Oshkosh.
Photo courtesy the Experimental Aircraft Association.

End of a Marriage and Lawsuits

Carolyn and Burt had their tiffs, but up to this time they had always gotten back together. In the April 1978 *Canard Pusher* newsletter, a picture shows her aboard one of Burt's *VariEzes* with her 13-year old daughter.

In June 1978 Carolyn threw a surprise 35th birthday party for Burt. All nine of the flying *VariEzes* showed up to help them celebrate. Over 80 people showed up at the Mojave Airport. In the July 1978 newsletter, Carolyn posed beside Burt and the caption names her as co-founder and co-owner of RAF.

Yet, the tension between the two grew and after a sharp exchange of words one day in the office in 1978, Burt and Carolyn separated.

Twelve years later I asked friends and family why Carolyn left. Some thought she was uneasy about the possibility of lawsuits that could take away the financial security they had gotten together.

There was a lawsuit. But, as Burt's father says, Burt has learned that he has the right to be faced with a plaintiff, on a monthly basis if desired. At these meetings, Dr. Rutan said, "Burt puts a dime in his hand and points to it and says, 'See this coin? This is more than you'll ever get out of me in an out-of-court settlement. I'll fight you all the way.'"

The confrontational meetings also gave Burt an opportunity to explain the situation to the plaintiff, how aircraft are carefully tested, what safeguards are used, and how every effort is made to keep the Rutan aircraft designs and their pilots safe. Often cases are dropped in the face of Burt's open sincerity and honesty.

But the possibility of a ruinous law suit did exist. Irene Rutan commented that this naturally worried Carolyn.

Even though Burt and Carolyn had their differences, it was a difficult time for them. They had shared so many happy and exciting experiences. They missed each other. Burt missed the two step-daughters, too. But they did not make up this time. They were to be divorced in 1979.

Years later, in 1990, Burt reflects on that time. "I certainly don't regret our marriage. We were a 'maw and paw' operation. She worked really hard, helped me get RAF started, did the accounting and flew everywhere with me. She married relatively soon after she left, in 1979, I guess."

Burt's Absorption in His Work

Work had so absorbed Burt Rutan that his marriage had fallen apart. He had a score of activities going at the same time: new designs, builder support, appearances, writing, and getting an approval from the aviation authorities of Canada and Australia for those who wanted to build his *VariEze*. He was also working with NASA on the skew-wing, on NASA evaluations of his unique *VariEze* design and continuing his test flying.

Whenever he had a moment to think, Burt was sorry to lose his companion of so many hopeful and happy years. He knew that he owed her a great deal for her support and encouragement in his Rutan Aircraft Factory days. He plunged into his work with his new designs, the *Defiant*, the completion of the *Quickie*, his solar hot water heater, work with NASA, and an idea, which was to become the *Long-EZ*.

In his still typewritten, "homebuilt" and homely newsletter, Burt included a photograph of the RAF staff.

Shown is Paul Striplin, who helped build the *Defiant* but then left to work on his own ultra-light project. Burt's brother, Dick, who was now working full time at RAF since retiring from the Air Force in April 1978 as a fighter pilot, after 20 years of service. Burt and Carolyn, founders and owners of RAF are shown. And finally, Marge Merrill, who had been with RAF since April 1978. A small and variable crew to do such amazing work. The photograph shows just a few people engaged in nothing less than revolutionizing aircraft design and building!

The Long-EZ Idea

Burt took a look at his operation in 1978. He saw much success with the *VariEze* design. He also noticed that due to the lack of power in the engine he had placed in the improved *VariEze* design, builders were often tempted to use a heavier engine, the Lycoming 0-235. This changed the weight and balance of the *VariEze*, making it over-weight and tail heavy. Burt saw this as a potential problem. [A tail heavy airplane tends to stall readily and is difficult to get out of stalls and spins.]

Reassessing the market and his work, Burt decided to build a new aircraft. He would design the new plane around heavier engines, the Lycoming 0-225 with starter and electrical system, or the 0-200 Continental engine could be used. These were available and reliable aircraft engines.

Longer range, good visibility, and slower landing speeds were looked for in the new design. Burt wanted to keep the stall and spin-free characteristics of the earlier aircraft, its elegant look in his new design, the *Long-EZ*.

National Geographic

Some exciting times were spent with photographers and writers from the *National Geographic Magazine*. NG photographer James A. Sugar set up some spectacular shots including one with remote cameras, mounted on the nose of the *Defiant* at dusk, strobe lights illuminating the cockpit eerily. A *VariEze* was shown in close formation behind the *Defiant*. The article was to be titled, appropriately, "Advances in Aviation," for publication in 1979.

Fatal Accidents

It was a blow to Rutan when on May 21, 1978, pilot Harold Reiss lost his life when his *VariViggen* crashed just a quarter of a mile off the end of the runway at Illini Airport, Indiana.

Burt sent Mike Melvill out to see what had happened. Mike found that this was probably caused by the canopy opening after takeoff. The pilot had struggled to close it but did not have time. Burt sadly reiterated his warnings to be certain that the canopy latches were locked before takeoff. Even with the canopy open, pilots were warned to keep flying the airplane as they tried to close it. It was a very sad day at RAF.

A mandatory second safety latch was immediately designed and required for all *VariEzes*.

On July 3, 1978 another life was lost. In this accident the pilot had limited flying experience, and almost no recent flying time. He was excited by his beautiful new plane and instead of making taxi tests and lift offs, could not resist flying the plane out of the pattern.

The weather, overcast with low clouds, was not good for first test flying. Rain showers were in the area. No structural failure was found when the FAA and Dick Rutan checked the accident site. There seemed to be no engine problem. The workmanship was excellent.

Investigators suggested that the pilot had become disoriented in low clouds and had lost control of the aircraft.

Burt was heartsick over the loss of life. Again and again he reiterated his safety warnings. The first flight was a most important one. It needed very careful preparation and execution.

Pilots and builders, however, continued to build the planes. They accepted the risks and most of them heeded Rutan's cautions and made careful first flight check lists. Almost every week now first flights were taking place.

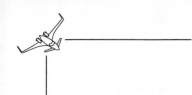

CHAPTER 19

DICK RUTAN

In appearance, Dick Rutan looks very much like his father, George. His face is craggy, with creases running from nose to mouth. Narrowed eyes look out from under thick, overhanging brows. His hair springs up in rough tufts. He is over six feet tall and is a lean, broad-shouldered, attractive man.

Like his brother, Dick sports the Rutan sideburns that tend to come and go with the seasons and the occasion. Dick is the oldest of the three Rutan children and was born in California. His sister, Nell, and brother, Burt, were born in Oregon.

Dick Joins the Air Force

At a very young age, he became interested in aviation. At the earliest possible legal age he soloed, after only five-and-one-half hours of instruction. While still a teenager Dick received his private license. He worked hard to earn money and poured his pay into buying time for his commercial, instrument, multi-engine, seaplane and instructor's certificates. This took a great deal of money, time and study.

Dick received his FAA powerplant license from Reedley Junior College in Dinuba, CA. "Mom says Burt and I were born with av/gas in our veins," he comments.

Dr. George Rutan, Jr. remembers advising Dick to train for a profession. "Well," he said, "Dick thought about this for about two weeks and then joined the Air Force!"

In any case, Dick joined the USAF in May 1958 and went to Lackland AFB in San Antonio, Texas, for preflight training. Unable to get into pilot training at first, he went to Harlingen, Texas, for navigator school and then on to Waco, Texas, for radar intercept officer training. He joined the Air Force to get into flight training, but it took seven years of other assignments with various aircraft systems, computers and navigation to get his wish. This later proved to be valuable background training. His main goal was pilot training. He wanted to fly and he never considered giving up.

In 1959, Dick married Geraldine "Geri" Tompkins in the chapel at Edwards Air Force Base. In 1961 Dick was sent to Keflavik, Iceland, and later was assigned to Travis AFB in California.

Holly Rutan was born in 1965. A 1967 photo taken in Del Rio, Texas, near the flight training base, shows Dick with Holly, just after he graduated from pilot training, first in his class. This graduation won for him what he had dreamed of—duty as a fighter pilot.

After gunnery school at Luke AFB in Arizona, Dick was sent to Phu Cat, South Vietnam and combat flying the F-100 fighter. In Vietnam he flew 330 missions.

In 1988, Irene Rutan wrote: "When he [Dick] came home from Vietnam he had flown 105 missions over the *North*, and 225 other missions, with many of them rescues. He was awarded the Silver Star."

Dick Rutan.
Photo courtesy the Experimental Aircraft Association.

After Vietnam, Dick served on-duty assignments in Italy, Turkey, and England, where his daughter, Jill, was born in 1970. Then he went back to the United States to Ohio [Wright-Patterson AFB] and later to Arizona [Davis-Monthan AFB]. At the age of 39, Dick left the Air Force.

Geri was furious with him. She had gone wherever he went, put up with military housing and problems. She had entertained and had worked hard to be an excellent military wife. Dick's career in the service meant a lot to her. That and other things caused them to drift apart. Geri and Dick separated in 1980 and were divorced in 1988.

Dick Joins RAF

In 1978, now 39 years old and retired from the Air Force, he went over to see what his brother, Burt, was doing at the Rutan Aircraft Factory in Mojave, California. He had been keeping up with Burt's work all along and found it fascinating. Before leaving the Air Force, Dick had done some flying in the *VariEze* prototype. In 1975 he had flown it to the EAA Convention in Wisconsin, and while there had set a distance record.

So, Dick went to work for Burt as his test pilot. Dick notes in the book, *Voyager*, that his brother needed a test pilot but didn't have the money to hire one.

Dick took to flying the light, fast aircraft like a duck to water. But how different these planes were from those he had been flying! Military aircraft weigh tons and cost millions of dollars. These planes he was now flying seldom weighed even one ton and were affordable enough for homebuilders to own.

Dick set several world records for speed and for distance. He flew the *VariEzes* and the *Long-EZs* on these record-breaking flights.

Fascinated and attracted by the fun the RAF people were having building aircraft, Dick built one for himself. He flew the plane around the country and put on aerobatic exhibitions. As an ex-military pilot he was well trained in aerobatics. Burt was not happy about his Rutan-designed aircraft being used for aerobatics and air show flying. He saw this as courting danger and inviting accidents. The brothers disagreed over this.

Voyager Idea Emerges

A few years later, the *Voyager* idea emerged while Dick, Burt and Jeana Yeager were lunching in a diner, the Mojave Inn, near Mojave. Burt drew the *Voyager* concept out roughly on a paper napkin and the fantastic story began (described in detail later in this book).

Dick is disciplined, his sister, Nell comments. Probably due to his 20 years in the military, she says, he is very tenacious and systematic. He has the ability to order and schedule his work. He has over 6,000 hours of flying logged. He has flown everything from military transports and fighters to the small *Quickie*.

The *Voyager* was built by Dick, Jeana Yeager and Bruce Evans. Burt, with John Roncz, did the concept, aerodynamics work and the design. Dick, Jean and Bruce, however, worked long hours, seven days a week, month after month and flew 68 flights before the "big one."

Dick and Jeana flew the flight. Burt hoped for the best but his faith wavered and he worried about them. He prayed that they could successfully complete that difficult flight.

Dick has been a constant in Burt's life. They grew up together, sharing long hours of talk and day dreaming. Burt saw his brother master complex skills in model building, motorcycle riding, automobile driving and mechanics, aircraft systems and mechanical maintenance. Burt heard the tapes that Dick sent back from combat where tremendous amounts of skill and courage were needed to survive the flying there.

"A Dynamo"

When I met Dick in 1990, I found him a humming dynamo of a man. He is very much the lean, tough, fighter pilot. He speaks urgently, quickly.

He spoke more gently, and with pride, about his daughters and noted that they had both married fighter pilots.

Dick is evangelistic in his advocating more advanced technology for aircraft control and air traffic control. After an hour-long interview packed with information, Dick dashed off. I packed up my recorder and notes as frazzled as though I'd just stepped through a propeller.

"Locking Horns"

Dick and his brother are very different, in spite of their many shared experiences and interests. They care about each other but compete, too. Burt loves to fly but continually seeks out the new kind of plane, the new challenge to unlocking the mysteries of the air. Dick loves to fly all airplanes and to stretch his skills and endurance to their limits. It would be simplistic to say that Burt is cerebral, thoughtful; and Dick is physical, geared for action—yet there is some truth in that opinion.

Dick and Burt's sister, Nell, says that the two brothers "lock horns" but there's a lot of love there. They've lived in a classic love/hate relationship—big brother feels a need to dominate, but little brother is sometimes the boss.

"Someone asked me," Nell said, "how I would assess my two brothers in one sentence. I told them, after thinking about it, that neither of them ever quit on anything. No matter what!

"Last evening we were sitting here in the hotel," [The Grand Hyatt Hotel, 1000 H St NW., Washington, D.C.] at two tables, talking. I could see Burt struck by an idea. Suddenly he was lost to everyone around him. He turned around in his chair and tapped Dick on the shoulder—and soon they were deep in talk—the party was going on around them, without them!"

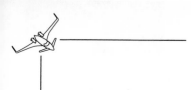

CHAPTER 20

THE RAF TEAM EXPANDS

Gradually, talented people gravitated to Rutan's company. Burt had reported in his October 1975 newsletter that engineer George Mead had joined them that month. He would be working at RAF on the planes in hand and in the future.

The Brothers Differ

When Dick Rutan came to work for RAF in April 1978, he enjoyed showing off the capabilities of the Rutan aircraft with aerobatics and flight exhibitions at conventions and air shows. Burt worried about this, for not everyone had Dick's training and skill. He saw the considerable risks involved. For one thing, if crashes occurred, the public would see small plane flying as unsafe. Also, FAA would be apt to tighten up homebuilding regulations. The Rutan designs might be blamed for accidents. Aerobatic flying added risk to the exposure.

Burt was not even wholly enthusiastic over Dick's record flights. In fact, he suggested that Dick work on those on his own time, not RAF's. Dick, the pilot and brother who enjoyed daring and self- actualization, clashed with his innovative but conservative designer brother.

The two also disagreed on which designs should be built and marketed. Burt was interested in solving design and performance problems. Dick looked for new commercial possibilities of designs. Naturally, Dick grew restless, for as an employee of RAF, his younger brother was the boss.

Then, too, Dick was leading a spare existence at the time, separated from his wife and daughters. His work was his whole interest. In 1980, however, life looked up when he met Jeana Yeager. By 1981 they were busy building a *Long-EZ* together. Dick wanted a plane of his own—one for which he didn't have to ask for the keys!

John Roncz

John Roncz, another member of Rutan's team of experts, is an airfoil expert. He is well-rounded, physically as well as mentally. Roncz's background included studying Egyptian hieroglyphics, classical music and computers. He had turned to airfoil design because he enjoyed it. The problems challenged him.

Roncz has worked with Rutan on the Beech *Starship*, the *Voyager*, and other Rutan designs. He is in his early 40s and has about 1,800 hours of flying time.

At the age of five, Roncz was a child prodigy and an able violinist, playing with the local symphony orchestra. By age 10, he had changed instruments to piano, and soon entered national and international piano competitions.

It was in the special high school for the gifted at Notre Dame University that he found his unusual talent for languages. Before long he was fluent in eight modern and ancient languages. He breezed through Notre Dame University, studying languages and particle physics. His degree is in Arts and Letters. Now equipped with these languages, knowledge about particle physics and Egyptian hieroglyphics, he set out to earn his living in Illinois. This odd collection of talent only got him a carpenter's job in an Illinois manufacturing plant.

Then, he supported himself by selling his paintings done in the style of Miro and Chagall to art galleries. Several well off mid-westerners hired him to paint murals.

Finally John went to work in his father's company learning to engineer specialized metal parts. He says he was fortunate not to have had formal engineering training since this would have predisposed him to standard solutions. Instead, his mind was free to search for novel solutions to problems.

He set up a company called Gemini Technologies, Inc. He provided special metals for his designs, including wind tunnel applications, that did better and less expensive work for his customers. But he had to be on the road several days a week. Sitting behind the wheel of a car was boring and wasted his time.

He long had an interest in flying. His father had flown as a bombardier in World War II. Early on John had built models and hung around local airports. While still in school he had earned money to take flying lessons. He got his Private Pilot's license in 1975. As a result, he bought a Rockwell 112 and got his commercial license, multi-engine and instrument ratings. Soon he was working in his business during the day and flying cargo in Cessna 310s and Navajos at night for a local operator.

After joining EAA, he began to study the theory of wing sections with the aid of a hand calculator, just for relaxation. Not long after this he bought a Heathkit H-8 computer kit. This was back in the days when you had to know some programming language in order to get the computer to work well. Once he had built his H-8, John, with his ability to master languages, soon learned "computerese," programming. Now that he had computer and programming skills, what could he attack with these tools?

The book, *Theory of Wing Sections*, offered some challenging work. Meshing airfoil theory and the computer was to Roncz a turning point. He was entranced with his new toy and its capabilities. Soon he was working on boundary layer flow, airfoil transformation and other aerodynamic ideas that could be mathematically expressed. The hours he spent on this were long—fortunately John is a bachelor!

At Ohio State University he met Dr. Jerry Gregorek, a teacher and aerodynamics expert. The two linked forces. Dr. Gregorek helped John to understand the parts of aerodynamics that his self-study had not revealed to him. Once past-known theories, John began to put forward ideas and concepts of his own. Professor Gregorek did not discourage Roncz for this. Instead, he looked into them with him, pointing out possible good parts and spotting errors.

John was outgrowing his small computer so he installed new circuit boards and worked out ways of enlarging the Heathkit! He called the improved computer, "Hal," after the one in the movie "*2001*."

Roncz knew of Burt Rutan and admired his work, what he knew of it then. He decided to order a set of *VariEze* plans. Of course he put the numbers for the airfoil used in the canard into his computer. To his amazement, according to "Hal," the canard was stalled at all angles of attack. Was this another case of bees flying when aerodynamically they couldn't?

Eventually he learned that the Glasgow University (GU) airfoil used on the *VariEze* definitely flies but in a strange way. The odd behavior of the GU airfoil sent John off into an intense examination of airfoils with low Reynolds numbers. Little work had been done in this particular area between the very low Reynolds numbers below a hundred thousand and those of around three million and more.

It took Roncz over two years to find his answers. He would work 24 hours a day when he was on the track of interesting findings. He analyzed scores of airfoils and possible changes in them. He worked out a way to analyze them, not by drawing them out, but on his computer with numbers. Each day he learned more, finding that he could read his columns of numbers and find out how an airfoil section would behave.

It was time for Roncz and Rutan to meet. It happened when John wrote a letter to Dick Rutan asking for the coordinates of an airfoil Dick had tried out on a *Long-EZ*. As an introduction, he sent along some information from his analysis of the GU airfoil. A call from Burt Rutan came along a few days later. He needed some work done on evaluating low Reynolds number airfoils for his project, the *Solitaire*.

Soon Roncz's detailed analysis was in the mail along with one of an airfoil and a tape to talk Burt through all the charts and diagrams. Typically, Burt put John's airfoil onto an airplane and tested it on John Murphy's *Long-EZ*. Next to fly was a canard on Mike Melvill's *Long-EZ*. The third Roncz airfoil to fly was on the *Solitaire*. This work made Roncz a justly famous airfoil designer, an authority on low Reynolds numbers airfoils, and welded Roncz and Rutan into a winning team. The rest of the story is history past and history in-the-making.

Roncz now lives in South Bend, Indiana, and comes to Mojave when needed.

Mike and Sally Melvill

As Burt's RAF business grew, his time was eaten up with business details. True, the details needed intimate design knowledge and of aircraft in general. He wouldn't, in fact couldn't, delegate them to just anyone.

His friends and homebuilders from Indiana, Mike and Sally Melvill, had built the first Burt Rutan design, the *VariViggen*. This part wooden and composite aircraft was always good for looks of astonishment and admiration when it arrived at an airport. The Melvills had handcrafted it into a beautiful example of the homebuilder's art. In the process, they often consulted with Burt. Both Melvills are excellent pilots as well as airplane builders.

Mike was working in an Indiana tool and die shop when he first met Burt. Sally was bookkeeper. Since Burt needed both a bookkeeper and a technical man, he talked the couple into moving to Mojave in 1978. It was to be a happy and rewarding time for them all. They ran the business for him. This gave him back his time to think, to innovate, to design. So, in October 1978 Burt reported that Mike and Sally had moved to California to work for RAF full-time. "RAF in 1978?" Sally smiles as she reminisces. "We had a ball. There were about a maximum of six employees. Everyone did everything. If you needed to fly, you flew; if the floor needed sweeping, you did that. Build it quickly, build it right, keep it simple, was the rule."

Mike became Rutan's test engineer and loyal friend. In the July 1979 newsletter there is a picture of Sally shutting down the engine of their *VariViggen* after her first solo flight on June 19. Mike is standing by "ready for a kiss!"

Sally Melvill, a slight, blonde, has fine eyes and is outgoing. She is easy to talk with. In February 1990 I asked her about herself and her husband. "Well, we were both born in South Africa," she said. It seems that she left there and went to school in London. Mike followed her to England and they were married there. Both of their boys (who are now in their mid-twenties) were born in England. Sally has a trace of England in her speech. Sally's father was born in the United States but lived most of his life in South Africa. Both her parents now live in the United States.

Mike is wiry, fairly tall, wears glasses and has (some) dark hair. He has been Burt's right-hand man for over ten years now. He has taken over writing the *Canard Pusher*, does test flying, and lends a hand whenever needed. Sally's title is now Facilities Security Officer and Personnel Administrator. She likes the work, even though in earlier days RAF and the Rutan operations were smaller, and they were doing innovative things—"firsts."

Mike and Sally now live in a small town called Tehachapi. Their sons, grandchildren and friends live near them.

Enter Patricia Storch

Patricia Storch was another early member of the RAF team, an important person in Burt's life and, later on, in the new company he was to form—SCALED Composites.

About the time same time Burt and Carolyn had separated (1979), Patricia Storch and her husband— states away—were divorced. Pat came to California for a change of scenery at the invitation of her friends, Mike and Sally Melvill.

Bruce Evans—First Meeting

Bruce Evans is shown in the January 1980 newsletter by his *Long-EZ* after his first solo cross-country trip. Evans was to play an important part in Rutan's life and in the *Voyager* project to come.

Saturday Shows Resumed

After RAF had its new building on the flight line in 1977 the airplanes were accessible to visitors and could be shown daily. Often, too, Burt and his team flew away on weekends to airshows so the weekend flight shows were discontinued.

In the early spring of 1980, however, a number of Saturday visitors were showing up. With the exception of advertised days when the team would be away, the Saturday discussion sessions and aerial airshow practice sessions began, weather permitting, at noon.

This would reduce the number of work interruptions during the week, and let Burt and his pilots talk to customers and show the airplanes in flight. Burt encouraged builders to bring parts that were presenting problems of any kind. Seldom, if ever, has such close support been offered to customers.

1980 EAA Sun' n Fun Fly-In

By April 1980, the *Long-EZ* had been shown off at the EAA's spring fly-in at Lakeland, Florida. Each year pilots from all over the United States and quite a few foreign countries, congregate at the Lakeland Airport. What a grand excuse to get away from winter's icy grip and fly into the sunshine!

This year Dick Rutan flew from Mojave, California to El Paso, Texas in one jump; then on in one more 1,500-mile hop of eight hours, to Lakeland, Florida. The entire 2,200-mile-trip might have been done in one record flight, but Dick carried baggage in one strake baggage compartment instead of fuel. Even so, with only 50 gallons of fuel aboard, these were respectable distance flights. Average speeds were 180 mph at a fuel consumption of only 5.5 gallons per hour.

At Lakeland, Dick was escorted in by a flight of *VariEzes*—"galactic wonders," he called them. There followed a week of bull sessions, builder seminars, flight demonstrations and an air race. The race featured nine *VariEzes*, with "the whole gaggle of them taking off within 40 seconds of each other," and two ending in a close finish, sizzling across the runway intersection at near and over 200 mph. (Even the "slowest" average speed was over 163 mph.)

Fifteen *VariEzes* and one *Long-EZ* attended the fly-in. This made the Rutan aircraft by far the most popular homebuilt design at the EAA event.

Dick flew a short but amazing four-and-one-half minute flight demonstration. He stressed that the plane was not built for aerobatic use but was designed to be a fast and economical cross-country airplane. Even so, pilots' hair stood on end as the plane performed steep, convolutions that, heretofore, had been virtually impossible for light aircraft.

We can see two forces at work here. Dick Rutan's delight in the strong and frisky airplane which let the fighter pilot fly brilliantly. Yet a disclaimer that the plane was not essentially built for the purpose of aerobatics did not quite override the exhibition given. This continued to be a source of disagreement between the Rutan brothers.

Burt knew that Dick could fly the plane into steep attitudes at low altitudes, but he didn't want to encourage the ordinary pilot to attempt these maneuvers. Burt feared accidents that would blacken the name of his designs.

Burt Rutan flying his *Long-EZ* over the Mojave Desert.
Photo courtesy Burt Rutan (RAF).

Burt Travels "Down Under"

In March and April of 1980, Burt went to New Zealand and Australia to meet with homebuilders and aviation enthusiasts.

He stayed with ten different EAA families. He was pleased to find his *VariViggen* and *VariEze* designs being built.

Australia has very strict controls on amateurs building aircraft. Materials, plans, and test flights are closely controlled and monitored. At an Australian fly-in, Burt reported, about 50 aircraft could be expected. [By contrast, in the United States summer convention as many as 12,000 planes arrive.]

Burt enjoyed his trip to Australia and the warmth of the "Aussies." He did not know it at the time, but in a few years he would be battling New Zealanders not in the air, but on the water!

Meanwhile, Back Home

While Burt was in Australia, Mike and Sally Melvill held down the RAF "fort" with Dick Rutan. All flew to air shows and fly-ins to show off the Rutan airplanes. Dick's airshow routine was a popular attraction.

Mike reports: "I took Bruce Evans for a ride in my '*Viggen*." Again anticipating the future, Mike could not know that Bruce Evans would be an important member of the Rutan team one day and take part in years of drama as *Voyager* was built and flown.

While on his fly-in visits, Dick was "dismayed at the number of *VariEzes* flying that have not accomplished the safety modifications." In spite of Dick and Burt's work with newsletters and seminars, the builders did not always heed their advice.

Long-EZ Plans Ready

Some builders had begun *Long-Ezs* before the plans were even ready. But, finally, in spring 1980, completely new sets of plans were available.

Burt warned builders who were trying to modify *VariEzes* into *Long-EZs* that this might not work and to please get the new plans. He offered a trade-in program to help them do this.

"We at RAF, of course, cannot enforce a mandatory change, as FAA can on a type-certificated aircraft. The regulations allowing amateur-built experimental aircraft recognize that the *homebuilder* is the aircraft manufacturer and that the aircraft does not need to conform to certification requirements. This allows experimentation by the homebuilder, giving him the freedom to develop new ideas. FAA achieves their goal of providing adequate public safety by restricting the homebuilder to unpopulated areas and to solo flight until his aircraft is proven safe." [Flown 50 hours]

RAF, however, voluntarily provided information to the homebuilder for flight safety.

Burt Discovers Computers

In 1978 Burt got his first Apple computer. It wasn't long before he found that the computer greatly extended his creative abilities. He was fascinated with what it could do.

Soon he had written a program for the computer to determine and print out many performance points for airplane performance. With certain data keyed in, Burt could bring up rate of climb predictions, for example: speed, power requirements, propeller efficiency and fuel consumption.

On a Wednesday visit with friend Peter Garrison Burt asked for some data on Garrison's aircraft. He tapped the information into his computer and a few moments later was able to hand over a printed-out copy of an amazing set of variable for more than 10 performance points. Garrison says, "I'd never seen anything like it!"

"We have two MacIntoshes here in the house, networked together. We use Write-Now and Super Paint and other programs, but most I write myself.

"I was on the cover of the Apple magazine in the early years. Bought my first Apple II in 1978, which was in the dark ages really. There wasn't an IBM PC then.

"I got so that when we got in our more capable computers, the IBM's, Apollos whatever, I was in an environment in which I was very busy and became a computer illiterate again. After doing three-quarters of my time writing software. In this DOS, you know, it's very capable but not for the occasional user.

"But I was spread so thin, I got so I couldn't even pull up a write-up program for putting in stuff. So then the Mac came along and the worm turned. The occasional user can come in and work it. I can now program much easier. Boy, I've bought three Mac IIs. Four of them actually."

Yes, computers were fascinating. But computers were not the only attractive and fascinating things around. Burt found himself depending more and more on Pat, enjoying her company, appreciating her pitching in at RAF. She fit into the desert life.

CHAPTER 21

THE FAMOUS LONG-EZ—FROM DESIGN TO SUCCESS

1979

The year 1979 saw yet another Rutan design. It was called the *Long-EZ*. With Burt's *Long-EZ* design, he was not just selling an airplane; he was selling a whole new way of life. An ordinary "Joe or Jane Doe" could become an aircraft builder, a pilot. Their planes could be featured in national magazines. They could even take part in improving the designs by relaying ideas and tips back to RAF. Burt was doing something very difficult—bringing an untrained population into aircraft design, building, and test flying!

The *Long-EZ* airplanes were a runaway success. More and more were built and flown. Five hundred sets of plans were sold in the first two months! Enthusiastic and appreciative letters came to Rutan. A cartoon shows the owner of a conventionally-factory-built Cessna in a hangar full of Rutan aircraft. He's saying, "Damn you Burt! Now folks say I'm the one with the weird airplane."

By the end of 1979, the *Long-EZ* had proved to be a tremendously popular homebuilders' design. His care in building and rebuilding, testing and re-testing throughout the year had paid off.

The First Long-EZ Flies

After just four months of building, the *Long-EZ* made its first flight on June 13, 1979. Test results, however, were disappointing.

In the June flight, the prototype *Long-EZ*, was flown with the *VariEze* outer wing panels attached to a larger center section (larger than the *VariEze*). It had a keel-like rudder under the nose.

Extensive modifications to the wings and controls were to be made in the months that followed.

Homebuilt VariEzes Fly!

While Burt struggled to get the prototype *Long-EZ* ready for the Oshkosh, Wisconsin EAA Convention to be held in late July, he was encouraged by the very large number of first-flights that builders reported back to him. By July 1979, there were a total of 126 *VariEzes* flying. "Now," said Burt, "If we all arrive at Oshkosh Saturday in formation...!!"

Safer Epoxy

As though designing, building, flight testing, modifying were not enough activity for

Burt, he was also busy that summer running a complete series of workability tests with a new epoxy that promised to allow sensitized people to hand-laminate aircraft. If builders are sensitized to the epoxies, they have a great deal of trouble ever handling the stuff again. The new SAFE-T-POXY was testing well.

Planning for Oshkosh '79

In the July newsletter Burt said that, "Oshkosh '79 should be a big year for canards. We expect that 25 to 50 *VariEzes*, *VariViggens* and *Quickies* will fly in to the EAA convention, July 28 to August 5. We will attempt to reserve two rows...so that we can all park together. We plan... a daily pilots' bull-session at the airplanes."

The Fun Part

Readers wrote to Burt that he published only builder support and modifications and when covering flying, and mentioned only problems and accidents. In response to this, Burt added a section of comments received praising the Rutan designs and those telling about the fun people were having with these unique and beautiful aircraft.

Oshkosh '79 Finally Arrives

After all the pressure and work, the day finally arrived. The RAF crew and Burt Rutan set off for the Big Event for homebuilders. It was a big event in every sense of the word, with thousands of aircraft and people converging on the small Wisconsin city. Among the people arriving each year are leading aviation writers, designers, federal aviation men and women and representatives from over a score of manufacturers.

"All of us at RAF flew to Oshkosh this year and had an enjoyable trip," reported Burt in the October 1979 newsletter. "We took two new aircraft—*Long-EZ* and *Defiant*—also the Melvills' *VariViggen* and a 180-horsepower Grumman *Tiger*, flown by Sally Melvill." They were scheduled to fly in the opening day airshow thanks to a comment made to EAA's talented writer Jack Cox in the spring. So they found themselves committed to a non-stop Mojave to Oshkosh flight with the *Long-EZ* and the *Defiant*.

On opening day, July 28, they fueled up the airplanes, stowed three people plus baggage in the *Defiant* and took off for a 1,780-mile trip. "The flight was beautiful," Burt said, "Excellent weather and good winds." After a refueling stop at Laramie, Wyoming, to be sure of extra fuel in case they were asked to "orbit" before landing at Oshkosh, they reached Oshkosh after 9.9 hours of flying time and had to orbit for an hour waiting for their slot in the airshow.

What a schedule of flying! The airplanes were made of composite but the pilots had to be men and women of steel! The speeds made by the *Defiant/Long-EZ* flight, *including* the stop in Wyoming, were 180 mph. [Most light aircraft cruise at around 100 mph with a few of the more expensive models attaining cruise speeds of 140 and 165 mph.]

Mike Melvill, who had flown out two days before in formation with his wife in the *Tiger,* joined the Rutan flight in orbit as they arrived. The planes were then flown through their rehearsed airshow, a three-ship routine before the largest crowds ever at the convention.

More exhilarated than tired by this demanding schedule, Burt, Dick and Mike flew all three aircraft many times during the week of the convention. They flew in the airshows, in "fly-bys" and flew demonstration flights. They talked to hundreds of people, and gave seminars and interviews.

"One afternoon the *VariEzes* literally saturated the fly-by pattern." Burt was to gleefully write later, "It was certainly exciting to see 41 *VariEzes* at Oshkosh.... The icing on the cake was when the Grand Champion Custom Built Award went to a gorgeous Canadian *VariEze* built by Norman Ross."

Flying Backwards?

After this exciting convention, Burt didn't rest but went back to work at his typical breakneck speed. In spite of the heavy workload, he took time to survey builders about a possible fuel/epoxy contamination problem and reported the results in the newsletter. In the October 1979 newsletter he reported not only the survey results, the Oshkosh events and other flying activities Rutan aircraft were participating in, but this odd incident, as well:

"Interesting problem," a reader wrote in, "flying a *VariEze* cross country. I was east bound level at 5,500 feet. Another aircraft appears to the right also east bound at the same flight level on a path that will cross slightly behind us. He thinks we are going backwards and since the aircraft on the right has the right of way, he turns to the right to pass behind us! I'd sure like to hear his version of what he though he saw and the evasive maneuver that followed!"

Long-EZ Modified

In the summer 1979 after more flight tests, Burt modified the *Long-EZ* design. He was essentially, redesigning the *VariEze* into a plane that would use the powerful Lycoming 0-235 engine with a starter and alternator.

He had tried to make the first prototype *Long-EZ* work. Finally, however, to get the gentle handling qualities, safe stalling performance he wanted, even 30 different modifications were not doing the job. So, in August, he built an entirely new aft wing.

In August he approved the final configuration. It had a new wing, larger winglets, rudders on the winglets. Fuel capacity was 52 gallons in two wing-strake tanks. There was no header tank. Baggage space was provided in the wing roots.

AOPA writer, Mark Twombly, reported that these planes were not hard for proficient pilots to fly, but were not to be for everyone. They have long range, he reported, and are fast, making it quite easy for a pilot to fly quickly out of good weather and into bad weather.

The instrument panel is tiny but builders have found ways to incorporate sophisticated electronics into the plane, he noted.

A new canard that does not change pitch in rain was offered by RAF—for experience had shown that the canard sometimes pitched down in rain and other precipitation. RAF also planned for the Long-EZ, larger rudders and better brakes.

Finally the modified *Long-EZ* was flown on October 1979. Flight characteristics were much better, notably the slower landing speeds possible. All through the fall, modifications, "tweaks" were made, tests were flown.

Complete flight tests in December 1979 were most rewarding. Burt now had an aircraft with excellent control characteristics, something he wanted for pilots who might have limited flying experience. The *Long-EZ* main wing airfoil was designed by Richard Eppler. The plane had a long range of over 1,250 miles, a 22,000 foot ceiling. The cruise speed was 183 mph. Either the 0-200 Continental or the 0-235 Lycoming engine could be used. There was a complete electrical system for the starter and for night flying lights and other equipment.

Long-EZ Record Flight 1979

At 7:27 a.m. on December 15, 1979, Dick Rutan took off from the Mojave Airport in the new *Long-EZ* prototype. He was attempting to break a closed course distance record held since 1959 by a Czechoslovakian pilot, Jiri Kunc, of 2,955.39 miles.

When Dick landed at 5:01 p.m. the following day, after many laps between Mojave and Bishop, California, he had covered a distance of 4,800.28 that was credited toward the new world's distance record. How far is that? It is as though Dick had flown in a straight line from Hawaii to Washington, D.C., or from Seattle to London.

The modified *Long-EZ*, just out of its cradle was modified with extra fuel tanks for the record. He broke the world's official closed-course distance record, for aircraft of the *Long-EZ's* class, by flying those 4,800.28 statute miles. It took him 33 hours and 33 minutes of solo flight.

The flight was blessed with perfect weather and wind conditions. It was, however, not only a long flight but a demanding one. He flew in a plane without an autopilot, with no directional gyro or attitude indicator. Dick had to remain alert all through the long hours of darkness to remain oriented and in control of the fast aircraft. The flight was over dark and sparsely populated areas which offered little visual reference. He landed with less than four gallons of fuel aboard.

Again, this was an example of a composite aircraft flown by an iron man!

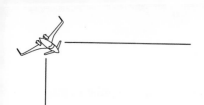

CHAPTER 22

A PIVOTAL YEAR

1980

There seemed no end to the vital work that needed to be done to design and market airplane plans. Few people would (or could) have attempted it.

Oddly, Burt Rutan seemed to thrive on the demands. He completed projects, tackled new consulting work. An owner's manual was now available for *Long-EZ* customers. He offered a book for sale, *Moldless Composite Sandwich Homebuilt Aircraft Construction.* Materials could be bought with the book sample. Many commentators say this introduction of composites into the homebuilding arena is his greatest claim to fame.

He believed in his customers' intelligence. He believed that they could undertake these revolutionary building materials and construct airplanes lighter, stronger, even faster than most aircraft made before.

"A Good Team"

Sally Melvill encouraged an old friend, Patricia Storch, to come to California for a change of scenery after her divorce. Pat began helping out at RAF, doing all sorts of odd jobs, including aerial photography of the new and beautiful airplanes being built at the Mojave Airport. She and Burt took a liking to each other and the two made a good team. They lived and worked together, meeting adventure after adventure on the way.

"We checked out and soloed two of our RAF low-time pilots," the July 1980 newsletter reports, "Sally Melvill [who was] 150-hour Private pilot and Pat Storch (Burt's girlfriend), a 24-hour student pilot.... Both were soloed after one-and-a-half hours of dual instruction."

Sally had flown a Grumman *Tiger*, a *Champion*, and the *VariViggen*. Patricia had flown alone only in the *Tiger*. "Both girls are exceptional pilots, better than average for their amount of flight time."

Patricia takes up the story: "Incredulous—that was my first feeling when they told me they wanted me to solo the *Long-EZ*. 'But I'm only a student! I've only soloed one other airplane! I have less than 25 hours!'

"But they would not be dissuaded, it seemed that I was the only one lacking confidence.

"The day came when it was time to give it a try from the front seat. The cockpit looked foreign, almost hostile. Instruments were not where my eyes wanted them to be. Throttle and stick were in the wrong hands. With my heart in my mouth, Burt and I started the pattern work. Soon I was too busy to be nervous, but I still felt I was reaching for an unattainable goal. Control of the *LongEZ* felt so different, and the full-stall landings I had practiced in the *Tiger* were to be forgotten.

"Then, amazingly, the pieces started falling together. Each landing felt better, the cockpit looked more familiar and a tiny seed of confidence started to bloom. Could it be? Would it really happen? Down to refuel and then..."

Earlier Burt noted that at no time in the checkout did he need to reach for the controls to save the airplane, as sometimes happens in check flights.

"And then came the words I wanted to hear, 'You're ready to go!'"

"My heart was racing once again but this time it was from anticipation and excitement. Lined up on the runway, alone, I took a deep breath and was rolling. The take-off was smooth and felt good. The plane felt fantastic.

"I played in the sky. Up, down, around, turns and steep turns up to 2 Gs. I never expected any experience to equal my first solo, but this surely surpassed it. Flying never felt so good!

"Then came the final test, the landing. It was a little long, but a good one. A *Long-EZ* pilot! I flew the *Long*! I wanted the world to celebrate with me. Flying had just taken on a new dimension.

"I may have landed," Pat wrote, "but I was still in the air and haven't come down yet. What a satisfying, exhilarating experience."

Grass Field Landings

The Rutan designs had small wheels and gear designed to be strong enough for runways, but not for rugged grass and gravel landing strips. Burt decided to develop a grass field/rough field capability for the *Long-EZ* so it could be flown anywhere.

Typically, after designing and installing a spring-loaded nose gear "shock strut" and larger main tires on the *Long-EZ*, Burt flew it into a typical grass field and tested the landing gear. He then announced that with the new modifications, the plane was approved for operation from average grass fields. He still did not recommend that the planes be flown off gravel or other rough surfaces. One reason for this was that the propeller damage would be unacceptable.

VariEzes, however, were not approved for grass landings. This plane landed and took off faster and could not use the larger tires needed.

Builder Trapped!

Funny things happened on the way to building the planes!

A builder wrote to Burt, who published the story in his *Canard Pusher* newsletter, June 1980:

"While doing some finishing work in the back seat of my *VariEze*, I decided to close the canopy to check the rear head rest. It felt great, so I went to open the canopy and, Lo and Behold, the safety catch in the front cockpit was working perfectly!

"There I was, all 210 pounds of me, locked in the back seat with no tools or anything to reach the four inches more required to release the catch. My wife had just gone shopping and was not expected back for nearly an hour.

"Did I panic? Hell yes, because I was getting warm (hot actually), and I decided to use my head and tried to use mind power to move the catch. After that failure, I started thinking some more and it finally dawned on my dulled brain that I had shoes on, which I promptly removed one of and was out in less than five more minutes."

And, the newsletter reported in another instance the builder had no shoes on. He removed his pants, rolled them into a stick and used it to reach the catch!

Amateur Design Work Lethal

Again and again Burt Rutan warned builders to have new designs and alterations checked by the RAF or other qualified engineers. Some builders did not heed his warnings.

One much-modified *VariEze* crashed on its first tests, injuring its designer/test pilot. Another look-alike Rutan design also crashed, killing an experienced pilot.

Rutan urged builders to get appropriate analysis and tests before risking their lives.

Dick Rutan and Mike Melvill Build a Long-EZ

Dick and Mike liked the *Long-EZ* so well that they decided to build two planes for their own use. They did the work on their own time to get a practical, fast aircraft to use. Frankly, too, Dick didn't like to have to ask Burt for the keys to the prototype aircraft. He and Mike set to work in a rented building.

By June 14, 1980, they had picked up the parts for the two airplanes. Twelve days later, working weekends and after work, they had two fuselages assembled and glassed on the outside and were laying out center section spar parts. They were aiming not at a craftsman's perfect Grand Champion airplane but rather for a "plain vanilla," excellent, flying machine.

Gearing Up for Oshkosh '80 and a "Birthday Surprise"

Prefabricated fiberglass parts were now available to builders with RAF approval, beautiful cowlings, strut covers and other parts.

Builders of the *Long-EZs* were pleased to read in July 1980 that Johnny Murphy of Cape Canaveral, Florida, had flown his *Long-EZ*. He and his son were planning to "fly off the test time" [50 hours] and then make a non-stop cross country to Oshkosh 1980, the EAA Convention in Wisconsin.

Murphy had built a *VariEze* and a *Quickie* before this third aircraft. As of July 2, he had eight hours on the airplane and had let three other pilots fly it because it is "so easy to fly."

RAF was busy getting ready for the huge EAA Convention. "RAF will be closed from August 1 through August 12 for Oshkosh," Burt announced.

But before leaving Mojave for Oshkosh, a surprise was in store for Burt Rutan. As May turned over into June, he had attended a Hospitality Club Fly-In, at Kernville, California. There he'd seen Dick take their 91-year-old grandfather, Mr. Goforth, up for the old man's first small airplane ride.

Burt, Patricia and Dick with Rutan family members and 25 airplanes full of builders enjoyed the fly-in. The weather was perfect, there was friendship, music. This was a hard to beat event. But an even more memorable time lay ahead.

On June 21 Burt drove onto the Mojave Airport at about 11 a.m. to find 25 *VariEzes* parked in front of the RAF hangar for a surprise birthday party. Unknown to him, planes had arrived from Canada, California, New Mexico and Texas. Over 120 people had flown and driven in to celebrate!

The next event was planned—a trip with the Rutan aircraft club to the Bahamas. Could this top the birthday party? And just ahead, what would Oshkosh '80 bring?

Oshkosh '80 and More!

Well, the only place it could happen would be the EAA's Oshkosh '80. There, parked together on the green summer grass were 62 *VariEzes*, both of the *Long-EZs* now flying, the prototype *Defiant* and a *VariViggen*.

It looked like a page out of the future. Yet the planes were there at the family-oriented EAA convention, and built by amateur builders, financed by homebuilders themselves. Amazing when you think about it. The builders were pilots, too. Many of them took part in the Oshkosh Air and Formula Races.

Mike and Sally Melvill flew in their *VariViggen* in loose formation out to Oshkosh with Burt and Pat, who were in the *Defiant*. "We had an outstanding trip, flying from Mojave, via Zion National Park to Page, Arizona. We then flew the length of a beautiful lake and directly over the Continental Divide to Denver, where we had lunch." It is interesting to note that flyers think little of flying hundreds of miles before lunch. "Oh yes," they may say, "I left Maryland and stopped for lunch in Georgia!"

From Denver the RAF flight went along to Omaha, Nebraska where they spent the night. The following day they flew directly to Oshkosh, arriving at noon.

As always, "Mom and Pop" Rutan attended the Oshkosh EAA Convention. They helped in the RAF booth, attended seminars and were interviewed regularly.

After a very busy week for the RAF team, the Melvills flew back to Mojave via South Dakota and Utah.

Patricia and Burt spent time with Fred Keller of Anchorage at Oshkosh. Keller won the Grand Champion Homebuilt Trophy. He had to fly a round trip of 7,000 miles to attend. This was the second year in a row that a *VariEze* had taken that award.

As a result of meeting Keller, Pat and Burt flew off to Alaska (in the world's only *Defiant*) to visit with him after the convention. The two young people reveled in this life of new adventure. They appreciated the warm hospitality and the gorgeous Alaskan scenery. Burt was mesmerized by the amphibians and floatplanes everywhere in the

Northland. Wouldn't it be interesting, Rutan mused, to plan within the next year a non-stop distance record in a *Long-EZ* from Nome, Alaska to Puerto Rico?

Bahamas For Christmas?

After the EAA Convention, Dick poured time into completing his *Long-EZ*. He kept the rented building and spent most of his leisure time working on the airplane, dreaming as he worked of the records he could set, the airshows he could fly.

Mike moved his building project over to his two-car garage to make more room. He and Sally pressed to get the *Long-EZ* ready to fly to the Hospitality Club's Bahamas for Christmas jaunt. Mike wondered if they would make it. They needed a lot of little parts, and each one had to be carefully installed to finish the whole project. They figured they had the plane very nearly complete and had spent 458 man hours on it.

Long-EZ Long Distances Flown

In the October 1980 newsletter, Dick reported, matter of factly, amazing long distance flights. He reported attending the Tullahom '80 fly-in. "Myself and my friend Jeana Farrar with baggage for two weeks, flew the 1,600 nautical miles (1,840 statute miles) non-stop."

This 11-hour flight included a detour so that they could see the Grand Canyon at dawn.

Dick also reported that in August 1980 they had flown from San Francisco to Oshkosh, Wisconsin, at over 170 mph, almost the same 1,800-mile distance. Dick commented that in a *Long-EZ* one could go three-quarters of the way across the United States at about 30 percent of the cost of airline fare and faster.

Long-EZ praises flowed in to RAF at Mojave. From France a builder wrote, "It is a wonderful machine." From England to British Columbia; from Ohio to Michigan, builders wrote to praise Rutan aircraft.

Yet Burt had the regrettable duty of reporting five crashes to his customers in the October 1980 newsletter. Two resulted in no injury but three were fatal. With each, Rutan doggedly investigated and made recommendations to help prevent repetitions of the accidents. His work to save lives seemed never ending. This business, he must have reflected, had both its incredible highs and heavy responsibilities.

"Because of the present ridiculous legal liability situation," Burt wrote in October 1980, "we at RAF would never sell any of our experimental aircraft. [Nor sell those built by others.] Both the *VariViggen* and *VariEze* prototypes were donated to the EAA Museum."

The Bahamas for Christmas—1980

Activity at Mojave Airport was at a fever pitch late in 1980. Burt was busy at a dozen known projects, plus a mystery project. Mike and Sally Melvill, with help from Burt,

Patricia, Bruce Evans and the others, pressed to get their *Long-EZ* completed and the 50 hours "flown off," in time to take the plane to the Bahamas for Christmas.

Mike mentioned casually that he was glad to see the engine of the aircraft start so quickly *since he and Sally had overhauled it themselves*! The plane had required 1,200 man hours of work.

Mike and Sally tested the engine and adjusted it carefully. Finally on Sunday, December 21, 1980, Mike taxied the plane out for taxi tests, a lift off and landing.

Then, back at the end of the runway again, with Dick Rutan and Sally in Burt's *Long-EZ*, operating just off his right wing as a chase plane, Mike took off. "It felt absolutely right," Mike reported. It's hard to describe, he said, but when you commit yourself and your new plane to the air for the first time, it's an incredible feeling. The plane was trimmed exactly right. Mike flew for 40 minutes and landed. Sally took it up for its second test flight. She, too, was delighted with it. Just before dusk Burt flew it and was pleased.

What lives these young people were living. There was friendship, contact with the weather, flight into Mojave Desert skies, work with their hands and brains, then the physical and mental challenges of flying the newly-built aircraft themselves!

For Dick Rutan, building his *Long-EZ* was to be a very different experience.

Bahamas Call

The Hospitality Club had plans set for Rutan designs to fly out to the Bahamas. Merrily the RAF contingent set out. Burt and Pat in the *Defiant*, Mike and Sally in Burt's prototype *Long-EZ*.

From all over California Rutan-designed aircraft took off, hop- skipping states, meeting other Rutan homebuilders in Texas and New Mexico. The Rutan aircraft joined up at the St. Lucie County Airport in Florida. The sky and parking area was full of *EZs* from all over the country.

Air traffic controllers sometimes called the planes "small jets."

Still the planes arrived. Three "flights" were set up to make the trip across the water to the Bahamas. Burt and Pat led the first flight in the *Defiant*. The radio channel they used was full of chatter back and forth, weather observations and progress reports.

All flights and planes arrived safely at the sleepy island of San Andros. There were nine *EZs*, one *Long-EZ*, and the *Defiant*. Then the pilots and co-pilots set out to have fun with much the same energy they showed in building and flying airplanes.

There was swimming and sailing in the beautiful waters, snorkeling by Burt and others, reported skinny-dipping by a couple of the feminine contingent, biking, walking, building not a sandcastle but a sand *VariEze* on the beach, partying, music, sight-seeing. "We went native," they claimed, but it was a 21st Century sort of native when you consider the snorkel equipment and aircraft!

Finally, replete with sun and water, after thanking their hosts on the islands, most of the people set out for the mainland. One plane, however, the champion *VariEze* "Pegasus" flown by Norm Ross and Glenne Campbell, went on down the island chain for more adventures and then returned safely to British Columbia after flying 11,000 miles!

Burt and Pat flew back across the nation to Mojave Airport in the *Defiant* to pick up work again. Burt was ready to unveil his mystery project.

Chapter 23

PATRICIA STORCH

I first heard of Patricia Storch when I met her attractive, vivacious mother at Oshkosh 1988. She mentioned that Pat's maternal grandmother had just published a book about coming to America from Lithuania. She and Irene Rutan went on to speak about "Patricia." Later I asked Irene about the name, "Patricia Storch? Who is she?"

"She's a chapter in your book, Vera," Irene replied.

I looked around for information and found that Patricia Storch, according to a Peter Garrison article, helped form the company, SCALED Composites at Mojave in 1982. She is described as Burt Rutan's friend. She was with Burt for five years—1979-84.

In March 1989, I managed to obtain an interview with Patricia Storch in Mojave. We were sitting in a booth at, Reno's, the Mojave eatery. [It was, when the tape was played back later, a very noisy place! Shrieks of children, clatter of dishes, waitress's calling and assorted clangs and bangs were recorded along with Pat's soft voice.]

Patricia and I were almost equally tense at first. After all, this was a reporter here to probe into the life of Burt Rutan and she was an important part of that life. She is a lovely, tall, slender, young woman with a beautiful voice, and clear enunciation. Her manner is gentle, courteous, somewhat tentative, as well it might be under the circumstances.

We both used small talk to get our conversation going. Her remarks helped a great deal to fill in the picture of the life and work of this remarkable man, Burt Rutan.

"I wasn't interested in flying originally for myself, although my father was in the Air Force in World War II. I came out to California to visit Mike and Sally Melvill. I had known them for years. When they first came to this country they were into falconry, and my (then) husband was a falconer. So we met. They lived just a few miles from us. Mike and Sally stood up for me in my first wedding out in Illinois.

"So I got a divorce in '79. Mike and Sally had come out to California, and I was upset, needed a vacation. So I came out for a vacation and Mike and Sally introduced me to Burt, who was also on the rebound from a divorce. We started up this long-distance romance, it got to be quite expensive, our going back and forth to see each other. So Burt convinced me to come to California for the summer.

"The Mojave Desert was a big change, but I liked it, the Western atmosphere. Incredible that we were out here in southern California and yet it seemed more like Arizona or Montana. I miss the winters, though.

"So I came out for the summer and I kid people that, incredibly speaking, the summer's never ended. We went together for almost five years, all through the establishment of SCALED. It's a story in itself. We worked long hours, worked hard, lived together. It was not that. We were both people on the rebound. It was just a relationship that wasn't meant to be. We got along together quite well afterwards.

"You asked how I happened to be at RAF, well they needed some help, so I started working there part-time, then full-time. Then and later at SCALED we always prided ourselves on doing whatever job needed to be done. That's right. I'm now treasurer and office manager. Before we grew to the size we are now I was also the photographer. At the Rutan Aircraft Factory I started out, taking photographs, then Burt needed someone to help out on computer programming, so I did that for a while.

"I feel that if you don't have the background, you can get busy and get it, learn it." Pat said she hasn't been to an Oshkosh Convention in several years.

"When the *Voyager* project first started I was their photographer. I took pictures at Oshkosh that year, 1984 that *Voyager* flew in. They went on later, when they got closer to the flight, to get a PR guy and he hired a photographer."

I commented that Pat had to learn quite a lot about photography.

"Well I'll tell you what, Vera, it was a case of ... the way I got started was at Rutan Aircraft Factory. There'd be a beautiful day with clouds and white buildings. Everyone would jump into airplanes and say, 'Let's take some pictures.' Well this was before I could fly. So when everyone got into a plane, I was the only one left. It turned out to be great fun. I did about 12 magazine covers. I just fell into it.

"I was at the right place at the right time, and willing to do it. I used to be in the baggage compartment, so I'd tie one of the baggage straps to my belt." [To prevent her falling out or being tossed out by turbulence.]

"I was working at Rutan Aircraft Factory when Burt was selling plans. Some of his projects didn't involve homebuilding. The NASA skew-wing aircraft, for example. Another project was a Fairchild Trainer (new generation trainer, NGT) demonstrator that Fairchild wanted to show to the Air Force.

"RAF built a demonstrator model on that. Those two projects were so successful that Herb Iverson, who was at that time vice-president of Ames talked to Burt, Ames actually built the AD-1 and the NGT, but Burt designed it back in California. But it was a long-distance relationship, between New York and California, and Ames told Burt that it would be a lot easier if another setup could be put in place.

"So we got to thinking that a separate company might be a good idea. The designing and the prototype models didn't really have anything to do with homebuilding the RAF's main work."

I comment, "I think Rutan really wants to design, be creative."

"Yes. Very much so. The original plan was for Ames to build a place in California, but then Ames was sold to a French corporation. They decided that they didn't want a place in California. Herb ended up leaving Ames, coming to California and helping set up SCALED.

I asked if Pat were a shareholder, an original investor in SCALED Composites. "No, we got outside investors. Herb and Burt are shareholders, along with our two investors."

"What is your job, Patricia—comptroller?"

"Well, in the very beginning, before we actually incorporated, we had the freedom to work together, to get the financing, then on August 16, we set it up. We've gone through a lot, I'll tell you.

The RAF "family" in the early 1980s numbered six—Dick, Burt, Mike and Sally

Melvill, John Roncz, and Patricia Storch. Jeana Yeager, though not officially working for RAF, was with them, working on the *Long-EZ* and generally helping out as needed.

When writer Peter Garrison arrived for his Wednesday lunch date, the group would adjoin in a body to eat, talk and laugh. They might linger over coffee and pie for an hour then work far into the night to more than make up for that relaxation.

The Mojave Desert location was ideal for such a small, close-knit group of people to operate their own "think tank." The empty land stretched for miles around. The RAF and SCALED Composites group hardly noticed the barren surroundings and lack of artificial entertainment. They were working with the stuff of adventure, of life—and death. Each decision about designs and each bit of advice given to builders was of vital importance to safe flying.

"Have you spoken to Jeana, Vera?" asked Pat. "She would make a good story to write a book about, too. She's a very unusual person, very unusual. She looks so fragile, but she was just driven. There were times during building *Voyager* when I'm sure Dick would have given up, but she would just not let him.

"Jeana has a very interesting history, too. She came out to be with Dick about a year after Burt and I had met. So we four went around together. They were living together and we were living together. It was almost as though she was my sister-in-law."

"When I first met Mrs. Irene Rutan," I told Pat, "she said that Burt had been married four times. Then she paused and said, 'Well three times officially.' "

Patricia smiled, "Mmmmmm."

We commented on the parents. We called Irene a dynamite lady. Pat said that the senior Rutans had always been supportive and fond.

"It must have been fascinating being with these vivid people."

"I certainly am not in their ballpark, but it was great just to be with them."

"Patricia, you are just as interesting but just with different skills and abilities. Say, shifting subjects here, was the *VariEze* an aerobatic airplane? I know Dick often flew it aerobatically."

"Well it wasn't really. It was strong enough, but it doesn't stall unless you go through all sorts of gyrations, so you can't do snap rolls. Also, it wasn't designed for a huge powerplant, so doing vertical things was out. It was meant to be a cross-country airplane. That was its mission."

"Patricia, what was your impression of the desert and all these unusual people when you first came to California?"

"Well, people are the same wherever you go really. I was very much in love with Burt when I came out here and took the desert to heart, and the people. During the relationship with Burt I had to get a lot of interesting and exciting things together. It was a good part of my life and now I'm into another good part of my life.

"When I first moved out here, I had applied to be a full-time paramedic for a firefighting company in Illinois. A couple of months after I moved out here, they called me. I had to reply that the commute would be a little too long! I'm happy the way it went."

119

"Working with these people, on the leading edge of technology must be pretty interesting?"

"I'm glad to have branched out. Not only with aircraft, but you know we did the sail for the America's Cup group and now we're involved in a space project."

Casting about for more understanding, I asked, "What do you think you taught Burt Rutan? Or, what did he teach you?"

"Well, he taught me that you can do anything. You just *do* it! I don't know if I taught him anything. If so, I hope it has to do with human relationships, to be more aware of that, maybe."

This interview helped me to understand of this unusual group of people in the Mojave. It gave me material for this and other chapters in the Rutan story. The RAF team and later the SCALED team, work with rare enthusiasm and dedication. They are in the business, not for the money, but also for the sheer fun of seeing beautiful machines take to the air.

CHAPTER 24

SURPRISING NEW DESIGNS—1981–82

Predator, Solitaire, Twin-Jet, Amsoil Racer,
Commuter Airliner for NASA

The Predator — 1981

Would you expect Burt to have time to even breathe with all the air shows, demonstrations, newsletters and trips—plus the *VariViggen, VariEze, Long-EZ* work to do? He did better than this, without leaking the work-in-progress to the press, Burt designed and built an entirely new aircraft, the *Predator*, his Model 58.

The *Predator*, (it preys on insects) is a proof-of-concept, large, turboprop agricultural aircraft. It features a unique joined-wing and is a strutless biplane. Its estimated hopper payload is an amazing 6,700 pounds.

It was designed as a feasibility study by RAF for an independent contractor, Mr. David Record. Work had begun in late 1978. Yet it was only in the January 1981 newsletter that the first announcement was made: RAF was ready to fly this new design, the agricultural aircraft, *Predator*.

Record's requirement was for an efficient, high-capacity aircraft using the PT-6-34 turboprop engine. It had to have a wide span to allow the spraying of a broad swathe of insecticide, fertilizer or seed. "Stall/spin resistance, visibility and pilot crash protection were also prime considerations," Burt wrote. This was vital since agricultural aircraft operate within a very few feet of the ground and are often heavily loaded. They spray fields that may be surrounded by trees or wires.

The plane had a new look! Burt, after evaluating several configurations, decided on using a connected-tandem wing arrangement. Rutan noted that the concept of joining tandem wings is not a new one. It was originated in the 1920s by Norman Warren and Rex Young of England. More recent work Rutan credits to Dr. Julian Wolkovitch, an aerodynamicist of Palo Alto, California, who used joined wings on a recreational glider prototype. Wolkovitch "has proposed several configurations of wing joining, to make maximum use of the structural benefits of the bracing achieved with large dihedral angles," Rutan stated.

This configuration gave the plane a long span and low induced drag. Locating the hopper to allow for changes in load as the plane works, dispersing its cargo, was an interesting design challenge.

Frankly the plane was one whose performance far exceeded that of other agricultural aircraft available.

NASA's Dynamic Stability Branch at Langley Field, Virginia, was interested in the design. NASA's Joe Chambers and Joe Johnson "who have had the foresight to keep alive an aging 12-foot wind tunnel to investigate many interesting aerodynamic theories and configurations," tested a model of the *Predator*. The NASA wind tunnel testing solved several stability problems and confirmed the performance of the configuration.

It is this kind of basic design research that Burt Rutan enjoys. The project reveals, too, that he was evolving a policy of not mentioning a plane in development until it was ready, or almost ready to fly.

The Solitaire—Rutan's Model 77

Yet, Burt did announce an unfinished design in April 1981. He told reporters that he was entering the Soaring Society of America's contest to design and build a "home-buildable, single-place, self-launching sailplane." At that time, there were 55 official entries in the contest, which had been announced in Sept. and Nov. 1980.

RAF, however, in keeping with its policies of secrecy during design, he kept the details "under its hat," and begged readers of the *Canard Pusher* [April 1981] not to ask for information until the sailplane had successfully been flown. Larry Lombard joined RAF in the summer of 1981. He had built, and was flying, a *VariEze* and had helped build several others in the Sacramento area. Burt told his readers that he planned for Larry to help the self-launching sailplane project along.

During the summer, Burt worked on the aerodynamic development of the sailplane. While at work on this, Burt also continued to refine his research on composite component assembly methods and structural arrangements.

Actually, the sailplane work was a smokescreen for still other secret projects in development that Burt was doing. He very much wanted to design a STOL "bush" airplane, strictly as a research project. It was not to be another homebuilt design. Yet, if word got around that he was working on a new design, builders might think that he was planning an improved *Long-EZ* and stop buying those plans to wait for better ones. Burt had been interested in sailplane design for some time. Now he had time and private space to work in his "skunkworks" on both his new aircraft.

In fall 1981 the sailplane gained a name—the *Solitaire*. The name was suggested by RAF employee, Roger Houghton. Burt also disclosed that it would have a retracting propeller. Flight tests were set to start in January 1982. "If flight tests planned are successful, the *Solitaire* will be offered for homebuilder construction. Please don't ask us about the sailplane," Burt pleaded, "we're very busy with the completion and test program."

Mike Melvill was in on the first sketches of the *Solitaire* that Burt drew on a yellow pad. Eventually, after changes, there was a forward canard, a straight wing, and pilot position was to be at the center of gravity so that no ballast would be required. The engine was to retract, propeller and all, into the forward fuselage.

Melvill said that construction on the *Solitaire* itself began in December 1981 and it was complete and ready to fly by May 28, 1982. Melvill was test pilot on the project. First flights went well. The engine worked smoothly and the controls responded fine. The innovative "spoilflap" worked as they had hoped it would. With canard designs, glide path

The Rutan motor glider, *Solitaire*.
Photo courtesy Burt Rutan (RAF).

control is a challenge, Melvill notes. Burt designed a device that trailed from the main wing, when desired, to add drag without a lift change, the "spoilflap."

At Oshkosh '82, the *Solitaire*, towed by car to Wisconsin, was towed aloft by Burt's *Grizzly*. (An experimental towing an experimental!)

A dreaded hazard with sailplane flying is when a tow rope breaks on takeoff. Burt's sailplane would not stall or spin. This was to be a great comfort to Melvill when the tow rope broke one day at Oshkosh. Melvill turned back toward the Wittman Field with only 200 feet under him. Would he make it?

Yes. The *Solitaire's* glide was more than adequate! He landed safely.

Mike and Burt, test flying the sailplane, had found that the risk of fire in a design with the whole engine buried in the fuselage, and the propeller only extended, was unacceptable. A better plan, Burt decided, was to cause both the engine and the propeller to extend into the airstream. As the RAF crew returned from Oshkosh '82, contest time was getting near. Back at Mojave Airport, Burt made his first flight in the *Solitaire*.

The Soaring Society of America (SSA) rules demanded that the sailplanes meet a static load test of seven G's. With the *Solitaire* upside down on a table, cushioned by foam blocks, bags of lead shot weighing 25 pounds each, were laid on its wings. After testing the canard for strength (at 4.67 Gs), it was then loaded for the ultimate strength (at 7 Gs). The canard took the strain (900 pounds of lead shot) without damage, and returned to normal position when the weights were removed.

Now for the main wing. As the wings were loaded with more and more shot, the tips bent toward the floor over 45 inches! In all 1932 pounds of weight were carefully taped onto the wing. "It was scary," Melvill said. "As it turned out, like the canard, the wing did not make a sound and returned to its normal relaxed position as soon as the weight was removed."

Dive speeds, full spoilflaps, loops, split Ss and wingovers seemed quite safe to Mike whenever he recalled the tremendous loads that the sailplane could stand.

The 1982 SSA contest was held in Tehachapi, California (20 miles west of the Mojave Airport) so the sailplane was flown over there. Burt and the *Grizzly* towed the sailplane and Mike over the ridge of the mountains near Tehachapi. While Mike loafed aloft, Burt went along into the Fantasy Haven Airport and landed. Mike arrived with three consecutive loops and a series of wingover turns to lose height. He then made a high speed pass and pulled up into the pattern and landed.

The sailplane was opened up to reveal its features to the judges. While at the SSA meet, Burt made his first tow-assisted flight in the sailplane.

Finally, on the last day of the contest, the *Solitaire* was declared the winner. Melvill says, "The whole purpose of our design was realized: to make the best homebuilt available to promote soaring."

"Later that afternoon," Melvill writes, "I fired up the engine and flew my first powered cross-country back to Mojave. The same week Sally Melvill and Burt's brother, Dick, flew the *Solitaire*. Both were delighted. Burt was invited to have the *Solitaire* fly in the Society of Experimental Test Pilots Air Show,... quite an honor."

Meanwhile, in Mojave in the spring of 1981 ...

Video Completed

As though still not busy enough, Burt supervised the making of a videotape on construction techniques used in building moldless foam/fiberglass aircraft structures. It ran for 96 minutes and showed every phase of construction including health precautions, foam preparations, hot wiring, damage repair, epoxy mixing and the use of micro balloons, fiberglass and much more. The tape could be purchased from RAF.

Apple Enters Newsletter Production

Other projects included putting the *Canard Pusher* on the Apple computer. This helped Burt keep in closer touch with his builders and the builders in touch with RAF.

Skew-Wing Aircraft at NASA

The RAF-designed AD-1 jet research aircraft successfully completed its initial flight tests with the wing being skewed up to its 60-degree limit. Flying qualities even at "full-skew" were better than anticipated.

Burt understandably gloated over the fact that the AD-1 airframe and its two engines had required no repair or unscheduled maintenance during the test program. "The 100 percent availability is unusual for a research aircraft," he commented.

A Rueful Dick Rutan

Dick reported in the April 1981 newsletter some advice for builders: "Keep it stock. Don't make modifications from the design."

He ruefully reported that he had tried modifications on the *Long-EZ* design. Whereas the one built by the Melvills was running as "smooth as a Swiss watch." Dick's plane was a disappointment to him.

He had installed a more powerful engine than the plans called for, revised the canard airfoil, made longer ailerons, and made several other changes. His plane, he reported, when he flew it in April 1981, had major problems. The big engine overheated, the revised canard airfoil lost speed-stability at high speed, and the aircraft had very poor stall characteristics. Also, the plane was not as fast as the standard *Long-EZ*.

It was hard for Dick to have to bring these facts out. Yet he did so in the April *Canard Pusher* in order to help other builders avoid his mistakes. "I'll fix the problems but it will take some time and effort. In retrospect, I wish I had stayed more standard.

"I don't recommend any of the changes I made and wish I had not," Dick reports honestly. He did not specifically say that his brother was an excellent designer and knew what he was doing with engines, controls and canards—yet the inference is strongly there in Dick's frank admissions.

He also announced that he was now deeply involved in a whole new project, the *Voyager* around-the-world program.

Irene at EAA's Sun n' Fun Fly-In

At the 1981 spring fly-in in Florida, RAF had an effective and slightly unlikely champion, Burt's mother Irene Rutan. This tiny woman moved briskly about the Florida airfield and recorded 24 *VariEzes,* and a *Long-EZ* that flew in to Lakeland to attend the event.

Irene and the builders of Rutan aircraft were mutually charmed with each other. She reported back to Mojave Airport saying that the pilots/builders were "the finest people in the country" and she was "proud to see so many beautiful ships flown in." She thanked those at the fly-in who were so gracious to her and admitted that she loved every minute of her stay.

She told RAF that people at the air meet are still asking [about the Rutan airplanes] "Where's the tail wheel?" and "What's that solar panel for?" and finally, "Where's Burt Rutan?"

She and George Rutan were also asked about Burt's new projects but smiled away the questions.

Twin-jet Research Aircraft Mentioned—Rutan's Model 73

Barely mentioned in the July *Canard Pusher* was "design support for a new twin-jet research aircraft being built for a major aerospace company."

Burt gave more space to an upcoming CAFE 250 Race (Competition in Aircraft Fuel Efficiency) held in June 1981 in Santa Rosa, California. There were 27 commercially-built aircraft and 20 experimental aircraft at the meet. The top nine winners were fiberglass aircraft—and the top five "did not have a horizontal tail."

Jeana Yeager was there, flying the Melvills' *Long-EZ*; Mike Melvill flew Burt's prototype *VariEze*; Dick flew the Rutan prototype *Long-EZ*; and Burt flew the *Defiant* with Pat Storch as his navigator.

Anchorage, Alaska to Grand Turk Island, British West Indies

Dick Rutan and Jeana Yeager left for Alaska on May 22, 1981, but had to wait in Anchorage for 14 seemingly endless days for wind and weather conditions good enough to make the record attempt.

Once aloft, Dick took his much-modified *Long-EZ* up to over 12,000 feet. He flew for 29.5 hours, over a distance of 4,690 statute miles. Once at Grand Turk, he loafed about in the air for another half-hour to make the time 30.08 hours! Commenting about this remarkable demonstration of endurance and flying skill, he mentioned only that toward the end of the flight his Arctic clothing became uncomfortable and that he had to fly through the night with limited instruments [a turn and bank gyro after his vacuum pump failed].

He would have liked to have flown on to make the distance 5,000 miles, but fuel and lack of landing sites prevented this. As it was, he broke the world distance record. Dick loved these record flights. Now that he had his own *Long-EZ*, he planned to make still others, try for the world altitude record and for some of the world speed records.

NA&S Museum Anniversary

In July 1981, the National Air and Space Museum in Washington, D.C., held a full week's celebration of the fifth anniversary of their opening. The museum has opened its doors on the nation's 200th birthday. Now officials invited the Experimental Aircraft Association (EAA) local members to place a display of five homebuilt aircraft just outside the museum. Builder Bob Woodall of EAA Chapter 4 was invited to show his *VariEze*. "I jumped at the chance," he said. "The five planes were flown into Andrews Air Force Base, outside D.C., and hauled fully-assembled on flatbed trucks through the city of Washington in the middle of the night to the museum. What a sight!"

The owners/pilots, with generous help from EAA Chapters 4 and 186, provided personnel at each aircraft for 12 hours a day to answer visitors' questions. Thousands visited the display. There was always a crowd around Bob's *VariEze*.

Bob will never forget one incident that week. Burt Rutan stopped by to chat and told Bob of an idea he had for an aircraft that could fly around the world without refueling, non-stop. "This was in July of 1981," Bob notes. "Then Burt proceeded to sketch the *Voyager* design on the back of a business envelope and left it with me!"

Bewildering Blaze of Activity Ends 1981 Third Quarter

Many an aircraft designer is proud to have one design, or perhaps two, to his name. In one paragraph Burt Rutan casually mentions a few of his activities going on in the October *Canard Pusher* that stagger the imagination. How could he carry off all these designs? This genius for doing the impossible is precisely why this biography is being written. It is, in actuality, an incredible story that nevertheless happened, and is happening!

Here's the October 1981 paragraph from the *Canard Pusher*:

"Since the last newsletter RAF Activity has involved: the Oshkosh Convention trip, builder support, development of our RAF Model 77 Sailplane, engineering flight tests of our RAF Model 73 Jet, flight tests of the RAF Model 68 Amsoil Racing Biplane, design of the RAF Model 78 and 79 commuter airliner for NASA wind tunnel testing, flying for several TV programs, laminar-flow flight measurements, flight demos, construction demos, and preparing a video tape to illustrate the flight test preparation of a new *Long-EZ*."

Only a Burt Rutan, known for his capacity for work and for generating loyal assistance from a team, could undertake even half these activities.

He enjoys this press of interesting activity. "There's just not time enough," he says, "to do all the interesting things I'd like to do."

Among other things, he reported, "Some very spectacular footage of *Long-EZs*, *VariViggen* and *Defiant* has been shot this summer and fall for several scheduled TV programs to be aired this fall."

In 1980 and 1981, personnel under Joe Chambers at the NASA Langley Research Center in Virginia, built a full-scale mode of the *VariEze*. They tested it in the 30-by-60 foot wind tunnel. One of the many tests they did was to measure the extent of smooth flow (natural laminar flow) on the airfoil surfaces. They found that the model was getting more extensive laminar flow—low drag flow—than theory predicted. Next they wanted to verify this in flight.

So, in September 1981, Langley officials contracted with Bob Woodall of Maryland to bring the *VariEze* he had built to Langley Field for a week of flight testing. Dr. Bruce Holmes was test director and flew in the rear set of the plane on most of the flights. Holmes was able to get good correlation with the wind tunnel findings. It was concluded that the extensive natural laminar flow of the *VariEze* is a significant factor in the excellent performance of the design.

NASA's Holmes and Phil Brown [test pilot] came to RAF to study the remarkable Rutan designs. They wanted to see with their own eyes how the wings and canards performed, and to find out how Rutan got the amazing results that he was getting with these innovative aircraft.

The NASA men were amazed to find the *Long-EZ* so docile in not wanting to stall, and refusing to spin. It is interesting to note that Burt was willing to let these pilots put his beloved aircraft through grueling programs of testing.

Fairchild Trainer—Model 73

"RAF," Rutan writes in his October 1981 newsletter, "is conducting an instrumented flight test program for a major aerospace firm." The new aircraft he tested was a scaled flight demonstrator for Fairchild Republic's proposal for the Air Force's next generation flight trainer (NGT) program.

The full-scale aircraft, designed by Fairchild Republic, was a two-place, fuel-efficient, twin-engine turbofan trainer. It was intended for modernizing the Air Force T-37 fleet.

In early 1981, Fairchild Republic contracted with the Ames Industrial Corporation to design, build and test the scaled flight demonstrator. Fairchild supplied accurate lofts of the external shape of their design. Ames turned to RAF to design the structure and systems of the 62 percent sized demonstrator, and to conduct the flight test program.

Ames had built the Rutan-designed AD-1 skew-wing aircraft for NASA in 1978. The skew-wing plane had then been shipped out to RAF for flight testing.

Within weeks, RAF had carried out initial flight tests on the NGT and prepared the plane for even more strenuous ones. The Fairchild Trainer flew nicely, Burt reported in October 1981. "Four different pilots flew the first four flights—one having no previous turbo-jet experience!" The entire (except spins) instrumented engineering flight test program was completed at RAF in an incredibly fast, 15-day time period.

The Model 73, scaled-down demonstrator of Fairchild's Next Generation Trainer proposal is small. At 842 pounds empty weight, the scale model has a 21.8-foot wingspan and is probably the world's smallest twin-engine jet.

"The all-composite, moldless-construction prototype flight demonstrator concept," Burt wrote in October 1981, "is proving to be a valuable, economical engineering tool for aircraft development." Burt pressed this point at every opportunity. Even though active in helping homebuilders, he flew to air meets, did test flying and designing, and had an eye on the future. He could see what a tremendous breakthrough this new type of aircraft construction was for testing new ideas.

By January 1982 Rutan reported that the design and prototype construction effort took eight months. "The aircraft was shipped to RAF in early September 1981. Within eight weeks, RAF flew it, instrumented it, and flew test flights including [after development of spin recovery parachute device] spin tests.

"The use of manned, scaled flight demonstrator produced higher quality data than other methods, particularly for areas such as spin susceptibility and departure stall recovery." Burt commented on the time and cost savings of this method of development. Further, actually flying a scaled-down prototype, with a test pilot aboard, much more data can be discovered than with wind tunnel testing alone.

Like the Wright brothers, Rutan builds the plane and then, if necessary, draws the detailed plans.

The Amsoil Racer—Model 68

Another canard-equipped aircraft, the *Amsoil Racer* was a sleek Rutan design with a T-tail.

Late in 1979, Burt Rutan had designed the *AMS/Oil Racer* design, which was built by a team in Sacramento, for customer Dan Mortensen, of Newcastle (near Sacramento), California. About 4,000 man-hours fabricated the racer. Over 40 members of EAA Chapters 52 and 526 at Sacramento and Roseville, California, worked on the project.

In fact, builders Mike Dilley and Larry Lombard worked so much on the project that later, both of them went to work for Rutan at SCALED Composites. These two men had started and operated a business called Revolutionary Propeller Manufacturing (RPM), which generated so much business carving propellers that, for a time, they had to refuse more orders.

The racing biplane had to fit racing specifications. It was designed to use a 160 horsepower engine, to go 250 mph on the straight and to sustain 4 G turns safely. In 1980 Mortensen received sponsorship from the Amsoil Company, a company marketing synthetic lubrication, to build and race a prototype *Amsoil Racer*. The aircraft was completed in August 1981 by the Sacramento team of builders.

Dick Rutan and Mike Melvill flew the initial flight test program.

The AMS/OIL Racer

In September 1981 it was entered in the Reno Air Races. It turned in several record-exceeding laps during a heat race but finished third in the final race due to several pylon cuts. After the race the pylon cuts were attributed to roll deficiency in the control system.

In October 1981, Mortensen brought the racer to RAF so that they could evaluate it and help him complete its development. Once the roll deficiency was corrected by giving the controls more travel and eliminating stiffness, the *Racer* proved to be "an excellent flying machine," Burt said. "With good firm flying qualities at its 240-mile-per-hour racing speed."

For the first time in his designs, Burt used a horizontal tail on an aircraft, a T-tail. He knew the racer would need excellent control to survive the 6 G vertical turns possible at Reno.

Later, the plane had its misfortunes. In 1983, Mortensen lost part of a propeller blade, suffered intense vibration but managed to shut down the engine, and landed on a National Guard airstrip. After a month of repair the plane was ready for Reno '83.

Mortensen qualified at Reno '83 at over 200 mph. Flying the race Mortensen found himself trapped when another pilot turned in front of him. He could not pull up without hitting other aircraft so tried to dive out underneath. He almost made it, but due to encountering propwash, hit the ground almost level at 200 mph. Mortensen, though black and blue from seat belts, walked away from the accident—a tribute to the materials, workmanship and design of the aircraft. It was a one-of-a-kind airplane. The University of Illinois is rebuilding it as a project that may take some years.

Ah! Oshkosh 1981

The high point in every homebuilder's year is either going to the EAA Convention at Oshkosh, Wisconsin, or reading and dreaming about it.

The RAF team was no exception. Burt sat down and prepared a lecture on basic ways to fly performance flight tests. The new videos were packed. Irene and George ("Mom" and "Pop") set out for Oshkosh.

Burt's RAF team took four planes to the convention in 1981. Burt and Patricia flew there in the *Defiant*. Larry and Janet Lombard flew the prototype Rutan *Long-EZ*, Sally Melvill and her son, Keith, flew the Melvill *Long-EZ*. Mike Melvill and his mother, Isobel, flew out to Wisconsin in the *VariViggen*.

As is true of the EAA organization itself and the convention each year, attendance is a family affair. Young and old mingle.

At beautiful Aspen, Colorado, Burt's four-plane flight landed around 11 a.m.—Too late to leave this "super place," Burt declared. As a result the team spent an afternoon and evening relaxing there. The next morning the departure was to be made from an elevation of 10,800 feet above sea level. So Mike Melvill decided that his mother should fly in the twin-engine *Defiant*. Mike by himself got the *VariViggen* off the ground successfully, but his rate of climb was a dismal 200/300 feet per minute! (Pilots always have to think about weight at high-altitude fields.)

Burt pulled ahead in his *Defiant* to scout the weather for the RAF flight. It was decided, via radio cross-talk, to cross the Continental Divide west of Boulder, Colorado and go to Hastings, Nebraska for a lunch break. From there it was an easy flight on into Wisconsin.

The EAA Convention was bigger than ever this year—more planes, more people. Irene Rutan set to work logging in over 60 Rutan aircraft that landed, and getting the aircraft registration number and pilot's name. She and George Rutan welcomed each one and handed them the new RAF shoulder patch.

As always the Rutan seminars were filled to overflowing and the sleek Rutan-designed aircraft generated intense interest. In fact, builders told them the *VariViggens* and other Rutan designs brought out scores of people to look longingly at the attractive planes at every airport. Pilots of big company jets and airline pilots all begged rides in Rutan airplanes when they saw them, not only at Oshkosh, but at gas stops everywhere.

After a hectic week of holding seminars, talking to builders, flying in the afternoon airshows, the RAF aircraft took off for home via separate routes. It was always a good opportunity to visit relatives and friends on the way back to California. All in all, after the convention, it was found that the RAF aircraft had logged 110 hours, 20,000 miles of flight, with no mechanical problems!

Tender Problem

How to tell aircraft builders about this? The only way was to just do it, Burt decided. So, in the October issue of his newsletter he warned that when mounting a transponder antenna under the front (pilot's) seat, one must be aware that a sensitive part of the pilot's anatomy is in very close proximity to some quite high powered microwave energy.

"To put it bluntly," Burt wrote, "it may be a little like sticking your fanny into a microwave oven!" He recommended that it might be prudent to laminate a sheet of aluminum foil under the seat to shield the occupant.

October 1981 News

The *Canard Pusher* for October contained a mass of data on changes, improvements, cautions, recommendations, news of the RAF activities and ways to prevent accidents. One correspondent wrote that he had not secured the gas cap and had lost fuel. He noticed it when he lost power over the Sangre de Christos mountain range.

Heading for the plains, the *VariEze* pilot, from 12,000 feet, spotted the distinctive shape of the Air Force Academy Chapel. He glided 20 miles, "straight into the Academy's north-south runway, unannounced, uneventful and followed by lots of red tape."

Secret Project Under Wraps

No leak to the press yet, but in 1981 Burt had another secret project being designed and built in his Mojave Airport hangar. He planned to roll it out in 1982.

CHAPTER 25

VOYAGER IDEA EMERGES

The Voyager Experience/Phenomena—1981-82

The *Voyager* story. It was one in which the aim was clear, a grand thing in today's rather unclear world. It was much like the World War II years when the fight was for freedom; like the search for a polio vaccine to save the children—the aim was clear, the danger great, the experience intense.

The *Voyager* idea took over our American imagination for the days it flew. It was a vindication of sorts of our times—often circumscribed, materialistic, boring—that the *Voyager* flew. In the face of formidable odds, the drama played. It starred a greatly gifted young aircraft designer, a young woman with enormous talent and courage, and an ex-fighter pilot with raw courage and a "velvet arm."

The aircraft was built with only grassroots money, not federal funds, donated industry money and equipment.

The Voyager People

What fate brought the three key people involved in Voyager together? Tiny, talented young Jeana Yeager met a lanky, ex-fighter pilot, Dick Rutan, and these two joined forces with the aviation visionary and designer, Burt Rutan.

Dick Rutan gives one the impression of an elemental force; raw power; he is almost unreasonably determined. His flying skills are tuned not only to the feel of aircraft in the air, an old-fashioned "seat-of-the-pants" talent, but also to today's complexities of numbers and electronics.

In Dick, the confidence or arrogance that is needed to attempt and carry out such a venture is strong.

Jeana Yeager—was there ever such a woman! Dedicated, loyal, a consummant flyer and systems operator. She demonstrated unstoppable determination. In the years that it took to build and fly *Voyager*, she showed brilliant organizational and business skills, too.

Hers were many of the innovative ideas for raising funds. She and Burt's mother, Irene, had faith in the grassroots forces, in American capitalism. She helped to hold together the people involved in the building project and the flight itself.

The male territoriality can be seen in the Dick-Jeana relationship. The masculine need to dominate, take center stage, to blot up attention without realizing that is what is happening—this was strong in Dick Rutan. It was a natural, but annoying and probably hard-to-live with, characteristic in him.

You can see this in the excellent book *Voyager*, by Jeana Yeager and Dick Rutan with Phil Patton. This gives in detail the trials and tribulations, the joys and achievements, of building the plane and of making the around-the-world flight.

Who designed the *Voyager*? Burt Rutan. Other names have been mentioned, and several designers had shown interest in the possibility of flying around the world, unrefueled, but *Voyager* was a Rutan design.

Voyager did not break the non-stop endurance record set over 30 years ago, which still stands. It was in the air a few minutes more than nine days.

Back in 1958, in a Cessna 172, pilots Robert Timm of Las Vegas and John Cook of Los Angeles took off from McCarran Airport in Las Vegas on Dec. 4, 1958 at 3:52:55 p.m. and landed back there at 2:11:55 p.m. on Feb. 7, 1959. Total time aloft, 64 days, 22 hours, 19 minutes and 5 seconds!

Fitted with a special belly tank that brought the total fuel capacity up to 140 gallons, the 172 has to be fueled just once a day. This was accomplished each morning on a blocked off section of public highway near Blythe, CA—from a hose passed up from a speeding gas truck! On the first refueling run, the airplane's tires were painted by a crew member on the truck so that the (then) Civil Aeronautics Administration (CAA) could determine daily thereafter whether a landing had been made during the flight.

"Comfortwise Timm and Cook fared better than Dick and Jeana were to do—they slept on a contour mattress, had a hot meal each evening and took sponge baths each day."

Voyager Background

The idea of going around the world unrefueled was not Rutan's alone. A competitor was working to try for the world's long-distance flight record (Tom Jewett and his associates).

Also, several other designers had talked about such a project. Paul MacCready, who had developed the manpowered *Gossamer Condor* aircraft series, was interested by the idea but saw that Rutan was well along. Jim Bede had mentioned the idea, and was reported to be working with Jerry Mullins of Oklahoma City, Oklahoma. Also, Terry Bloodworth of Memphis, Tennessee was thinking about a U-2-like design. Julian Nott of London had ideas for a balloon flight.

Dick and Burt had sometimes talked about the possibility of making an around-the-world record flight, but had not given it any more weight than a score of other interesting projects they discussed, until ... one day Burt, Dick and Jeana were having lunch at a now-vanished eatery, the Mojave Inn.

Dick had been talking to Burt about his dissatisfaction with his present work at RAF. Why not take one of his brother's designs and produce it, pay Burt a royalty? Jeana and Dick agreed they would like to produce an acrobatic plane designed by Burt. They would call their company Monarch Aviation (but that name proved to have been taken, they learned later).

Seated in a horseshoe-shaped booth at the (then) Mojave Inn, Burt made a counter suggestion. Burt said: "Sure, you can do Monarch, but why don't you just do this round-the-world flight first? It won't take very long—six months or a year."

134

The three looked at each other. Was Burt serious? He was. They thought for a moment and then said, "Let's do it!" Burt laid out the basic design ideas. On a paper napkin he drew a sketch showing an extremely long wing. There were two engines. The occupants of the plane had a central cabin. There was a canard out front. Composite materials would make the plane light enough to carry fuel for the entire flight without designing unusual engines.

Dick comments in the book, *Voyager*, that he had been thinking about his career to date, and where it was leading, about what he would be remembered for. He was thinking, with the *Voyager* project, about this last frontier to be conquered, and thinking about posterity.

By the time the trio walked out into the hot California sunshine they were dazed with excitement. Voyager had well and truly begun that day in February 1981.

Burt took the napkin, stained with teriyaki sauce, and went back to his desk to work out more details. He called it #76. It was the seventy-sixth design in his notebook.

Voyager Design

Rutan has often been heard to say that the entire design of *Voyager* was made up of only 11 drawings. This was not a popular statement with Dick and Jeana whose whole lives for years were dedicated to the *Voyager* project.

Some very strict design requirements had to be met. Enough fuel had to be placed somewhere in the aircraft to last around 28,000 statute miles. Two engines would be needed. A crew of at least two was necessary with room for one to sleep at times. Weather and winds had to be considered.

By March 1981 the design was completed. Burt had used his computer to good effect. The plane now had two long booms which would not only help carry fuel but would strengthen the aircraft and stabilize it. The canard now helped brace the twin booms. The vertical stabilizers were moved to the rear of the booms. The flying wing idea was discarded in favor of a long, very slender wing. The passenger compartment housed a pusher engine and a puller engine.

Formula and computer work showed that the flight would require around 1,500 gallons of 100-octane aviation gasoline, around 9,000 pounds of fuel. How this fuel was to be stored—used so as not to disastrously affect control, weight and balance; and equipped with valves simple enough to operate during a very long and very demanding flight—that was the main and essential question. The pilots would need to know where their fuel was, how the weight was distributed and how many gallons were left.

When the news of the *Voyager* project came out in the spring of 1981, Tom Jewett, building the *Free Enterprise* for a long-distance flight record attempt, was incensed, saying that *Voyager* was taking his idea for around-the-world flight. Both teams continued to work at the Mojave Airport on these similar missions.

Burt, at first, left to his brother and Jeana the long, drawn out task of building the huge aircraft, raising the money and finding the equipment. He had a dozen projects going at the moment.

This was somewhat provoking to Dick and Jeana. They had hoped Burt would devote more energy to the project, but they carried on, never relenting.

Even though Burt retained a considerable share of ownership in the project, for a time, he had less and less to do with it as other projects claimed his attention. He saw it, ultimately, as a money-making undertaking. Later, however, Burt sold his interest to Dick.

The brothers grew cool towards one another. Dick resented the fact that Burt was too busy and gave so little time to the building of *Voyager*.

Building Voyager

Every lay-up and connection of the *Voyager* construction was of vital importance. Each was actually a matter of life or death.

Burt, himself, was awed by the size of the aircraft and the required effort.

A corporation called Voyager Aircraft was set up to carry out the project. Sponsorship, however, turned out to be very slow indeed. For one thing, the Rutans turned down cigarette advertising sponsorship. They do not smoke. They also didn't want to advertise tabloid newspapers, fast foods or sodas, nor did they want *Voyager* to become a government project. They wanted their *Voyager* project to represent energy, health and American enterprise.

The first corporate sponsor and most important aid came from the Hercules company, which donated Magnamite graphite composites which made up 90 percent of the airplane. Teledyne Continental engine makers and the builder of King radios (avionics up to a value of $250,000), did come through, but even so, the bulk of the funds raised had to be scratched for over the months, as Dick and Jeana toiled. After about two years, it was apparent that corporate sponsorship was not to materialize. The effort expended to attract backing and the disappointments they experienced were almost unendurable.

Voyager people then turned to the EAA and its members. "Grassroots" money did come in. These people understood what the Rutans and Jeana Yeager wanted to do. They also understood the heroic flying and the heroic fundraising and building needed.

"Mom" and "Pop" Rutan pitched in with their time, work, energy, encouragement and other support.

Dick and Jeana flew their *Long-EZ* on several record hops during 1982. This was done, in part, to build up credibility for their *Voyager* flight.

Big Bird/Free Enterprise

On the clear, bright morning of July 2, 1982, the plane built to try for the world's long-distance flight record and its designer, was approaching the Mojave Airport to land toward the north, northwest. Suddenly the airplane rolled steeply, the nose went down, the plane dove almost vertically down and crashed.

The *Voyager* group, despite their uneven relationship with Jewett, were depressed and saddened. This was a great loss. Gone was a gifted designer and pilot, a brave and able man.

It pointed out, strongly, the hazards that faced pioneering designers and pilots.

Bruce Evans

One day in 1982, a man who was to be a pivotal person in the *Voyager* program, Bruce Evans, landed at the Mojave Airport. He was curious about the rumors that an around-the-world airplane was to be built. Planning to stay a few days and look around, he ended up agreeing to work on the *Voyager* and stayed over four years. He became indispensable as the *Voyager* ground crew chief and Dick and Jeana's best friend and honorary brother.

Evans is an interesting man. His way of taking a break from his work was to fly down to Baja, Mexico. He often wore a shirt that had a slogan printed on the front: "Everyone has to believe in something, and I believe I'll have another beer!" Above his desk at Mojave was the Zen saying, "To travel rather than to arrive." Evans, seeing the obstacles in the way of the success of the *Voyager* flight, had serious doubts about it.

Jeana and Dick say in their book, *Voyager*, that Bruce did most of the building on the airplane. A craftsman, he worked at full throttle. He served, too, as a calming force when nerves frayed and tempers flared. This was especially helpful in serving as liaison between the two Rutan brothers.

This serving as a liaison was often needed. There was a constant struggle between the pilots who wanted more equipment, a radar for example, and the designer, who stood firm against adding any weight to the plane. The *Voyager* team began to wryly say, "If you can throw it up and it comes down again, it's too heavy!"

Burt succeeded in impressing on the team the need to carve away the ounces and keep the weight down. Dick and Jeana gained concessions on radio and radar equipment—needed for survival.

Would they be able to do it? Where would all the dollars, equipment and man hours come from? Amazingly, the *Voyager* project was only one of a dozen or more Burt was concerned with.

CHAPTER 26

SCALED COMPOSITES COMPANY

1982

SCALED Composites was founded in 1982. It is located near the original, small Rutan Aircraft Factory shop at the Mojave Airport. SCALED occupies a roomy hangar-office building on the flight line.

As these past pages have shown, ideas, designs, and prototype aircraft were proliferating from Burt Rutan's mind and computer. He had financed, after that first loan from his parents, all the designs and other work himself. He operated at a profit. This in itself may seem to many to be a remarkable achievement!

Yet, if he had even more money and room, Burt knew he could bring more of his own designs to life. He could take on more projects to build test-of-concept, research and test scaled-down prototype aircraft for the industry. How could this expansion be achieved?

The January 1982 *Canard Pusher* made the first announcement of the formation of the new company:

"New Company, SCALED, Inc., will do research projects. Since the successful completion of the Fairchild 62 percent NGT program in November '81 there has been a great deal of interest in RAF's capability to design, develop, fabricate and flight test new aircraft concepts at low cost and short schedule. Because of this interest, Herb Iversen, general manager of Ames, the company that built the NASA AD-1 (Skew-Wing) and the Model 73 (twin-jet research aircraft), is forming a new company to deal exclusively with this new type of business.

"Burt will do the design work and the flight testing for the new company.

"No changes are planned for RAF. RAF plans to continue to support builders of RAF-designed homebuilts and to develop new designs for homebuilders.

"The new company will be called SCALED, Inc. The SCALED is, in fact, an acronym for 'Scaled Composites: the Advanced Link to Efficient Development.' Pat Storch spent several late nights and the better part of a carafe of white wine to come up with that name.'"

"SCALED will be based on Mojave Airport next door to RAF. The new facility will conduct the entire program of contracting, design, fabrication, testing and reporting. Proposed customers for SCALED include any agency requiring aerodynamic, systems or structural research data early in the development cycle. To date, proposals include next-generation general aviation designs, commuter airliners and military applications."

Burt closed his short description of the new company with a request for personnel: a French-speaking secretary, a computer fanatic, instrument technician.

"If you are more concerned with interesting, challenging work than in civilization and culture, you might consider a move to our Mojave Desert to get in on some real stimulating projects."

This last note was later to have its ironic echoes when Burt was affiliated with the Beech Aircraft Company.

Early SCALED Composites Days

Talking to Patricia Storch in Reno's Restaurant in March 1989, I asked her to think back and tell some anecdotes about the start of the SCALED Composites Company. She smiled.

"I was reminded of a story the other day. When we first met with our investors, these people just wrote us out a couple of personal checks that were in six digits! And we were impressed, well, floored really. We had never seen any check for that much money, let alone a personal check for that amount.

"Anyway, Burt and I, Herb and his wife, had a wonderful time at dinner that night and Burt handed the cashier one of the checks, 'Will you take this?' I really think she thought it wasn't real. It took her time to recover from the shock."

Aviation writer Peter Garrison, reported on the formation of the new company this way: "In 1982 Rutan, together with his friend, Patricia Storch and a new partner, Herbert Iversen, with a few investors, formed SCALED Composites, a job shop whose purpose was to produce, quickly and economically, scaled-down flying prototypes of new designs for other companies."

The first work carried out by SCALED was for the Fairchild Aircraft Company, building a scaled-down version of the Fairchild "New Generation Trainer (NGT)." This new design was Fairchild's proposal for the USAF competition for a design to replace the T-37 Trainers. Fairchild was the successful competitor.

The next assignment for SCALED was a design for the Lotus Company, a two-place canard design, the "Microlight."

This was a two-place, side-by-side airplane of the 300-pound empty weight class (to meet British microlight requirements). It has a slightly swept-back canard forward and swept back wings with winglets at the tips.

This brand new European Microlight was developed for Colin Chapman, former director of the Lotus Company. Unfortunately, just before the plane had completed flight tests, Chapman died of a heart attack. Later a new company was formed to manufacture the aircraft in England. Rutan shipped the prototype with its drawings to England. It was not to be offered in the United States. It was, however, to be a future source of legal headaches for Burt.

Another development assignment for SCALED was one called the California Microwave CM-44. This was an aircraft based on the *Long-EZ design.* It was larger than the *Long-EZ* and powered with the Lycoming turbocharged T10-360 engine. It was a plane that could be used as a manned or unmanned reconnaissance vehicle.

Now Rutan has development money in hand. He didn't throw it around on grandiose schemes, but used it to build a roomy hangar with adequate shop and office spaces.

There was room now for work for customers and room to work on Burt's own designs. Just when he seemed to have "done everything"—he changed direction.

(Above) Interior view of Reno's Coffee Shop, Mojave, California, 1991.
(Below) The Chamber of Commerce trailer, Mojave, California, 1991.
Author photos.

CHAPTER **27**

THE GRIZZLY, MODEL 72—1982

The Grizzly Rollout

On January 14, 1982, the latest Rutan prototype, RAF Model 72 *Grizzly*, was to be shown. It had been shielded from public anticipation and speculation by Rutan's announced involvement in the sailplane contest with his *Solitaire*.

A plain announcement landed on the desks of about 20 of the top aviation writers in the United States. It was from Burt Rutan's RAF and announced the rollout of a new plane was set. The veteran aviation writers were completely in the dark as to what this new design could be. It had been a very well kept secret. They gladly came to the Mojave Airport from the leading aviation journals of the land. There, they found a wine and cheese buffet ready for them. The weather was fine.

In the hangar on the flight line Rutan held a pre-inspection talk. He introduced Herb Iversen of Ames Industrial Corporation and announced that this company was coming to Mojave from Bohemia, New York, to build new scaled-down models of aircraft for flight testing.

While reporters were inside the hangar, with its doors closed, the new plane was taxied onto the ramp out front. At 2:30 p.m. the doors opened and the writers rushed out to see the new machine.

The idea behind the *Grizzly* was to provide a rugged bush aircraft. Design 72 was to be an experimental STOL (short takeoff and landing) aircraft.

The new plane was a proof-of-concept prototype. It was to be tested and used to see what short takeoff and landing (STOL) capabilities could be gotten with a canard/tandem-wing design. First trials were with four low-pressure tires on the main gear. Two wheels were mounted on each landing gear strut. This would allow the plane to be used on rough and soft surfaces. The fat tires were a departure for Rutan, who had used the smallest and slimmest ones he could get on his other models.

Reporters, family and friends circled the plane on the ramp at Mojave Airport.

They saw a four-place plane with a large baggage compartment. It had a 180-horsepower Lycoming engine and a constant-speed, two-bladed propeller in the nose. It was substantially larger than Rutan's previous designs, the *Long-EZ* and the *Solitaire*.

There was a forward wing with an interconnect, an outrigger, at the end which reached back to the rearward wing. This unique plane was a very new and obviously very sturdy. Once again Rutan had come up with a departure from the conventional aircraft of the day. Reporters admired the bulging side windows. They could see that these let the pilot have excellent visibility below and ahead. The pilot sits high in the airplane. With the rear seat folded, there was a long 78-inch area available for two people in sleeping bags.

Safety features included fuel carried in the wing interconnects to keep it away from the cabin.

Burt told the crowd that he also wanted to experiment with making the plane amphibious. He would like to make it possible to land the aircraft on the water and then taxi onto a beach. If the initial tests of the aircraft were promising, Rutan then hoped to design floats for the plane with wheels and brakes a part of the float system and not retractable. Would this be possible?

Three floats might be used, Rutan told reporters, "Just like Glenn Curtiss did back in 1910."

He said that he just didn't know exactly what floats would be used at present, except that they probably would be made of low-density foam sandwich core, covered with fiberglass and carbon fiber facings. He stressed that the *Grizzly* concept was strictly for research and to be used at first as a test bed for finding out what this tandem-wing design could do. Previous aircraft had not been designed for short field operation, so there was much to be learned from the *Grizzly*. With the knowledge base gained from this airplane Rutan would find his technology expanded.

Its wings were the research items aboard this first *Grizzly*. Rutan pointed out that the right wing was of a hollow, sandwich-skin material, while the left wing was the full-core construction technique first pioneered on the *VariEze* back in 1975.

Rutan hoped to develop his new aircraft into a tough "rugged bush airplane that will fly just about like a Cub, except maybe slower. If the *Grizzly* proves not to be a good slow-flying airplane, we won't go ahead with it. That's what a flying test bed is all about."

Reporters learned that the *Grizzly* had been built in Rutan's "back room." It had never been run or taxied until the evening before the press conference. This shows the confidence Rutan held in his design. He expected it to operate well for the start up and taxiing, and it did! In the middle of the night it had been moved from the back shop into a T-hangar, to keep it out of sight.

The Rutan designs had, to date, a fairly high landing speed for light aircraft, though well within the capabilities of most pilots. The planes needed, however, a long rather flat approach to prevent the build-up of excessive speed and a resultant non-landing or "float."

Burt realized that other aircraft, say the popular Cessna 172, could make a steep, slow approach. The *Grizzly* was a reaction to this. Here would be a plane that could approach to land at a steep angle and a fairly slow airspeed.

Using his computers, Burt applied a new aerodynamic design program. It handled the complex aerodynamic relationships of the high lift devices and the tandem wings, in several flight and near-the-ground situations. His goal was an ambitious one: to use large Fowler flaps on both of the wings. For this flap configuration, Burt needed to know how the plane would best operate in many flight situations. It was a complex aerodynamic design problem.

Burt announced this new plane, which had been a well kept secret, the *Grizzly*, with a simple mimeographed announcement sent to about 20 of the nation's top aviation writers, saying that a roll-out was scheduled January 14, 1982.

Some months after *Grizzly's* first flights, Burt took a writer for a ride in the plane. A typical Mojave Desert 25-knot crosswind was quartering across the runway. The plane handled the wind easily on takeoff and landing. The writer commented on the fact that Burt was "a surprisingly good pilot," and "maintains his proficiency well." This is an interesting aside, for many of us somehow believe that a person can really do only one thing well. It comes as a surprise to find a person with several fields of expertise. Rutan is a designer, a pilot, and an excellent businessman.

Rutan's work has precluded his experimenting with floats for the bush airplane. It sits tied down at Mojave, awaiting his pleasure, used on occasion.

Writers left Mojave on the day of the rollout feeling a breath of fresh air in the world of general aviation had blown in. It was good to see something really new in the air. Whether *Grizzly* ever claws its way into acceptance is yet to be seen, but it has great potential, they agreed—trust Rutan to spring a great idea on us!

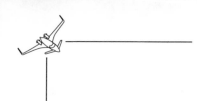

Chapter 28

RAF & SCALED ACTION—1982

Cozy First Shown

The *Cozy* is a side-by-side modification of the *Long-EZ*. It was developed by Nat and Shirley Puffer of St. Paul, Minnesota. Puffer wanted Burt to take over the design and market it, but Burt was too engaged with other items at the time. He did look over the design for Puffer. The Puffer's *VariEze* and *Cozy* were shown at Oshkosh.

No designer likes to have their designs changed. Burt has had many sad experiences—disasters for the builders changing his elegant and carefully balanced aircraft designs. In two cases, however, Rutan cooperated with builder-designers who wanted to modify his designs, because they were doing so with care and with an appreciation of the engineering involved.

Nat and Shirley Puffer's side-by-side modification of the *Long-EZ* was one of these. Originally this was to be a personal plane for their own use, a one-of-a-kind project. Later, however, several homebuilders bought Puffer's plans.

Nat Puffer had begun a BD-5, but when the *VariEze* was shown he eagerly changed his efforts to building a conventional *VariEze*. The plane was completed after almost two years of work. Puffer now looked for another project to build. Why not, he asked, build a modification of the *Eze* so that it would be a side-by-side aircraft?

Puffer sent a barrage of questions out to Rutan. Finally, even though he was too busy to personally help Puffer, Burt said that the design might be acceptable. There were problems with possible overloading with two large people sitting side by side and possibly that old bugaboo, center of gravity problems, might arise.

Puffer purchased a set of *Long-EZ* plans and began work. Rutan and Puffer talked about marketing the plans. Even though working long hours and busier than ever before, Burt took the time to check the drawings and to evaluate the probable flight behavior of the *Cozy*.

It took Puffer about three years to finish the *Cozy*. It was a thrill and an achievement when he was able to show if off at Oshkosh in 1982.

Advantages of the side-by-side configuration are: larger instrument panel, easier dual instruction, more enjoyable cross-country flying with two people (handing maps back and forth, talking), and a larger luggage compartment.

Since he was too busy to take on another marketing effort, and realizing that Puffer was a uniquely experienced person, Burt offered him a license to sell *Cozy* modification plans with *Long-EZ* plans and RAF technology. Due to retire from 3M, Puffer, a chemical engineer and World War II Naval aviator, took Rutan up on his offer. He now sells the plans and lends builder support to *Cozy* builders.

The Gemini, Another Co-Design

The design "went the other way," with Dave and Kathy Ganzer's *Gemini* design. They changed the seating arrangement of Rutan's four-place *Defiant*, to that of a two-place, side-by-side aircraft. Hence the name "Gemini," third sign of the zodiac, "the twins." They kept the twin engine, pusher-puller configuration.

They call their plane, "a pusher with pull," and built it on a bare-bones budget in San Diego, California. Inspired by the beautiful twin-engined *Defiant*, shown to the public in 1978, they set to work with a dream of building a plane with a speed of 165 mph and a range of over 1,200 miles.

The engines that can be used in this design are not expensive. They are the Type IV Volkswagen engines often used in vans, or the 914-4 Porsche engine. Both have to be modified for aircraft use (dual ignition and independent electrical systems).

Rutan admired the couple when he saw what they wanted to achieve and took time to help them almost from the beginning. The Ganzers, aided by Ganzer, Sr., had built a *VariEze* and liked the performance, but wanted more room, side-by-side seating and added luggage capacity.

Ganzer, like Rutan, had grown up around airplanes. His father owned an *Ercoupe*. When only 19, Ganzer built and flew a hang glider and by the age of 20 had earned an FAA license.

The *Gemini* was completed, and the hours flown off, just in time to fly to Oshkosh in 1982. This completion was achieved with the help of fellow builders' generous contributions of elbow grease and sweat. It didn't win a new design award at Oshkosh, but it did generate a great deal of interest.

RAF (and Rutan) "On the Covers"

By April 1982, seven national magazines showed Rutan aircraft. The first three listed were photographs taken by "our own RAF photographer, Pat Storch."

The magazines were: *Popular Science, Aviation Week & Space Technology, AOPA Pilot, Plane and Pilot, Private Pilot,* and *Homebuilt Aircraft.*

Was this to be Burt's peak year? He seemed to be everywhere.

Whimsical Test

While in Florida in February 1982, to speak at EAA (Miami) Chapter 37's Annual Banquet, Burt and Mike Melvill hobnobbed with dozens of builders of Rutan aircraft. They drove up to the Fort Lauderdale Executive Airport for a composites materials seminar for about 300 people.

Just before the seminar, in an antic mood, Rutan called for people weighing 175 pounds. He carefully positioned 18 people on a rejected composite canard in an effort to find out what the failure, the ultimate strength, would be. The canard survived with only minor cracks, not major failure, under a load calculated at 11.54 Gs!

This illustrates both Rutan's ability to seize on wild ways to demonstrate his points and his understanding of the strength of composite materials. No wonder he was, and is, the darling of editors in America and abroad. He thinks up these pranks that have serious purposes and that demonstrate his points. Also, he is a "great interview" with a talent for telling a story, making it fascinating and liberally larded with many quotable quotes.

RAF Women at Work in '82

Sally Melvill often flew the Melvill *Long-EZ* to airshows. She went along to a 99s meeting [the 99s is an association of women pilots] held at Bullhead City Airport, on the banks of the Colorado River, early in 1982.

Sally regularly flew a plane to Oshkosh.

Irene Rutan, too, was a valuable team member. She and George went east for the Florida "Sun 'n Fun EAA Fly-In" held in the spring of 1982. She logged in the pilots of Rutan-designed aircraft and answered questions. George contributed with information on the technical and pilot's side.

Jeana Yeager flew in with Dick Rutan in their much-modified *Long-EZ* to the EAA Sun 'n Fun Fly-In. Dick put on an aerobatic exhibition each evening, along with other airshow participants.

Dick, Jeana and Bob Woodall, a *VariEze* builder, met Johnny Murphy for dinner one evening at a restaurant near Cape Canaveral. It was just after the Sun 'n Fun Fly-in at Lakeland. Murphy is a former major of Cape Canaveral and a builder of the *VariEze*, *Quickie*, *Long-EZ*, *Defiant* and a *Glassair*. The group planned to see the launch of the space shuttle the following day (March 1982 launch).

In fact, Woodall hoped to photograph the launch from his airplane. At the dinner, Dick talked about their problems in trying to get financial support for the around-the-world *Voyager* flight. It was then just in the design and planning stage. He dominated the conversation.

Near the end of the dinner, Dick and Jeana became involved in a minor, playful tiff. Suddenly, Dick blurted out, "What more do you want from me?" Jeana shot back, "More front seat time in our Long-EZ." Woodall was to wonder later if she felt the same way about the *Voyager* flying.

New World Records Set by Long-EZ

Dick Rutan, who had set three world distance records to date, in early 1982, set out to break more speed records. With Jeana Yeager in their *Long-EZ*, in spite of mechanical problems and weather, the two pilots set these speed records: Two "absolute" speed records for Dick at over 200 mph; and an "absolute" speed record for Jeana at over 200 mph. Also Jeana broke two records for female speed flying of over 200 mph.

The 2,000 kilometer record, Jeana's "absolute" required a full-throttle dash at low altitude of a distance equal to a trip from Los Angeles to Dallas!

Around the World

RAF received letters from "down under" in Australia, France, Switzerland, England, and from homebuilders praising the sleek *VariEzes* and *Long-EZs*.

Private planes are not very numerous abroad, and these ultra-sleek Rutan designs were even more unusual. Wherever they landed, builders reported that groups of people gathered to admire them.

Before Oshkosh 1982

Just before the RAF team left for Oshkosh this year, there was good news. The Fairchild Republic NGT (new generation trainer) won the Air Force Trainer Competition. And once again Rutan designs had swept the winners circle at the Santa Rosa Fuel Efficiency 1982 Competition Race.

AMES/OIL Rutan Racer

The *AMS/OIL* Rutan *Racer* was also in the news. Dan Mortensen of Duluth broke the world speed record in the *Racer* in the C-1-B class for the National Aeronautics Association 3-kilometer course. He flew an average speed run of 234.62 mph, breaking an old record that had stood for 16 years.

Also, at the spring fly-in, EAA's Sun n' Fun, the *Racer* was named the "Best Original Design," of the fly-in.

Light Moments

Appearing among serious reminders about landing gear, carburetors, and other builder's concerns were sight jokes in the *Canard Pusher*. An airplane part is shown protruding from a house window. "*EZs*," the caption reads, "Can be built in a living room if you have a perfect marriage and a window in the right place!"

In this business of designing flying machines with life and death hanging on every design decision and builder's work, comic notes did intrude.

"It doesn't seem possible," Burt wrote in early 1982, "but there are still *VariEze* and *Long-EZ* builders out there who apparently are not aware of the fact that this configuration of aircraft *will* fall over on its tail if it is left unattended with the nose gear extended. The pilot is *required* in the front seat to balance the airplane to the correct center of gravity. Should the pilot climb out and let go of the airplane, it *will* fall over on its tail.... This is the main reason the nose gear retracts. This allows you to park the airplane nose down, a very stable way to park and avoids the requirement for a wheel chock when untied in winds up to 35 knots."

The July 1982 *Canard Pusher* shows a delightful photograph of Sally Melvill, Pat Storch (and a teddy bear) snuggled down "Snug as a bug in a Grizzly." This demonstrated the room available in that bush airplane for camping out.

On the Way to Oshkosh '82

All seemed to be well. The new SCALED building was going up near the RAF facility. Plans were to include a jacuzzi and other amenities in the building. "There's really not much to do in Mojave," Burt jokingly explained.

A big development, discussed in detail elsewhere in this account, was announced briefly: "RAF has agreed to join with *Voyager* Aircraft (Dick and Jeana) to build the *Voyager*. This will be an interesting project due to the very latest state-of-the art technology being used." Yes, all seemed to be well.

The Rutan designed aircraft were prepared to leave: the *Solitaire* Sailplane, the *Grizzly* STOL aircraft, the *Amsoil Biplane Racer* and the *VariViggen*, *VariEze*, and *Long-Ezs*.

Under wraps for years, in 1982 the *AD-1* skew-wing test airplane would also be flown at Oshkosh and displayed there.

Gleeful excitement was high as the RAF team sorted out the ferry plans. Later they would look back on this time with fond memories. How together they were, how happy they were.

Burt and Pat flew the *Defiant* out, stopping at Salt Lake City and at Wichita. Dick flew his *Long-EZ* and Jeana ferried the Melvill's *VariViggen*. Michael Dilley and Doug Shane drove a van pulling the *Solitaire* on its trailer. Sally Melvill flew their *Long-EZ* out while Mike ferried the *Grizzly*.

Interesting, Mike said later, the agricultural plane cruised at about 107 knots and burned 10 gph; while Sally in the *Long-EZ* burned only about 3.6 gph, which included occasionally having to circle the lumbering *Grizzly* to keep her speed down to his.

After skirting storms and flying under low ceilings in rain, the entire flight arrived safely at Oshkosh.

Immediately people flocked to see the new Rutan designs shown at the convention for the first time: the *Grizzly*, the *Solitaire*, the *Amsoil Racer*, also the *Cozy* and *Gemini*. The *AD-1* Skew-Wing was there.

Added to this were now 64 *VariEzes*, 16 of the new *Long-Ezs*, and two *VariViggens*.

There followed the usual happy, crowded days of the convention with interviews, seminars, gab-fests, dinners and flying. A high point for Burt was when all of his designs were gathered around the *AD-1* in front of the announcer's stand for a photo session.

After "the incredible week" Burt reports in his October news, "All the RAF folk pressed on home. The only change being that Burt traded with Mike and flew the *Grizzly* home, stopping at several small grass strips. While flying into the teeth of a 20-knot headwind, Burt was heard muttering something about wanting his *Defiant* back!"

"The annual trek," Burt reported, "to and from Oshkosh every year is a major undertaking for RAF and although it is always fun, it is also very tiring. It was good to be home and all had a safe journey."

From Hawaii to Oshkosh—Alone

The day he first began work on his *Long-EZ*, [March 12, 1981] W.A. "Rodie" Rodewald began to plan a 4,500-mile non-stop flight to Oshkosh from his home state of Hawaii.

The dream occupied (obsessed?) him, and his wife, Rosemary, his daughter, Ann, and many of his friends. All pitched in to gather together not only the entire airplane and engine but electronics for navigation, a spare gasoline tank and a thousand other items.

"Rodie" had built two other composite homebuilt aircraft. This was his third. "*Long-EZ* construction went along very easily," he reported in the October 1982 *Canard Pusher*. But what a feat—to build a plane, fly off the hours, equip it, and plan the trip in a little over a year! By mid-July 1982 Rodie was still looking for an adequate bladder tank for the back seat. His radios and navigation gear gave him headaches.

Finally, after an all-out effort by his family and friends, the tiny plane was ready to launch out over the immense Pacific Ocean. He slept for a few hours then planned to depart at 4:30 a.m. He wore special stockings to prevent blood clots in his legs on the long, long flight. Also, he had taken aspirin as prescribed by his doctor for a week before the flight for the same reason. His daughter, Jill, had made him velcro-fastened, removable sleeves for his down jacket. Otherwise his clothing was simply ordinary, loose and comfortable.

Takeoff was delayed until 5:45 a.m. Once off, the hours passed with Rodie encased in his small cockpit world. The Loran tracked well. Then came the shock of the flight. It was time for landfall—but where was the land? The Loran showed him right on course so there was nothing to do but keep going. "The moon had come up and it went down," he wrote. "It was dark and lonely out there all by myself." Two hours overdue. What had happened?

"Then," he understates, "the engine quit!" You might think that he was so numbed by the long flight and the tension of being hours overdue that he might falter. But he didn't, hands moving efficiently, he quickly changed gas tanks and the engine started right up again.

He arrived over the West Coast four hours overdue. In any other airplane this would have exhausted the fuel and landed him a long time ago in the water. "Lucky you to fly the *Long-EZ*!" he told himself. He still had hours of fuel left! The engine purred on.

Yet, he realized that he had flown into headwinds, rather than the forecast tailwinds, and the planned non-stop to Oshkosh was no longer practical. As pilots say, "It would have been fuelish." [sic]. Also, he didn't fancy flying over the Rocky Mountains in the dark, so he landed in Sacramento, California.

After a night's rest, he set off on the 12-hour flight to Oshkosh, the Loran ticking off the way points beautifully. "This is really living," he exulted. Seemingly he gave not a thought to the watery miles behind him. Nor what might have happened had he run into icing or storms. Blithely this remarkable man flew on to Oshkosh, aviation's Mecca.

He arrived near Oshkosh to find the field closed due to a thunderstorm, so diverted to land at Fond-du-Lac Airport. Were crowds gathered to greet this brave man who had just flown nearly 5,000 miles in two jumps? Not really. In fact, he couldn't even find a room for the night and tried to sleep in the airplane. He tossed and turned with nightmares of lost headings and suddenly stopping engines. He would awake in a sweat, throw open the canopy and "let in more of those damned Wisconsin mosquitoes."

This was an amazing flying feat, yet except for his fellow pilots, it was little noted! He even reports the return trip this way. "The trip back to Honolulu was not uneventful!" Understatement again. Events included having to land at Oakland, California to get his back seat fuel tank repaired. Thank heavens he wasn't on the watery part of his trip. And, the return trans-Pacific flight was delayed more with another fuel leak and repair, which meant defueling the plane and then having to refuel again. A long process. But he decided to take off across the Pacific for home.

Later, Rodie was to chide himself for pushing on this late in the day. It was going to mean a night landing after a long, long flight. He thought about this as he approached the islands with storms building up in the night sky. He was running two hours late on his planned arrival time at Honolulu. The *Long-EZ* bounced in rough air, flew through rain in the storms.

Rodie knew, too, that he was shooting for a much smaller target going home than he had been outbound. "I knew I was on track," he wrote, "I just didn't know where." He was in touch with Air Traffic Control Center and had 12 hours of fuel left. "Hey relax," he kept telling himself! But it was not really a very relaxing situation. Was he to land in the water after all this effort and planning?

Then the Hawaii VOR stations came up, the instruments awoke, one after the other. "It all ended well. But I made it a lot harder on myself than it needed to be."

The flights were astounding, but again, the man flying these amazing flights in a plane he'd built himself, got little notice! Yet he says, "As I was planning and getting ready for this trip, I was often asked 'Why?'" Was it for fame? He replied, "It's not why, it's 'why not!'" Mountain climbers are, for the most part, forced to climb mountains others have already climbed. In a *Long-EZ*, you have countless originals to climb. Lucky you fly the *Long-EZ*!"

This is (somewhat) understandable. But it is hard to understand why these amazing flights were so little noted in the press. These were historic achievements in flight. Certainly, too, these were historic examples of a man's courage and endurance.

Rutan reported the feat in his *Canard Pusher*. He must have been gratified at this demonstration of what his design could do.

Worrying Rain and Lift Considerations

An aircraft in the treetops, destroyed, but owner/builder well enough to write to RAF asked, "What happened?"

Could rain on the airfoil of the Rutan designs alter the lift and affect the aircraft's trim?

Dick Rutan had run into this earlier. Owen Billman in a *Quickie* was the man who ended up in the tree tops. Burt wrote in his *Canard Pusher* that RAF had been investigating the effect of rain on trim and performance for several years. Rutan had conducted wind tunnel tests at the NASA Langley Facility.

He concluded that "The trim change of the *Long-EZ* and the *VariEze* in rain is generally mild. Most trim down in the rain, but about 25 percent of the *VariEzes* trim up. There have been several reports of a strong nose down trim change, outside of the pitch trim capability. In general, these have been fixed with a correction of canard incidence or elevator shape. I know of no rain-induced accidents with the *VariEze* or *Long-EZ*, however several have reported extensive increases in takeoff rotation speed and takeoff distances.

"Again, there are variances from one airplane to another. We have done low-level aerobatic maneuvers in driving rain with our *Long-Ezs* without noticing any major difference in maneuverability. We have no operational limitations for flying in rain except to throttle back to save the propeller leading edges from erosion."

"It appears that the transition effect on maximum lift [in the *Quickie*] is more severe. Since the *Quickie* was not an RAF plans-built aircraft, Rutan advised the Quickie Aircraft Corporation of the problem and referred *Quickie* builders to them.

Accidents and Incidents

Routinely, Burt reported accidents in the *Canard Pusher* to warn his builders of possible hazards and to plan ahead for safe flights. Many of the accidents reported were a result of pilot error. Even these were reported, however, to increase safety.

Building and flying puts the builder and pilot in a position of great authority and responsibility. This is a part of the charm of flying—skirting danger with experience and skill. Burt's detailed advice was to check this, check that, and always be wary lest the aircraft "bite you."

The dialogue between Burt and builders of these very light planes continued. Burt was, however, now looking at the design of larger aircraft.

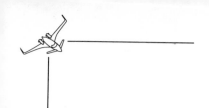

CHAPTER 29

ENTER BEECH AIRCRAFT

The Starship

The unveiling of *Starship* in September 1983 marked a turning point in Rutan's career. He was now famous outside the homebuilt community. He had arrived.

SCALED Composites now had its chance to show what it could do. The world watched as it tackled one of its first big projects—to build and flight-test an 85 percent scale prototype of the Beech *Starship*.

"... later came a windfall," aviation writer Peter Garrison said in an article. "Beech Aircraft, then under the leadership of Linden Blue, asked Rutan to further develop design proposals produced by Beech engineers for a new twin-turboprop business airplane."

Garrison saw the Rutan-refined design as resembling the *VariEze*. He asserted that, like thousands of home hobbyists, Beech executives fell for "the rakishly swept aft-mounted wings with finned tips."

The 85 percent scale *Starship* prototype was built in a remarkably short time period. The work was done with tremendous secrecy, by a RAF talented team of 18 workers. Garrison wrote that Rutan made great and sometimes tyrannical demands on his team and that they reacted with the "generous alacrity of religious zealots."

Beech Aircraft was later to buy SCALED Composites, some say for as much as seven million dollars, and to name Rutan to Beech's board of directors.

National Limelight

SCALED Composites continued to operate, with Rutan as its head, as an independent subsidiary of Beech Aircraft. Soon, Rutan was made a vice-president of Beech.

This was a time of great stress and change for Burt Rutan. He was suddenly in the national limelight both in and out of the aviation field.

Beech Aircraft executives, heading one of the best and oldest firms in the business, announced to the world that the company planned to follow the *Starship* with a whole line of new airplanes, all made of composites/plastics and all featuring Burt's futuristic and beautiful designs. This prospect had to have an effect on an energetic and ambitious designer.

Suddenly, now he had much more to lose. He had "deeper pockets" for suits. Burt saw that he needed to consider no longer selling plans at the Rutan Aircraft Factory. Instead, he could dedicate himself to servicing customers who had purchased plans. In this way, he could reduce his liability responsibility and the prospect of possible lawsuits.

After the dramatic and successful debut of the *Starship* design in September 1983, there seemed no limit to Rutan's rise in success and fame. SCALED Composites grew and

The Beech *Starship*, 1990.
Photo courtesy Beech Aircraft Corporation.

grew. Eventually, the janitorial staff was larger than the team that had built the 85 percent prototype *Starship*.

Worldwide, aviation was depressed and several companies building aircraft, particularly general aviation aircraft, were closing down assembly lines and going into bankruptcy. But, at Beech, Rutan was making more new designs and prototypes than most companies would consider in many years!

Not only civil aircraft, but military designs were in his shops. His mind seemed endlessly inventive. He looked for aviation niches that were not being satisfactorily filled and set to work to solve problems, to design useful aircraft.

CHAPTER **30**

1983 AND CHANGES

As 1983 came around at Mojave, change was in the air. Yet the *Canard Pusher* continued without interruption, selling plans, churning out advice, planning changes, and giving useful information to builders and pilots.

Prop Windmill and Forced Landings

An *EZs'* prop, the newsletter calmly advised, will windmill at flight speeds above 65 to 70 knots. "However, while practicing slow-flight or stalls at 60 knots or less, if your engine's idle speed is set too low, or you run out of fuel in one tank, the engine may not only quit running, but the prop may stop. Should this happen and you do not have a self-starter [many of the *VariEzes* had to be hand-propped on the ground] *keep calm*, switch tanks, verify mags on and mixture rich. Push the nose down and build up a least 135 knots (155 mph). The prop will begin to windmill at 124 to 135 knots and the engine should start.

"A windmill start uses less altitude if you initially dive *steeply* to rapidly attain the 135 knots. If you are faced with a forced landing for any reason, pick out a smooth spot and execute a *NORMAL* landing. Extend the nose gear and speed brake and land as if you were on your home field. *DO NOT* try anything fancy. Make a normal landing. If there are obstacles in the field, guide the fuselage/cockpit between them."

Now many people might not engage in building and flying an airplane of any kind, with this kind of possible problem in mind. Yet, pilots of both "Spam Cans" (manufactured aircraft) and homebuilts find this not normal, but a possible situation that lends a spice of danger to flying. They prepare for it and think about it. Should it ever happen, they want to know how to deal with it.

Burt and Pat Storch Part Company

Changes in the desert "family" were ahead. There were no mentions of Patricia Storch in the 1983 newsletters, no photographs with her credit line. Indeed, Burt himself was not so evident in the newsletters. He was occupied with the new Beech Aircraft work at SCALED, *Voyager* after work, and scores of builder demands.

Patricia Storch had decided to move out of Burt's personal life after five years. She said recently that the relationship was not meant to be, that perhaps they had both been on the rebound from divorces in the late l970s and so had joined forces. Five productive and fascinating years later, they parted as 1983 ended.

"Mom" and "Pop" Rutan admire Pat. "Isn't she lovely?" Irene Rutan asked me. "She's lovely inside and out!" The reasons for her leaving were not revealed me. Patricia says they had met on the rebound and had grown apart, but it had worked out well for them in any case.

Did Burt too openly admire other women and remark on them to Patricia? Or was it simply time for the two of them to separate?

Some things remained the same. As the year wheeled around, EAA's Sun 'n Fun Fly-In time arrived at Lakeland, Florida; the Soaring Society of America's Convention; and the EAA annual Convention at Oshkosh, continued. Rutan planes and people were featured on magazine covers across the country. Builders wrote in enthusiastically praising Rutan planes from Australia, South Africa and England.

Again a fly-in birthday party was held at Mojave Airport with a luncheon and friendly faces around the RAF and SCALED shops. A gusty day did not prevent 43 aircraft from flying in to wish Rutan "Happy Birthday." It was different this year, but the "tradition" continued.

Burt Rutan's life continued its pressured pace. Without Patricia he was at a loss for a time. He and Pat had been very close for five years. Suddenly he no longer had her to turn to. She was no longer at his side for the many business and personal hours they had formerly spent together. This year she did not fly a plane to Oshkosh for him.

Solitaire Plans About Ready for Sale

In the spring of 1983 Burt continued to develop aircraft for the purpose of selling plans to builders.

By April 1983 the plans for the *Solitaire* were promised to interested homebuilders. As always, freezing the design and executing the carefully-detailed drawings and directions took time. By Sun 'n Fun, Mike and Sally Melvill were able to begin preparing distributions for the *Solitaire* program.

Solitaire shone like a jewel, too, at the Reno, Nevada Soaring Society of America's Convention. Sally Melvill and Michael Dilley drove the van towing *Solitaire* to Nevada. Mike Melvill and Burt flew there in the *Defiant*. "What a sight—tons of snow," they reported after flying up the Sierra Nevada Mountains.

Finally, *Solitaire* plans went on sale at the EAA Convention. Aviation writers flew the sailplane and wrote articles in *Flying, Sport Aviation* and *Air Progress*.

The Military Investigate Rutan's Work

Over at Edwards AFB, two *Long-EZs* built by the U.S. Army at Fort Lewis, Washington, were tested. The Army wanted to know if Burt's all-composite construction would be suited for future Army aircraft. Also, the military wanted to determine the feasibility of using the latest civilian technology in a military environment. The tests began in May of 1983 and ran for six months. ("Does this mean," Burt smiled, "that we can park our 'replicas' with the War Birds at Oshkosh??")

A Long-EZ Spin?

Rutan designs are normally spin-proof and almost stall-proof. But in 1983 one experience of a harrowing flight was reported. The warnings that Burt had been issuing were correct—keep the center of gravity near the center or slightly forward! Here's the story:

An experienced 63-year-old pilot, approached a stalled condition in his *Long-EZ*. The left wing dropped and the plane dropped into a spin. The pilot had spun many aircraft before and knew what was happening.

He made the traditional spin recovery moves—*with no response*. Would he spin into the ground? The plane was whirling toward the earth. Fortunately his good sense and experience paid off as he frantically tried one control move after another to get the plane out of its spin. Finally, by using his engine, he was able to regain control and pull out of the spin.

Normally engine use only tightens the spin, but in this case it seemed to give more control authority and enabled the pilot to recover control. The builder realized he had an "aft CG" problem, so he installed 10 pounds of lead in the nose of his EZ and experienced no further spin entries.

Oshkosh 1983—Solitaire and Defiant

This year Burt talked in his seminars about his new sailplane, *Solitaire* and the *Long-EZ*. He even held a "Design College" with information about flight testing the Rutan aircraft. He had the satisfaction of seeing 87 of his aircraft at the convention.

At one of his seminars he introduced John Roncz, designer of the airfoils used on the *Solitaire*. After the presentation Burt and John returned to Mojave in the *Grizzly*.

Several times that week the Rutan aircraft were flown in the airshow: in formation to show off the various designs; aerobatically in the airshow by Dick Rutan; and in fly-bys each afternoon.

At Oshkosh, the biggest news of the week was Burt's announcement that *Defiant* plans were to be made available to homebuilders. Burt did not have the time, with *Starship* and *Voyager* and a score of other commitments, to develop the plans. But Fred Keller of Alaska agreed to build a prototype and to document it as he went for Burt.

Keller and his wife, Sharon, flew "their absolutely beautiful *Defiant* from Anchorage to Oshkosh. It was without a doubt one of the most popular aircraft on the flight line.

"Fred's achievement in completing an airplane the size and complexity of the *Defiant*, in the time he did is incredible, especially when you stop and consider that he was not only building virtually every single part himself, he was also keeping accurate records, drawings and photographs of his progress in order to be able to put together plans for the homebuilder."

RAF planned to market the plans as usual but builder support questions, requiring interpretation, were to be referred to Keller. *Defiant* plans were to be available, RAF announced, by March of 1984.

To be able to build a four-seater airplane would fill a real need among homebuilders. Families grow; airplanes do not.

"Thank You for the Strong Design"

A *VariEze* crashed near Lake Winabago. Rumors flew through the convention grounds about the accident, but it was determined that no fault was due to the Rutan aircraft. Rather, sand was suspected in the fuel.

The homebuilder/pilot wrote the true details to Burt. He had lost power and made an emergency landing in a cornfield. The plane flew and landed perfectly but the surface was so rough that on roll-out it turned and then flipped over.

The pilot was trapped inside and smelled gasoline. He had called for help, digging the headset out of the mud. He then cut the switches and hung on his belt, awaiting assistance. Burly firemen arrived and lifted the plane, about five feet up, still inverted.

"OK," a slightly-built fireman advised, "let go the belt." "Are you ready to have 215 pounds come tumbling down on your head?" the pilot objected.

"Whoa!" he said, and several other firemen came to catch him. Afterwards, the pilot praised the quick action of the rescue team, but wryly commented: "I could just see me surviving the crash unscathed only to break my neck in the rescue!"

"Thank you, Burt," the pilot wrote, "for the strong design of that aircraft that let me get out unhurt."

Burt's Son, Jeff

Burt and his son, Jeff Hiner, worked together in the summer of 1983. This contact was good for Rutan. He found his son to be an agreeable and intelligent young man. In fact Jeff came up with a new computer program for RAF to use for the newsletter on the Apple computer.

Jeff improved the program so that subscribers could be located in seconds by name. He also added capacity to the system.

"I see Jeff more than I see Dawn," Burt told me in February 1990. "He comes up here to Mojave. Dawn is busy getting her family going, she's expecting her third child now. Her first was born during the *Voyager* flight!"

By 1990 Burt was helping Jeff (now Jeff Rutan) through college, California State University at Fullerton. Jeff is going after his engineering degree in computer science. "He is a good programmer," Burt comments.

"Jeff has been working at Hughes Aircraft and has gone about as far there as he can without a degree. He's very good at computer programming, so I'm sure he'll do fine. He comes to the Antelope Valley less often now, working part-time at Hughes, going to college, married. I'd like to see more of him."

As '83 Ended

By the end of 1983 RAF and SCALED were full of interesting projects, some of them secret. The *Voyager* was nearing completion. Burt often "commuted" to the Beech headquarters in Wichita.

CHAPTER 31

1984—RAF'S TENTH YEAR AND VOYAGER'S FIRST FLIGHT

There was the usual number of complex activities going on in 1984 as RAF neared its tenth anniversary.

Test Flying

Mike Melvill was now doing a great deal of the test flying for RAF. He was apt to don his parachute and take a modified aircraft up to 12,000 feet above the desert to see what the changes had done to the airplane's flight characteristics. In this way he checked out new and larger rudders for the *Long-EZ*. Plans for the change, once tested, were offered for only $18.

"We sincerely hope that the builders and flyers out there in the field appreciate the amount of time, effort and not a little risk that RAF puts out for continued support and improvement where possible for the RAF airplanes."

Little Demon

"Fred Keller is working like a little Alaskan demon," reported the newsletter in January 1984, "on the *Defiant* plans. We are still shooting for March for availability."

Solitaire News

The *Solitaire* Owner's Manual was now at the printers after much detailed work in completing it. An article on the sailplane appeared in 1984 in *Soaring* magazine. So far 13 *Solitaire* kits were ordered, according to the January 1984 newsletter.

Smaller?

What could be smaller than a Rutan aircraft? A radio-controlled scale model. In December 1983, RAF gave St. Croix of Park Falls, Ltd. the rights to develop this. It was brought to Mojave Airport and flown by Jim Schmidt, manager of the St. Croix's Model Aircraft Division. RAF people had to agree it looked and performed much like the real thing!

More Proof of Builder Appreciation

Rutan would not have had the heart to continue his "pressure-cooker" lifestyle but for the heartening input from his friends and builders. These conversations and letters showed him that he was appreciated and that his work was contributing to their lives.

For example, Loren Glaser wrote from Ohio, "Dear Mr. Rutan: Well, what do you know, on July 16, 1983, six years after I obtained my prints and serial number #690, my N999TT came to life and flew off into the blue just like it was meant to be.

"Six years seems to be quite a span of time to build a plane, but maybe not too bad considering the wife's position when she said,'A home is the most important thing in our life and you had better get your priorities in order.' This cost me two years of time out of the six. [He built his own home!] Now we are both happy. I have my *VariEze* and she has her home...

"Now 74 years of my life have come and gone. Of those I have enjoyed 53 years as a pilot ... and now I'm cruising at near 200 mph. Sakes alive, what's happening!"

"On my way to Albuquerque, NM I stopped at Addison to pick up my son. About a mile ahead of me in the pattern, I saw what I thought was a *VariEze*. I was surprised to see later that it was the Beech *Starship*. What a beautiful creation. Keep on surprising us, Burt, with your marvelous creations."

Vortilons

Work continued on improving the RAF designs. It was found that by installing "little wing leading edge fences" with assistance from *VariEze* builders Chuck Richey, Gary Hertzler and Bruce Evans, with little or no speed penalty there was a noticeable improvement in takeoff and climb performance. Stall characteristics improved. Also, it was easier to see over the nose during rotation for lift off and during the landing flare.

Tests continued on the John Roncz-designed canard for the *Long-EZ*, after several disappointing tries to improve the performance of the canard in normal and bad weather flying. This fifth attempt was to be the charm, the success, the answer sought.

Changes were everywhere, but research continued at Mojave.

RAF's Tenth Anniversary

With the April 1984 issue of *Canard Pusher*, RAF celebrated its tenth year in business.

Achievements? Rutan, after founding RAF, had put out unique designs for 12 different airplanes. Eleven were built and tested at RAF in Mojave.

But that was not all, Burt had designed at least four other airplanes that have been built and flown. The future at this point held more airplane designs.

An interesting comment appears in the newsletter: "We, the employees of RAF are very proud of our boss and friend, Burt Rutan. We are proud to work for him and proud of his and RAF's record over the last 10 years. We look forward to many more years of exciting, rewarding and innovative work at the leading edge of aviation technology."

1983 and 1984

The year 1983 was devoted to construction. Hangar 77, *Voyager's* new home, was being completed. The move to Hangar 77 began in December. Burt was rather put out when he learned that they had a hangar of their own. Again, communications had broken down between the two brothers.

Homebuilders dropped by to see what was going on in Hangar 77 and stayed to help, sometimes for months and even years. There was a "seven-minute rule," that work could stop for a chat with a visitor for only seven minutes, then the visitor was put to work and progress continued.

Among the talented hard workers that helped so much with *Voyager* were: Lee and Diane Herron, Fergus Fay, Glenn Maben, Doug Shane, Neal Brown, Gary Fox and Dan Card. Wanda Wolf took over much of the office work, often assisted by "Mom" and "Pop" Rutan.

The airplane was nearing completion. The money situation was so tight it squeaked. Dick and Jeana had hoped for more help from Burt and his RAF people.

Voyager Looms in Hangar

By now the *Voyager* team had put together a huge aircraft. It was an imposing sight in the hangar. Wings 110 feet long, long fuselage, it looked insubstantial and fragile—yet was designed to carry 10 times the weight of the airframe—around the world!

Dick, Jeana, Bruce Evans and others labored to try to get the plane into the air in time to fly it to the 1984 EAA Convention at Oshkosh. They needed the grassroots money that would be donated by generous aviation enthusiasts, once the plane was a reality. The obstacles yet to be overcome were tremendous, but step by step they worked. This next step was to get the plane into the air and show it off in Wisconsin.

Once there, "this last great milestone in the history of atmospheric flight," would surely attract backing.

Voyager's First Flight

Using engines borrowed from Burt, "on June 22, 1984, early in the morning before the desert warmed up or it became windy, the *Voyager* taxied out from Hanger 77 and began a series of taxi runs," said the July 1984 *Canard Pusher*. "Each run was made a little faster. Soon, daylight was seen between the tires and the runway—the *Voyager* was airborne!"

[Shortly thereafter] "Dick taxied into position on Mojave Airport's runway 30. He sat alone in the *Voyager* at the end of the runway. Jeana put the canopy on over his head and secured it. The engines were ticking over. Jeana ran over to the chase plane and crawled quickly into the back seat behind Burt and Mike Melvill. They took off in the *Grizzly* to fly chase and to document the event on videotape.

There had been taxi tests but the plane had never been flown. How would the controls react? Would they be able to manage the aircraft? How would such a long wing behave? Would the weight and balance be safe enough? Dick pushed the power forward.

"The *Voyager* began to roll. The acceleration was amazing! It rose majestically into the air. 'It just slipped right up into the air,' Dick marveled later. It looked incredible. Dick climbed out straight ahead, gently feeling out control and stability. The *Grizzly* moved underneath to check. Mike called Dick on the company frequency, 'You have a major oil leak on the front engine.' Dick calmly replied that he was shutting down and securing the front engine. 'That's why we put two engines on airplanes,' Burt commented. After a quick discussion it was decided to continue the flight but to remain in the immediate vicinity of the airport.

"The air was glass smooth and the *Voyager* was an awesome sight to see. The wing tips were bent up like a huge bird. The impression Mike had from the *Grizzly* was that the airplane was sailing across the sky. It was a very exciting and satisfying feeling to see *Voyager* fly for all those who worked so hard to reach this point." Dick flew for 40 minutes then returned for a perfect touchdown.

"Of course, everyone was elated. The aircraft had performed aerodynamically flawlessly. Burt had predicted how it would fly and once again, he was exactly correct." Dick was pleased with the handling qualities of the plane on the first flights.

Later, the airport celebrated their "glad-to-be-alive party." It was more than three years after the start of a program they had expected to take only one year.

An official press day was held on July 3, 1984. *Voyager* was seen on all three major TV networks and many local TV stations.

On subsequent flights they found out how strange an airplane this specialized aerial device was. In turbulence the long wings would flail the air. The entire aircraft flexed. It was certainly a disturbing sight for the pilots.

Now, to generate more funds and interest in the around-the-world venture, it was decided to take the Voyager to Oshkosh, during the EAA Convention in August 1984.

Test flights showed the plane was a brutal one for the off-duty pilot in the prone position and very difficult to fly properly for the one in the pilot's seat.

There was a control problem in running through rain in which the canard lost lift and the plane plunged toward the ground. This was "bad news."

They called on John Roncz, airfoil expert, who set to work with Burt to solve the problem. With computers and wind tunnel tests at Ohio State University, the airfoil guru found the problem. He found that when raindrops hit the canard and spattered, the air flow treated the interruption as though the raindrop were a solid. Just like rough ice on a wing, the rain would destroy the lift.

One of the directors of the wind tunnel, Dr. Jerry Gregorek, suggested "vortex generators." These are little "teeth" that prevent the splatter of the rain, keep the airflow smooth, and so retain the lift. One tremendous hurdle to a successful flight was removed.

Variety of Projects Continue

Work went on with the Army *Long-EZs*, *Solitaire* builders, and improving the *Long-*

163

EZ canard. Fred Keller had the plans for the *Defiant* almost completed. "It is easier," Fred said, "to build two airplanes than it is to write one set of plans!" Once he finished the plans, he and RAF would have to get an owner's manual ready.

Annual events continued with RAF participation, the International *VariEze* Hospitality Club Fly-In to Jackpot, Nevada, where pilots gravitated to the swimming pool in the desert. RAF people attended various efficiency races and fly-ins as usual. How all this was fitted in can only be explained by the youth and energy of the RAF team.

Letters came in from Patrick Colin who had built a *Long-EZ* on the former U.S. atomic testing ground, Enewtak Atoll in the southwestern Pacific, 4,500 miles from Mojave.

When transferred, Colin flew his plane out to the Island of Kwajalein, over 360 nautical, watery miles away. From there he flew on to Papua, New Guinea via several island stops. He and his wife, Lori, plan to travel in the plane more—even to Australia!

RAF and SCALED were working at full speed to ready aircraft for the EAA Convention in August.

Jeana's Record Flight

On Friday the 13th of July, 1984, Jeana Yeager took off in Gary Hertzler's *VariEze*, from Bakersfield, California, to try to break the C1-A Closed Course Record held by Leon Davis in his Dave DA-5, of 2,262 statute miles.

She left at 6:40 p.m. and flew through the night on a course that lapped Meadows Field and the Merced Airport. She landed with a credited distance of 2,424 statute miles to break the record. [Her actual miles flown was about 2,700 miles.]

Hertzler Breaks a Record

Right after Jeana's flight, the plane was serviced and checked. Then Gary Hertzler took off from the Mojave Airport heading for the East Coast. He planned to break Al Lesher's 1975 record for a straight line distance flight in the C1-A class (maximum gross weight 1,102 pounds).

Gary fought headwinds, then bad weather. After "a nasty experience" with a thunderstorm over the Smoky Mountains, he decided to call it a day and landed at Martinsburg, West Virginia, 14 hours and 50 minutes after leaving Mojave. He had flown without stopping for 2,227 statute miles, thus returning the record to Rutan-designed aircraft.

London to Paris Record

News came to Mojave that a new World Record had been set in Europe in a *VariEze*. Henri Christ flew, with a passenger, from London to Paris, at over 167 mph.

Accidental Art

When water is calm and the airplane being flown is not near a shoreline, it is very hard to estimate how high the aircraft is above the water. Many a seaplane pilot has slammed into the water for this reason.

Mike Melvill was flying the *Defiant* so that photographs could be taken by Steve Werner over Koehn Lake. The water was absolutely calm. Wouldn't it be great, they thought, to get a reflection of the twin-engined airplane from the lake in the photo? Mike dipped lower and lower when to Steve's horror, and to his own surprise, the wheels touched the surface. Luckily Mike felt the drag and was able to react quickly enough to add power and climb away.

Fortunately, too, Steve had not frozen but had clicked the picture. The subsequently sold poster shows the *Defiant* skimming along on the surface of a mirror smooth lake, with two rooster tails of water trailing from the main gear.

The Predator—Tests Continue

The October 1984 RAF newsletter comments: "RAF has also provided test pilot support to SCALED Composites for Burt's latest airplane, the *Predator*." So work was continuing on this new agricultural aircraft design. [The plane was first announced in 1981.]

Oshkosh 1984

The biggest event of the EAA Convention in 1984 was the spectacular arrival of the long-awaited dream ship, the *Voyager*. It arrived flying out of the summer heat, a dream realized. It was so sleek and graceful that its size was not apparent until it flew close to the crowds waiting at Wittman Field, Oshkosh.

The crowd murmured when Dick moved the controls to show how much flex the 110-foot wing had. [What a difference between this graceful craft and the B-24 *Liberator* bomber, which also has a 110-foot-long wing.]

The *Voyager* was parked on the flight line. This around-the-world project of Rutan's design, joined a registered 48 *VariEzes*, 33 *Long-EZs*, 3 *VariViggens*, 2 *Defiants* and a *Solitaire*.

The flight to Oshkosh was the end of Burt's phase of the program, which was to provide an airframe with the capability to do the job. Now it was up to Dick and Jeana to furnish the aircraft with the proper engines, radios and other systems needed. A set of support teams on the ground, too, would be necessary. A tall order.

The *Voyager* flew several times during the EAA Convention and generated tremendous interest in the EAA members and in the media. This, Dick and Jeana hoped, would help get backing for the second phase of the project.

Once back in Mojave, the plane was tested with increasing loads of fuel. Burt turned the airplane over to Dick and Jeana, satisfied that it had the capability to do the job. He specified the power requirement. Now, Dick and Jeana faced the huge job of getting the engines and equipment for the flight and needed money. It was a promising prospect in 1984, but as told elsewhere in this book, and in their book *Voyager*, it was to be a heart-breaking and disappointing effort. "Mom" Rutan and others promoted a "VIP Club" so that grassroots support for the around-the-world project could be generated.

After Oshkosh, Alaska!

Mike and Sally Melvill in their *Long-EZ*, joined Fred Keller flying his *Defiant*, and others, for a trip to Alaska after Oshkosh '84. The weather wasn't always wonderful, but with care they made it safely. They brought back memories of flying very close to the 20,000-foot Mount McKinley one crystal clear day.

They returned to the Mojave Desert describing Alaska and its people as nothing less than "awesome!" "What a fantastic trip," they exclaimed.

CHAPTER 32

1985 ADVENTURES AND CHANGES

At SCALED and RAF on an early January 1985 day, decisions were being made by the Melvills. Later in the year, Burt, too, was reassessing his goals.

Melvill's VariViggen Donated to Museum

Mike and Sally Melvill stood in the hangar and looked at their *VariViggen*. The plane was seven years old and had "flown almost 650 hours of fun flying," with no major problems.

Number N27MS just wasn't being flown much anymore, however, and rather than let her sit in the hangar, the Melvills decided to give her away. They decided in January 1985 to donate the *VariViggen* to the Museum of Flight in Seattle, Washington. There it would be preserved and displayed for everyone to enjoy.

The plane had been the start of so much for the Melvills. It had led to their friendship with Burt, with moving to Mojave and a completely changed life and work.

Only about 18 or 20 of the *VariViggens*, Burt's first design, had been completed and flown. Their builder/pilots were a select group of people.

In fact, later, as of May 1, 1985, the *VariViggen* and *VariEze* plans were no longer available. RAF continued, however, to provide builder support. Plans for the *Defiant*, the *Long-EZ*, and the *Solitaire* continued to be offered for sale.

Since a homebuilder is, in effect, the manufacturer of the aircraft built, many choose not to sell the plane and assume the liability. Manufacturing carries a strict liability that has no end date. Several owners can have a plane, maintain it in various ways or not at all, then if an accident occurs, the original manufacturer may possibly be accused of some defect and sued.

Bird Talk

The "latest flying model" that Burt Rutan showed off was on the back page of his January *Canard Pusher*. Pensively Burt is looking at a large bird held on his arm. "Rusty" is a blue and gold macaw.

Burt looks in the picture as though he has serious things on his mind. This was no more than the truth. He was newly married, involved deeply with Beech Aircraft, wondering whether to move into the high-powered executive "rat race," which was interesting; or should he decide that this was not for him?

1985 Sun 'n Fun

Sally and Mike Melvill left Mojave on a Sunday morning, March 17, bound for Florida.

About a thousand miles later they landed in Elk City, Oklahoma for lunch. Another 700-mile jump brought them to Muscle Shoals, Alabama, flying at a speed of around 173 mph.

There they spent the night with a *Defiant* builder and saw his project. As mentioned many times in this account, the RAF people and the builders of Rutan designs often grew not only to be customers but friends, bonded by the common interests of building an aircraft and flying it.

In the morning the Melvills climbed to 13,500 feet, picked up a 51-knot tailwind, and in only two-and-one-half hours reached Lakeland, Florida, over 500 nautical miles away.

For the first time at the EAA Sun 'n Fun Fly-In, there were more *Long-Ezs* than *VariEzes*. The airplanes constantly came in and then departed, bound for Key West, the Bahamas, and for home ports.

The Melvills basked in the Florida sun, talked to builders, and watched the Sun 50 Race, originally started by Dick Rutan as an *EZ* race.

They noticed that almost all the *VariEzes* at the fly-in had the recommended vortilons installed on the leading edges of their wings.

"Where Do We Go From Here?"

You could almost hear Burt's thoughts as you read the July 1985 *Canard Pusher*. In the newsletter he recapitulated the history of the RAF and listed the dozen models flown since 1969 when he began the company as a part-time business.

"RAF," Burt explained, "has never entered the homebuilt kit market. From the onset, I have limited RAF's marketing to that of plans and support items. It is easier for me to assure the quality of those items. As you know we have been open and candid about the deficiencies that have been found after plans are out and responsive toward developing improvements to fix problems and pass important information on to you homebuilders in the *Canard Pusher*."

The decision not to get into the kit business, had stemmed from Burt's desire to stay small and to also reduce his liability exposure. With low overhead, RAF had managed to build a healthy cash base. The *VariEze* and the *Long-EZ* proved to have been the profitable designs. The others did not return Burt's investment.

"The *Voyager* project was done primarily because I decided that this significant accomplishment would be worth more in terms of the feeling of accomplishment by achieving an aviation milestone, than the more obvious financial income to be received by introducing a new homebuilt."

"Where do we go from here?" To answer that question, Burt explained to his customers and friends that the market for homebuilt plans was declining, the public's first excitement had waned, and he had found that the more homebuilts he brought out, the more builder support was required.

"I have decided to significantly curtail our overhead to a level to do only builder support. This allows the remaining cash to be available for a longer period to support builders."

He promised to be at Oshkosh 1985 but was no longer to be doing Saturday demonstrations at Mojave, aerobatic airshows, advertising and offering rides.

Mike and Sally Melvill, his valued associates, were to stay with RAF and also assist with projects at the SCALED Company.

"It is a difficult decision, of course, to retreat from the homebuilt plans business, since it has been a tremendous amount of fun working with people who also are having a lot of fun. It was a decision made necessary by the nature of the business and our success in the last two years. Also, I have been spread so thin on time, conducting the other business at SCALED Composites, that I have been unable to meet the schedule I had wanted on the next RAF aircraft."

Not quitting, he was simply shifting emphasis, it seemed. Burt was soon advertising for a mechanical engineer and structural composites engineer, composites fabricators and people with electronics experience.

RAF was trimmed back to an office in Building 13, no shop space. An independent division of SCALED was formed called Composite Prototypes and installed in Building 13. Burt described this as a smaller version of SCALED.

Still Busy, Still Flying

Still the flying events went on.

On June 8, 1985, at Mojave Airport, Burt and his team threw a party. Homebuilders and pilots were invited. The first game of the day was the arrival "spot landing" contest. A judge listed the aircraft landing closest to the white line drawn across the runway. Eighty-three Rutan-designed aircraft arrived for his party!

Around 400 people came to see the demonstrations of composite construction, see the landings contest, enjoy the lunch and generally enjoy being together, even in the 105-degree desert weather.

Oshkosh 1985

"Mom" Rutan counted 117 RAF-type airplanes at Oshkosh '85, far and away the most numerous homebuilts at the convention.

Warbirds were featured and the beautiful *Concorde* was flown and shown. The valuable "bull-sessions," the dinners, the seminars carried thousands of aviation enthusiasts through the week. Burt vowed that RAF would continue to attend Oshkosh Conventions to help homebuilders.

Dick and Jeana were honored everywhere they went for their magnificent achievement of building and flying the *Voyager* in preparation for the around-the-world-unrefueled record.

After Oshkosh Dick and Jeana, Bruce Evans, Sue Bowman, Wanda Wold and Mike and Sally Melvill all flew up to just west of the Yellowstone National Park for a rest and a visit.

Finally everyone was home again, tired but satisfied with their annual Oshkosh adventures. The round of fly-ins, air races and builder support (for RAF) continued at Mojave.

Voyager—Phase II

Dick Rutan reported in the *Canard Pusher*, October 1985, "When are we going? I wish I knew!" He appealed to homebuilders to keep up the grassroots help needed to finish the *Voyager* testing and to get it ready for the record attempt.

Dick reported that King Radio had volunteered to provide the avionics. Teledyne Continental Motors agreed to provide the two engines. The front engine was a standard 0-240 air cooled (130 horsepower) engine. The rear engine, however, was a newly-developed 10L-200 liquid-cooled engine of 110 horsepower. These two donations were vital to the continuation and success of the proposed flight.

RAF Now Support Only

It was in July 1985 that Burt Rutan announced that Rutan Aircraft Factory (RAF) would no longer sell homebuilder plans for any of its designs, including the *VariViggen, VariEze, Long-EZ, Solitaire* motorglider and *Defiant* centerline-thrust twin.

The reasons, he explained to his homebuilders in the *Canard Pusher*, were the decreased sales and threat of product liability suits. And, he told them, another reason was that he wanted to devote his work and time to SCALED Composites.

Today, RAF still provides support and a newsletter to its customers.

CHAPTER **33**

A SOCIETY WEDDING!

"What is the big news at RAF? New canard for the *Long-EZ*? New project in the shop? No, No, No. *Burt is getting married*!! On November 16, 1984, Burt will be tying the knot with a lovely lady named Margaret Rembleske."

Burt met Margaret Rembleske, daughter of a vice-president of Beech Aircraft Company, on a business trip. He was introduced to her at a dinner while in Wichita. Burt was, at the time, looking over the corporate landscape with its power meetings, its country club life, its many "perks," with interest. What a new world this was. His intelligent eyes looked at the people, the plant, the Wichita area. Interesting.

The *Canard Pusher*, not only the technical newsletter of the Rutan Aircraft Factory, but a newsy letter to his friends and a sort of a personal diary, too, announced:

"He calls her 'Sunshine' as she always has a smile and sure makes Burt smile a lot!! Congratulations Burt and Margaret." [In retrospect this enthusiasm is rather embarrassing, but at the time it revealed the sincere wishes of Rutan's RAF friends for him.]

The next *Canard Pusher*, January 1985, in a like vein of "happy puppy-dog" friendship, reported:

"As announced, Burt was married to Margaret in Wichita, Kansas on November 16, 1984. It was a beautiful wedding with a large crowd of friends at the church and the reception. At the reception we were treated to something very special, a piano solo by airfoil whiz, John Roncz. What a talent!"

It was an exciting event. The sunburned Mojave Desert RAF friends mingling with golf-bronzed Wichita society people and executives of Beech Aircraft. What was the best treat that Burt could imagine for his friends? A tour of the *Starship I* Manufacturing Facility, of course. And the RAF people loved it. The technology and the equipment was fascinating to them. They were used to homebuilt ovens and "can-do" hand lay-ups. At Wichita they were staggered by the amount of money being spent on buildings, tooling, autoclaves, ovens and manpower.

Typically, RAF friends flew to Wichita in a Rutan aircraft, the *Defiant*. They overflew states and dropped down casually from 12,000 feet to have lunch, hundreds of miles from Mojave.

Burt brought Margaret to the Mojave Desert. She found that she couldn't fully share his delight in the Joshua-tree-strewn, lunar-like landscape of the Antelope Valley floor. He would have liked to have moved to the barren desert near Mojave Airport, but compromised by buying an elaborate house in Palmdale, not far away. There you could, with elaborate care, have a few green plants.

Margaret would really have preferred that Patricia Storch didn't continue to work at SCALED. But Herb Iversen wanted to keep her on the payroll. She knew the company and was an excellent worker. Later Pat was to say, "Well, you really can't blame Burt because he was trying very valiantly to try to make the marriage work."

Margaret Rembleske Rutan and Burt Rutan cut the cake.
Photo courtesy George and Irene Rutan.

I mentioned Burt's remarks to Pat during a recent interview [March 1, 1989], that he'd gone out to Wichita and bought a pin-striped suit, but finally decided he'd be happier out here in Mojave.

"That's very true," Pat said.

Employees of SCALED watched Margaret's reaction to the desert environment. When he and Margaret first got married, she bought a poodle. She placed a gold chain that had been given to Burt around the dog's neck.

Margaret strolled through SCALED offices one day, dog in tow. When Patricia noticed it she complimented Margaret with, "Oh nice, that dog has good taste in jewelry." And walked on by.

When Margaret, not yet 30, had come to Mojave, she found it a far different place from her beautiful home in Kansas. She had gone to excellent schools and had moved in social circles that were interested in the arts, social affairs. She looked around at the little desert town and found that it had no Junior League. Few of its inhabitants knew what the League was, probably. So Margaret insisted on living in Palmdale where at least there were Junior League members and a golf course.

Margaret and the Mojave Desert turned out to be oil and water. It is a difficult environment and must have been a very strange one to her. "She hated this area," Burt admitted in a 1990 interview. "Didn't care for my friends, my family. And after about 20 months we separated."

This was not a peaceful separation. Margaret brought in expert legal representation. Margaret served Burt the divorce papers while the *Voyager* flight was in progress. No more "Sunshine," apparently.

CHAPTER 34

RUTAN AND THE HOMEBUILT MOVEMENT IN THE U.S.

Looking at Burt Rutan's work in homebuilt aircraft, we see an overall picture. He plugged into to a network of very interesting and able people, the nation's homebuilders. These people constructed planes made of tubing, fabric, wood, metal in their basements and garages. They changed designs and merrily altered engines and propellers to suit their own decisions. Into this wave of interest in do-it-yourself aircraft building came Burt with his startling new designs and materials.

When he flew his first plane to Oshkosh, Burt admits that "we just blew them away. We were amazed at the interest there was for this new plane."

This was one of the few parts of aviation in which an unknown, with practically no capital, could make such fast progress and become a star overnight. By pursuing something he loved, "building models on a full-size scale," Rutan was soon famous in aviation. His enormous talent and his radical willingness to try new ideas and materials were soon apparent. Aviation magazines reported his story.

The Experimental Aircraft Association was his natural home. His unassuming ways and his integrity made him a welcome EAA member.

I asked: "Were you thinking of going with EAA as an engineer after you graduated from college?"

"You mean go to work for them?"

"Yes, as an aeronautical engineer."

"Oh no. I never really seriously considered anything like that. I don't think a designer would fit into their organization."

"Did you quarrel with EAA at one time?"

"[Peter] Garrison printed that in *Flying* magazine. I don't know why he did that. Let me tell you what he was referring to. Since '71 I've flown my own airplane into Oshkosh every year. (He flew his homebuilt *VariViggen* in 1974.) The *Catbird* flew last year [1988].

"Homebuilders bring in their airplanes there. It's their show. Homebuilders are what EAA is all about. The flight line used to be open for them, you could take people for rides. When I first went out to the EAA Conventions, I would fly a dozen times during the day, giving people rides, showing off the airplanes. It was a fun fly-in. Then, EAA got mixed up with Warbirds, the Air Show, Classics. EAA wanted to be everything and it was. The *Concorde* coming in to fly. Military shows. We then felt that EAA was too big. You know they own all that property and we felt that we [the homebuilders] should have two weeks, then the Warbirds could have two weeks.

"We bring in our airplanes from all over the country. We're there, we *are* the show. People come from all over to see the homebuilts. They can bring their kids in, bash their cameras against your plane. But to do that, to bring your showpiece in there for them to see, EAA charges you 40 to 50 bucks for a flight line pass to get back out to your airplane! But not the Warbirds, EAA would buy the gas for them to get them to come in. *Then* they started cutting out the casual flying. Oh if there's Warbirds coming, if arrivals, no you can't fly. There was an accident or two and they cut out the flying. Now EAA guys go in there and they can't fly.

"At any rate, I made a little bit of noise. 'Listen we need some help, we need some changes around here.' I made some constructive comments. I was hearing from my homebuilders. They would write to me and say 'I'm not going to Oshkosh this year.' I would write about it in my *RAF Newsletter*. Have you a copy of those? I'll get a set for you. It'll drive you crazy, there'll be more in there than you can read! I was very open in the newsletter, discussed a variety of things.

"Every three months, four times a year, I've put them out every since 1974. The newsletter essentially tells my history from 1974 to present [1989]. Even since I got out of the plans business [1985], Mike Melvill who runs the RAF support functions, writes the newsletter and tells what we are doing currently.

"At any rate I published all this in the newsletter, 'Listen EAA needs to do this.' Garrison wrote that I had this big fight with EAA and that now I've returned to EAA. Well, I've never left. He said some very strange things. We had lunch together every week for years. We haven't in recent years, however, and he wrote this article in *Flying* as though he were still that close to us. He made some speculation there almost as though he had it in for me. Garrison, next time I see him, I'll give him a hard time!

[Speaking about Garrison's *Flying* article...] "He wrote that I made a lot of money selling my company to Beech, and I don't like that—the homebuilders hear this and think you're rich ... !" [Deep pockets!! Burt is sensitive to the way some lawyers attack like sharks when aircraft are involved! In fact he got out of the business of selling plans because of this strict liability situation.]

"At any rate I never left EAA. The very next year the *Voyager* stuff was building up and EAA actually has treated me much better since those comments that I made, than in the old days before I did. They take very good care of us now. First the *Voyager* and then the other planes. They want my *Starship* scale model for their museum." [The *Starship* scaled down prototype design that Burt designed for Beech in 1982 and 1983.]

Burt's voice changed: "Beechcraft wants me to cut it up, [the *Starship* 85 percent scale model] destroy it! And I refused. Because if a museum wants a history piece, it's theirs. 'Listen,' I said, 'A museum wants that. You don't go and destroy something that museums want. As long as there is some kind of appeals going on there, you can go pound sand.'"

"'You're not going to have that airplane.' They want it cut up because they don't want the history of the *Starship* connected so much to Burt Rutan. They won't admit that. They say it's because its a sub-scale airplane and they don't want the public getting the wrong idea of the *Starship's* real size. Anyway, we're fighting this thing. Probably get lawyers involved. [The word lawyers seems to sit bitterly on Burt's tongue.] If you go up there tomorrow, you'll see it on the ramp.

"It's prettier than the full-scale one. But at any rate, we've been asked to destroy it. This history piece which is the evolution of the *Starship*! If we lose that fight and they send someone out here to pick it up, or to destroy it, I'm goin' to have a media wine and cheese party and let them film the event.

"No we're very close in the last month or so to resolving that."

From that first plane built in his garage, Rutan has come a long way. Homebuilding has been forever changed by his sleek designs and by the new ways of using composite materials that he has pioneered in just a few years.

Rutan and other designers of homebuilt aircraft are altering the designs of future business aircraft, airline transports and even military aircraft.

It is a modest group, the experimental aircraft builders, but it has proved to be a very effective one. Rutan is certainly in the forefront of this activity.

CHAPTER 35

JEANA YEAGER

"Quiet, Shy, Introspective"

America hardly knew what to make of the second *Voyager* pilot, Jeana Yeager. She looked so quiet, so retiring, so slender. How could such a girl learn enough, have experience enough to be a record-breaking pilot? Particularly since the flight obviously would require endurance and skill that most men and women could never attain.

In early photographs showing the construction and test flying of the strange and beautiful airplane designed by Burt Rutan, Jeana's dark hair swept down over her shoulders. She was often pictured looking shyly at the camera while Dick Rutan explained some aspect of the plane or the flight.

At a Washington, D.C. seminar, after the magnificent *Voyager* flight was over, Jeana Yeager, Dick and Burt Rutan spoke to an audience of aviation historians and other Smithsonian experts. Dick gave a talk, brought Burt in to explain certain details of the design, and only once was Jeana asked for her views. It was to answer a question about the food they carried.

Obviously there is more to Jeana than this picture of a quiet, retiring young woman.

"Jeana Lee Yeager," her biography from the Voyager Enterprises Corporation says, "was born May 18, 1952 in Fort Worth, Texas. Most of her early years were spent in [the Texas towns of] Garland, Commerce and Houston." She is the daughter of Lee and Evaree Yeager.

Many people ask if Jeana is related to the famous test pilot "Chuck" Yeager. They say not. Yet research by Irene and George Rutan, Jr. leads the Rutans to believe that the two may be distant cousins.

Jeana is quiet, shy, introspective. She grew up in and around the Dallas-Fort Worth, Texas area, with the exception of three years in Oxnard, CA. She learned to ride horses when she was only three and soon began to handle her mounts with skill and confidence.

In junior high school, Jeana joined the school's track team. The principles of tenacity, discipline and stamina she learned there were to stand her in good stead later. Also while still in high school, she found that she had a talent for drawing.

By the age of 10 Jeana had become an expert in training and riding horses. This love for the beautiful animals continues to this day. Another very famous woman pilot had this gift for training horses—Beryl Markham, the first woman commercial pilot in Africa. Markham, too, grew up with horses, and became a respected trainer and earned her living training race horses in East Africa. Markham flew commercial charter, game spotting and rescue flights from 1931 to 1936 over mostly uncharted wilderness. In 1936 she became the first person to fly the Atlantic solo from east to west. She made the flight in a small single-engine aircraft.

All who know Jeana are impressed by her unrelenting determination to succeed, once she is convinced a task is worth doing.

Just before she was 20 she married Jon Farrar. After five years she decided to go to California to be with her sister, Judy Lindberg. She still cared for Farrar, even though they were divorced. Shortly after the divorce she was greatly saddened to learn of his death in an automobile accident.

Her drawing skills had proved to be useful when she moved to Santa Rosa, California in 1977 and qualified for a job drafting and surveying for a geothermal energy company. She is a commercial and engineering draftsman.

Jeana kept in touch with her father, Lee Yeager, and his present wife, Frances. She also wrote to her mother, also remarried, Evaree Winters and her husband, Douglas.

Jeana Takes to the Air!

Deciding to learn to fly airplanes was next for Jeana, as a first step toward flying helicopters. All this energy and determination is in a small package—she weighs in at less than 100 lbs. [To fly the *Voyager*, later, she had to use extensions to reach the rudder pedals.]

Her interest in aviation began in California. She was at first primarily interested in helicopters and but then found she enjoyed flying fixed-wing aircraft. By 1978 she had earned her private pilot's license.

Soon afterwards she met Capt. Robert Truax, U.S.N. (Retired). He was working on rocket launching systems. She began working for him as a draftsman and later with him in rocketry and systems engineering. In 1979 she posed in front of Truza's garage — home of Project Private Enterprise. [A play on the name of television's "Starship Enterprise."]

Jeana is described by writer Peter Garrison as being "... a futurist air-and-space buff."

She worked for a program which hoped to develop a way to safely launch private persons, one at a time, into space. The program was designed to launch these people for a ride of a lifetime and then recover them right away.

Jeana Meets Dick at RAF

It was in 1980 that Jeana stopped by the Rutan Aircraft display while attending an air show in Chino, CA. She met Dick Rutan at that time. Dick says that when he met her he had found a wonderful person. The two, as the romances put it, "fell in love," which is interesting—one falls! Yet it is a very descriptive and apt phrase.

Jeana came out to Mojave to be with Dick in 1980. They lived in a little house there. Irene Rutan and her husband helped the couple fix it up. Irene remembers doing interior painting with Jeana through the Mojave's dry weather, making the house bright and livable. Dick retains this home in Mojave.

Not long after getting her license, Jeana broke and set five new F.A.I. and N.A.A. world records for speed and distance flying. She set the records flying *VariEzes* and *Long-Ezs*.

The two couples—Burt and Patricia, Dick and Jeana—often went out to the local restaurants for the evening. They all look back on this time as one having the glow of youth, romance and zest for life. Subsequent achievements, disappointments and experiences were yet to come.

A World Flight Without Refueling?

One day, Dick, Burt, and Jeana were lunching at the Mojave Inn [now gone] and Burt brought up the subject of world flight without refueling, "the last first." All three were enthralled by the idea. Tom Jewett, a rival engineer and aircraft designer, had plans for a plane to break the world's long-distance record. Dick and Burt planned to do their rival one better and design a plane that would not only break the record but fly around the world without refueling.

So it was, just that simply, that the famous *Voyager* phenomenon began.

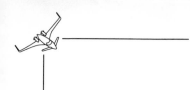

CHAPTER 36

THE YEAR OF THE *VOYAGER*—1986

Voyager Nearing Completion

Mike Melvill was invited to fly co-pilot on a *Voyager* test flight in the spring of 1986. Excitement was mounting. The around-the-world attempt date had been set—for September 14. Would they be able to make it?

Jeana was in the Midwest, adding a couple of ratings to her pilot's certificate, in preparation for the world flight.

No RAF at 1986 Sun 'n Fun

With the press of the *Voyager* and *Starship* work and a score of other projects, RAF people were not able to get to the spring EAA Fly-In at Lakeland, Florida.

Again, however, there were more composite type airplanes there than any other kind. In just a few short years, Rutan and his team had literally changed the homebuilt aircraft way of making flying machines.

July '86—Voyager Record

To test both the *Voyager* and themselves, on Thursday, July 10, Jeana and Dick took off from Vandenberg Air Force Base (where they had landed to solve a problem with the back propeller after seven hours of flight).

They flew up and down the coast of California, about 20 miles out to sea, around a closed course of 500 nautical miles per lap. It was also a good opportunity to get media coverage to build up the fund to help pay for *Voyager* and the equipment and people that would be needed for the world flight.

At dawn each day a chase plane left Mojave and joined up with *Voyager*, and again each day an hour or so before dark. The photographs from these flights were spectacular.

On Monday night George and Irene Rutan went up in the chase plane with Dick's daughters, Holly and Jill. "Mom" Rutan said, as she watched her older son with Jeana flying the plane designed by her younger son, that this was the "greatest day of her life, so far!"

On Sunday night, Burt, back from the midwest, came into the trailer that was monitoring the *Voyager* record attempt. He was frustrated to find that the detailed records he'd wanted were not being kept. Without the fuel data Burt had no way to figure the fuel needed for the world flight. He felt desperate and tightened up—the airplane was going to have to be so loaded with fuel for the world flight takeoff that is was going to be a most hazardous event.

Meanwhile, this long (long!) flight helped work out the transfer of pilots from one seat to the other. Jeana got in some flying time to get better acquainted with *Voyager* and its systems. Both managed to snatch some sleep. They had hoped to run through some rain in order to test out the behavior of the airplane in precipitation, but this was not to happen.

They did run into horrendous turbulence not far from Mojave and the three chase planes quickly broke away to give Dick, at the controls, a chance to fight the *Voyager* back to level flight. The crowd on the ground at Mojave Airport watched until they could see the four specks in the sky that soon turned into aircraft.

Both Jeana and Dick were exhausted. They had not really taken in enough liquids during the flight. This, too, was something they learned. Dick felt his attention stray during landing! But finally they were safely down at 6:37 a.m. Pacific time, July 15, 1986. They had proved that they could fly nearly five continuous days. Jeana found that she was dehydrated and standing for the interview that followed the flight, staggered and almost fell. Arms reached out for her valiant 98 pounds. She was soon made comfortable, with water poured over and into her.

They had flown 111 hours and 44 minutes. The distance traveled in the record laps was 11, 857 statute miles, plus the distance to and from the course. It was about the same distance as that from Paris to Tokyo! Amazingly, after the flight when the plane was weighed, it was found that it held enough fuel for a flight on to New York.

Oshkosh Again

This year Burt Rutan stock was higher than ever, if that were possible, at the 1986 EAA Convention in Oshkosh. Over 127 of his aircraft were parked on Wittman Airfield. The *Voyager* had just made its five-day record flight and was in training for the world flight attempt. There had been a serious set back in the *Voyager* program with the damage to the plane when a propeller failed. Yet, as worrying as this problem was, and delaying the world flight, it seemed to be on the way to being solved.

Burt was busy with Beech Aircraft, a vice-president, a star of design for both civil and military aircraft.

Reports kept coming in from all across the United States, from Europe, Africa, South America and Australia—of successful flights of homebuilt Rutan-designed aircraft—records flown.

As always, pell mell, life was going on. His mother, father, sister, Nell, and his brother Dick, were busy helping him into the record books. Jeana and the RAF and SCALED teams were working with him and they were his friends.

Melvills Celebrate

What? Could it be?

Sunday dawned and Sally Melvill prodded Mike to get up and go out to Mojave Airport. "No, no. It's Sunday. I've worked eight weekends in a row and I'm *not* moving."

So Sally had to admit that "a few people were flying in." They were coming, she announced, to help them celebrate their 25th wedding anniversary.

"Well," Mike wrote in the *Canard Pusher*, October 1986: "It turned out to be an absolutely beautiful day in Mojave." They counted 48 composite aircraft on the ramp. Friends had flown in from "all over" to spend a few hours eating good food and swapping tall tales. "It was great," Mike reported. "I had a ball. It was absolutely the neatest anniversary present any pilot could wish for."

"An Exciting Job for You"

If you would prefer to build a composite airplane instead of going to work, RAF wrote in January 1986, then we have an exciting job for you.

"Come to Mojave and challenge yourself while helping build some significant new research aircraft. We are in need of two good bodies to work with Mike Melvill and Bruce Evans."

RAF on Two-Days-a-Week

Only working two days a week, yet RAF readied a new 180-horsepower engine and three-bladed, feathering, constant speed propellers, installation for the *Defiant*. Mike Melvill made the first flight to test the new engines and propellers. He reported that the acceleration for takeoff and the climb were dramatically improved. He found level flight cruise speeds and attitude to be smooth and quiet.

RAF learned that the first homebuilt *Solitaire* had been flown and reported this in the January 1986 *Canard Pusher*.

The Smithsonian Calls—Doug Shane Answers

The historic *VariEze* prototype had been sitting quietly at Mojave Airport for a year and a half when Walter Boyne, curator of the National Air and Space Museum, called. He wanted Burt to donate N4EZ to the NASM.

"No problem," said Burt. The RAF and SCALED team gathered around the little airplane. Who would take it to Washington, D.C.? Doug Shane volunteered to fly it there in December 1985.

Doug got in some familiarization flying after the *VariEze* was inspected and put into flying shape. "Pilot proficiency," said Doug, preparing for the long flight to Washington, D.C., "Vari Important."

Off went the Californian covered in layer upon layer of clothing. He battled headwinds all the way. First stop was Las Vegas, then an overnight stay in Wichita. The following day he repositioned the aircraft, flying to Beech Field, Kansas City, where he waited out a cold front passage—"and enjoyed his mom's cooking," he reports.

Then off to Washington, D.C., with many a comment about the cold. The improvised cabin heater wasn't working and there were icy air leaks in the cabin. These kept the windshield clear but froze the pilot. At Louisville, Kentucky, Doug opted to land at Bowman Field, "I was so miserably cold that I couldn't stand to go any further."

"I think the people in Kentucky were taken aback at the monstrosity that climbed out of the funny little white plastic airplane," Doug said. "I was wearing electric socks, wool socks, down socks, moon boots, long underwear, blue jeans, sweat pants, flying suit, jacket, two pairs of gloves and a wool cap. And I was still cold!"

From Kentucky to Washington, D.C. [Hyde Field in Maryland] was an easy flight, once Doug warmed up. At Hyde Field, Doug pulled the mixture control, shutting down the faithful *VariEze's* engine for the last time. "It certainly had its glory," he writes of the prototype. "Its lines and performance caught the eye of thousands of people, and its siblings have brought thousands of hours of joy to their builders."

Smithsonian craftsmen from the Paul Garber Restoration Facility at Silver Hill, Maryland, arrived to disassemble the plane and drive it to the facility. Doug liked these dedicated men and women at Silver Hill. They shared the same love for their work as did Rutan's teams back in California. With some regret, Doug left "the fine, fine traveling machine," behind him to take its place in the history of flight. He returned to California in a well-heated McDonnell-Douglas MD-80.

Roncz Orders a Tailwind

While on a trip from New Orleans to Chicago, John Roncz walked into the Jackson, Tennessee Flight Service Station and said in a loud, steady voice: "I'd like to order a tailwind."

"We don't give tailwinds to Yankees," said the FSS man, and sure enough, he didn't.

Voyager Work Goes On

Work on the *Voyager* was an always present reality. The project was a presence behind the work on new designs being researched and behind Burt's work with Beech Aircraft Company.

CHAPTER 37

VOYAGER TAKEOFF ROLL—WOW!

Voyager Flight and Aftermath—1987

There was no time to even think about the usual three-week process of getting a January edition of the *Canard Pusher* out to RAF customers. The *Voyager* flight in December had absorbed time and energy and much of the RAF team's attention. It was early in 1987 that *Canard Pusher* reported on the Voyager flight to its readers.

Very early in the morning, December 14, 1986, Burt, flying a Beech *Duchess* and carrying Mike and Sally Melvill, took off from Mojave Airport for Edwards Air Force Base. It was so early that when they arrived over the base, the tower had not yet opened for business. But, after contacting Edwards Approach Control, runway lights were turned on and the *Duchess* landed.

They taxied over to the "hammerhead" ramp area of Runway 4. *Voyager* had been parked there overnight. Bruce Evans and his crew had worked practically all through the night to fuel the airplane.

Voyager looked homely, not historic, because to prevent frost from forming on the wings and controls, household bed sheets were draped across the wings and canard. Homeowners in the town of Mojave had donated these very useful items.

Voyager Flight Remembered

"The take-off roll! Wow!" reported the April 1987 *Canard Pusher* in an eye-witness account by Mike and Sally Melvill. "We lined up on Runway 4 [in the Beech *Duchess* chase plane] off the right wing of the *Voyager*. Burt was ready with his video camera as Mike eased in the power. The *Duchess* slowly rolled with the *Voyager* as she started on what we think may be the longest take-off time ever!

"At the 7,000-foot marker, we still were not going fast enough to lift off in the *Duchess*! The *Voyager* wingtips were dragging on the runway, Jeana was calling out indicated airspeeds each thousand feet, and the *Voyager* was behind schedule on speed.

"Finally, we lifted the *Duchess* off and continued following the *Voyager* while we were a few feet off the ground. The end of the runway was rapidly approaching, the end of a 15,000-foot runway! Finally, Jean called 87 knots, the speed Burt had predicted the *Voyager* would need to fly. Dick began to rotate and slowly, magnificently, the wingtips rose off the runway and the wings bent into a graceful arch—she lifted off with less than 1,000 feet of runway remaining!

"The take-off roll lasted for an unbelievable 2:04 minutes! The excitement in the chase plane was short-lived when we realized that the winglets were failing.

"There was a frightening moment as the winglets failed and fluttered off, ripping the top and bottom wing skins inboard to the outboard wing tanks.

"Then, [a little later] there was the beautiful sight of the *Voyager* crossing the coast at Point Mugu and heading out over the Pacific. Those were unforgettable moments.

"We followed in close formation until we were almost 300 miles off the coast. A last careful look at the engines, wings—everything but the wingtips looked optimum. We said our tearful 'good-byes,' waved to Dick and Jeana and, with difficulty, turned 180 degrees and headed back.

In the days and nights that followed there was to be a night rendezvous over Hawaii, a storm east of the Philippines, autopilot failure as they approached the Philippines, and weather south of the Malay Peninsula.

Southwest of India there was a coolant seal leak. Over Kenya they had a daylight rendezvous with another plane. Later, they had to fly across Africa's mountains avoiding squall lines and dangerous thunderstorms. Daylight and dark succeeded each other.

The crew fought to keep the *Voyager* flying, to keep themselves alive. They had to remember to drink and eat, to get rest. Dick, the most experienced pilot, stayed in the pilot's seat as long as he could and at one point suffered hallucinations from lack of sleep. Somehow Jeana managed to maneuver the big man over into the cabin to sleep and then flew the plane on course for hours. Then she waked him to cope with hazards ahead.

They alternated flying the plane. Together they made up the team that saw it make its way successfully across the broad and stormy Atlantic west of Africa.

They skirted the northern coast of South America, crossed Central America at Costa Rica, and began to fight headwinds home up the coast of the Baja peninsula, and then the coast of California. Then it happened. Off Baja Peninsula, Mexico, at 2 a.m., they lost power at only 8,000 feet. So near to home and to lose the fight? Somehow they got the engine started again. Now it was a matter of fuel and distance.

It was in the air that the brothers were reconciled. With Mike Melvill, Burt flew out to meet his brother and Jeana, as they came up the coast of California in the darkness, very early on December 23, 1986.

Burt was talking into a recorder to be sure the moment was preserved. As he saw the navigation lights of *Voyager*, valiantly flying home after its amazing and dangerous nine-day flight around the world, his voice choked off. He couldn't speak. Aviation writer Peter Garrison so well put it: "Perhaps Dick felt for Burt at that moment what brothers in storybooks are supposed to feel toward one another."

After 10 days in the cramped cockpit of *Voyager*, Jeana gladly put her feet back on earth. Burt hugged her then hugged his brother. Jeana said that she "... felt like a duck—calm on the outside but paddling like hell underneath." She found herself able to stand. Dick, walking stiffly but making it, was shaking hands all around. [Well meaning people placed Jeana in the ambulance. Actually, she wanted to be outside shaking hands, sharing the excitement of the successful end of the flight.] Finally Dick joined Jeana in the ambulance that was to take them over the base hospital for a medical check, a longed-for

Dick Rutan and Jeana Yeager pose in front of a *Voyager* museum exhibit commemorating their historic flight.
Photo courtesy the Experimental Aircraft Association.

shower and then the welcome home party. *Voyager*, left on the vast ramp/hangar area, had just 18.3 gallons of fuel left in her tanks.

Burt's design, the *Voyager*, had made it around the world on one tank of gas.

Against All Odds!

Long ago, the trio had stood in the National Air and Space Museum in Washington, D.C. They had vowed to make the around-the-world flight, and to do it their way.

Against all odds, this is just what they managed to do.

"The Burt to whom we returned was a very different man from the one we had left," Jeana had said. "He had become more and more concerned about us in the weeks before we took off and more and more conservative in his calculations for takeoff. And during the flight we heard that he had become more and more emotional."

"He couldn't work at all," Mike Melvill said.

"And not long after we landed," Jeana reported, "Dick and Burt went off together for a weekend in Las Vegas, the two brothers having fun together for the first time in years, probably since they were kids in Dinuba, California."

"...and the Tears Flowed"

Memories, highlights from the ground point of view came to mind, as Sally wrote later, they were to remember: "Working in the Communications trailer at Mojave ... threading the needle when Len Snellman guided *Voyager* around the cyclone "Marge" out in the Pacific; Dick, fighting sleep near Sri Lanka; trying to persuade Dick to quit flying and go to sleep; trying to figure out what was going on in the fuel system.

Mike remembers: "The storms and unfriendly countries in Central Africa; oil starvation in the middle of the Atlantic at 4:00 a.m.; the right side fuel transfer pump failing; both engines stopped, gliding for a *full five minutes* off the coast of the Baja peninsula at 2:00 in the morning on the last night!

Jeana replumbed the fuel system and *then* they could pump fuel from the right side, both engines now running. "Burt and Mike leaving the trailer at 4:30 a.m. to take off in the *Duchess* to greet the *Voyager* and escort her in."

Burt and Mike flew out over the black Pacific, probing for the *Voyager* in the night. Suddenly, there was a small strobe light, and, "Yes, it was the *Voyager* and tears flowed." Slowly we stepped closer, and like an apparition there was the dark shadow of the *Voyager* with its wings almost perfectly straight, "appearing against the background of clouds over the Los Angeles Basin."

"The emotional join-up was something Burt and Mike will never forget. There, after completely encircling the globe, was *Voyager* containing Dick and Jeana, so close we felt we could touch them. It was incredible."

They sailed over Los Angeles, across an almost solid cloud deck, at 10,500 feet. An airliner curved by, TV camera planes came up, a Grumman flown by Doug Shaen, a Beechcraft flown by Crew Chief Bruce Evans, all joined up on the *Voyager*.

"The excitement of flying off the edge of the clouds and seeing Edwards and Rogers Dry Lake far below, clear and calm; the talk over the radio...then the sight of all the thousands of people who had gotten up at two and three o'clock in the morning to line the edge of the dry lake ...." Dick and Jeana flew several passes over the crowd then landed. "These are the memories. What an incredible achievement, what real live heroes, Dick and Jeana. And what an unbelievable airplane. "Success at last! Congratulations to Burt, Dick and Jeana and the whole team of *Voyager* volunteers."

Voyager Flies "One More Time"

Bruce Evans, exhausted and drained by the years of effort and the anxieties attendant upon the flight itself, now told Dick and Jeana that the plane actually shouldn't have made it successfully. There were so many things, smoke, electrical arcing, failing seals, that could have downed them. "... and it should never fly again." Bruce said.

But it did fly one more time. Keeping over the desert, not using any more electrical devices than absolutely necessary, wearing parachutes, on January 6, 1987, Dick and Jeana flew the plane on its last flight, for photos, and to return it to the Mojave Airport. On landing, they found an engine coolant seal completely failed. But, in spite of everything that could have happened, the plane had brought them through, failing seal and all. That specialized, strange, unique and amazing aircraft had done its job, as they had done theirs.

Mojave Residents Celebrate

The town of Mojave seems to crouch to escape the winds and dust of the Mojave Desert. All during the building of Burt Rutan's RAF and his SCALED companies, the people in the town had been fascinated with his work.

When the *Voyager* project began, the townspeople watched with concern. As testing proceeded, they supported the team in every way that they could. Volunteers from across the country found hospitality in Mojave.

When *Voyager* landed, Mojavians were out by the hundreds to wave flags and cheer Jeana and Dick. On its last flight, Michele Gardner Behrens, Jeana's mother, local realtors, their family; the people of Mojave, again turned out to cheer. At this last landing of *Voyager*, after its four-hour photographic mission, Larry Caskey, the general manager of the project came up to Michele. "Well, this project is over, do you want a new one?"

"Anything you want!" Michele smiled.

"How about raising funds to purchase the communications trailer?" He was referring to the VMC (*Voyager* Mission Control) trailer, located by the Voyager Hangar. It had been leased in August 1986 back when plans were to fly the mission in September. Due to the propeller accident, the flight couldn't be made in that month. When they did fly, it was decided that the VMC would be placed in the Smithsonian so that not just the airplane itself but the whole project could be preserved.

Michele takes up the story: "The trailer was going to cost about $8,000; all the maps were going to be left just as they were; all the computers gutted but with their faces, consoles left in place.

"It would be set up so that people could walk through it. There would be videotapes going to show exactly what happened. (We had taped the mission operation.)

"It was a very exciting time, *Voyager*. Every minute. Living only five blocks away, we drove out there to the trailer every day. So when Dick and Larry Caskey came to me, it was decided to let just the community of Mojave donate funds to buy the trailer.

"A barbecue dinner would be best, with Burt, Dick and Jeana present to thank the community and an opportunity for the town of Mojave's residents to thank them for all the publicity! We started early in February of 1987 and the date was set for February 27, 1987. The main problem was getting a place—and then the problem of how to feed 500 people at once. We sold tickets all over town and across the Antelope Valley area.

"We ended up borrowing chairs from every church and community building in Mojave. Fifteen women helped get it together, yes, me too. We washed potatoes, volunteered home ovens to bake them, from 8:00 a.m. until noon. We had to get county clearance for that home cooking aspect.

"A local caterer did the steaks for us. The girls from Mojave High School cut up the lettuce for a giant salad. Then the high school choir came to the dinner and sang for us.

"At the dinner we had video messages from the volunteers who lived in Florida. Lots of people out of Los Angeles came who had been on the mission control team as volunteers. The dinner was from 7:00 to 10:00 and then they all had a big party.

"You see, it had been six weeks since they'd seen each other in many cases. They'd had a big hallelujah party after the landing and then had all scampered home for a late Christmas. So this was a great time to swap tales, relive the mission. We were all happy about that." Yes, she said, they made several thousand dollars and the trailer was bought. It sits in a hangar now waiting to be put on display at the Smithsonian or elsewhere. The townspeople had succeeded in saving a vivid part of aviation history.

Jeana Yeager After the Voyager Flight

Jeana, after her world flight, was honored with Dick and Burt in many ceremonies. She went on the lecture circuit. A popular book, *Voyager*, was written by herself and Dick Rutan with Phil Patton. Nell Rutan, Burt's sister, wholeheartedly admires Jeana. "She is so focused and so determined. She really deserves a large share of credit for the success of *Voyager*." She, like the Rutan brothers, never gives up on a project, but in spite of obstacles, tenaciously carries on.

Dick and Jeana had met and had been strongly attracted to each other before the *Voyager* project began. They had worked together for years to get the plane built, to equip

189

Friends for
Voyager's Mission Control

FUNDRAISER
BARBECUE

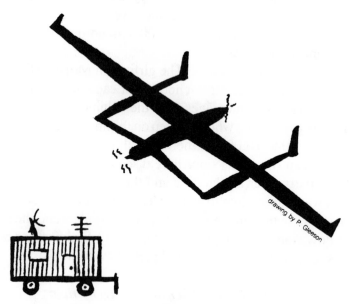

February 27, 1987
Mojave Airport
Aerotest, Inc. Hangar #68

Program for the 1987 Fundraiser Barbeque.
Photo courtesy Michele Behrens.

it, to finance the whole venture, and finally to make a flight that had tested both of them almost to the limit.

Oddly enough, at the moment of their triumph, they also felt lonely. They were to go their separate ways in their personal lives. They would appear before many a camera and crowd together in the months ahead, but a unique and magical time was over. True to their natures, they went ahead with their work and their lives. But the desert time, the planes, the hours spent together, that supreme adventure of the *Voyager* flight, was now a memory.

In a BBC broadcast, after the *Voyager* flight, Dick was to say that the project destroyed the relationship between himself and Jeana. There was so much pressure, such hope, such disappointments. Finally, as Jeana said, she chose the *Voyager* over her relationship with Dick and let it absorb her energy and attention entirely.

It might have been that the only way for them to get the project done was to abandon everything else, to press to the limit of their strength toward their goal.

Today Jean and Dick are no longer together. Jeana operates Voyager Enterprises, Inc., in Nipomo, California. She is giving a great deal of time to working with young people to instill in them an interest and some knowledge of aerospace subjects.

Horses continue to claim her love and attention. She has tried harness racing. She has traveled, to India and to Africa, and elsewhere. You can see her reaching out for life, for experiences. The Voyager Center, a museum that will show the world flight and give hands-on scientific projects experiences to visitors is planned for "kids of all ages."

You can see Jeana Yeager still reaching out for new horizons, new knowledge. In this she is still the young girl in Texas that broke out of the usual routines to ride, to draw, to run.

Citations were to follow. Dick and Jeana and Burt were national heroes, world famous.

Burt was on a roll at Beech Aircraft Company, busy with the futuristic, beautiful *Starship* design.

Honors and Awards

With Dick Rutan, Jeana has received:

Presidential Citizen's Medal of Honor	The Collier Trophy
Gold Medal from the Royal Aero Club (England)	Medalle de Ville Paris and the Grande Medallion from the Aero Club of France

Other honors include:

The Daedalian Distinguished Achievement Award	The Spirit of Flight Award
The Patriot of the Year Award	The Golden Plate Award
The Iven C. Kincheloe Outstanding Test Pilot Award from the Society of Experimental Test Pilots	The Edward Longstreth Medal from the Franklin Mint
The Flying Tiger Pilot Award	The Jaycees TOYA (Ten Outstanding Young Americans) Award

Honorary Doctorate Degrees:

In Science and Technology from Central New England College
In the Humanities from Lewis University

Thousands of people have visited this *Voyager* exhibit at the EAA Air Adventure Museum.
Photo courtesy the Experimental Aircraft Association.

Final Numbers

When the *Voyager* flight was over, flown from December 14-23, 1986, with pilots Dick Rutan and Jeana Yeager, the numbers they had piled up were impressive:

Total flight time, 9 days, 3 minutes and 44 seconds
Total flight distance, 25,012 miles
Takeoff weight, 10,000 pounds
Takeoff fuel, 1,207 gallons
Average fuel consumption was 16.9 miles per gallon

Patricia Storch Remembers the Voyager Flight

"Where were you during the *Voyager* flight?" I asked Patricia Storch in March 1989.

"We were all out here at Mojave at SCALED, business as usual, trying to keep things rolling. We'd go down to the press briefings to see what Burt was saying and just to check in. Very, very many of SCALED employees had volunteered their time to the project, so we were all very concerned.

"The press office during the flight was located in the *Voyager* hangar, here at the Mojave Airport.

"At the landing at Edwards, every family member was to be in the family trailer and they had their spouses. Nell Rutan had asked me to be her guest, since she had no spouse. There was some political problem.

"It was very, very kind of her to invite me. she knew how involved I'd been in the project from the beginning, how much it meant to me. Well, somebody took great exception to my being there. It may have been the *Voyager* PR person, he didn't care for me."

"Nell got upset that had happened. They were going to have a photographer—taking pictures of the family as they went through the emotions of the landing. So Nell said she didn't want a stranger taking pictures, she wanted me to take the pictures.

"She was really insistent. So I was very fortunate to be with them at that time and take some pictures. It was a very, *very* emotional time. Oh, God! I can't even describe it. My own personal emotions were upset for weeks surrounding that whole flight. Tension kept building and building—it was two years!"

CHAPTER 38

THE INSIDE STORY OF VOYAGER

Burt Rutan Reflects

"If you dig out some of these references, say, on the *Voyager*, let me caution you, [laugh] don't necessarily believe that they're factual because they're in print. A lot of things in the book were written more so that they'd be entertaining for the general public," Burt Rutan said in a March 1989 interview at his [then] Palmdale home.

"One of the basic issues, well the story has been told many places but, the thing that hasn't been published, and the appropriate place would have been the *Voyager* book which purports to be the document for the history of the *Voyager* program. What really happened there is an interesting story in itself.

"My brother served 20 years in the U.S. Air Force as an officer. When you do this you have this impression that you're a good business manager. Though if you really look at what your real responsibilities are, it's limited. At any rate, my brother got out of the service, checked the want ads, couldn't find 'Lieutenant Colonel'—I guess that's a kind of a joke." He looked around.

"He wasn't a test pilot. He'd done some flying for maintenance, FCF flying, that's Functional Check Flight. He'd been a fighter pilot. But he wanted to be a test pilot. You don't get to be a test pilot for a big company unless you get to go to the U. S. Air Force or Aerospace test pilot school or Navy Test Pilot School in the service, and he never got to do that, you have to have an engineering degree. So anyway, I agreed to hire him as a test pilot, but I didn't have much test flying to do, I did most of it myself, only on the agreement that he'd also do the floor sweeps, help me build airplanes. Now there's four people, two in the shop, well maybe five people [working at RAF], April 1978.

"Well, he came to work for me. It was a tough thing to do. I'm five years younger than he is, a successful entrepreneur, running a business, making good money and enjoying myself, building airplanes. Well Dick came into that environment. He thought 'I'm a lot smarter than my brother as a businessman, and I've had this Air Force experience.'" Burt smiled. "So you know, he thought that I should to bend over and change my ways of doing business, start promoting the airplanes like he thought they should [be promoted]. So I, on many occasions, told him 'No.'"

"He wanted to put on demonstrations to promote the airplanes, and I didn't want the airplanes demonstrated to customers with aerobatics. I wanted to discourage the homebuilders from doing aerobatics because I think it's dangerous for them.

"He had this awful desire to be a successful entrepreneur and businessman without ever getting a grasp of what it takes to do that, how much work. So anyway, he worked for me a couple of years. During that time period that I transitioned over from being the chief test pilot to letting somebody else do it. Mike Melvill and Dick Rutan during that time did the first flights. After Dick came to work for me he helped me to build the *Defiant* and I did the first test flight on that."

I asked Burt: "It must be hard to turn your airplanes over to someone else to fly?"

"Well, not really. Tell you why, the last airplane I made the first flight on was the *Defiant*, and it was the fifth new type that I'd made the first flight on.

"I found myself out there in a dive test once, a very dangerous thing to do. It didn't take a lot of skill but it takes a lot of guts because as the airplane goes faster and faster sometimes it may have a flaw. And if it does, it may develop a flutter and the airplane disappear around you and you may not get out of it. Very dangerous.

"A friend of mine had just been killed in a flight test accident, and another one a month earlier. And I realized on that *one* flight, at that *moment*, really, 'Why am I doing this? This is absolutely absurd! There are youngsters that *want* to do this!'"

"You were not so much interested in being a pilot as you were in being an aircraft designer?"

"Well that's been published, but it's not really true. I enjoy flying. I pride myself on being a very good pilot. But, no, I was into *flying* airplanes as much as Dick. Model airplanes, real planes. Mostly into something new. Whereas Dick wanted to fly anything. He'd go out and fly, fly, fly. But I wanted to fly different planes.

"But at any rate, I decided, 'I'm not going to do this anymore.' I'll fly my airplanes but within the envelope that other people take the risks. I knew that maybe twenty, fifteen or twenty people, maybe I knew them just from meeting them at Oshkosh, designers, friends, test pilots and whatever. And out of that twenty there were three, then four, that were killed. The odds here are much worse than Russian Roulette. I can't imagine putting a bullet in a barrel of six and going and trying that! And really I realized that I was doing that.

"When I was flight testing in the Air Force, I came very close to having to eject from an airplane. It was the only Air Force aerobatic flat spin that ever got out of it. On the next flight the plane crashed.

"So, the success rate of the ejection seat the F-4 was identical to Russian Roulette, one in six was a fatality. At any rate, I realized that it was just a matter of time, I'd had some tough breaks, some very close calls. 'I'm not going to do the dangerous stuff anymore, let someone else do the first flight, the dive tests, the spin tests. I'll fly the airplane when it's all through those.'

"As it turned out, it wasn't a good call, because we've developed a whole bunch of airplanes since then and none of them have crashed. I get to fly them but I don't get the glory of the first flight, but I don't need that now.

"OK, so at any rate, here's my brother working for me as test pilot, but he want's to run his own show, do his own thing. He met this girl and she moved in with him. Jeana. And here I was running the show and I was his younger brother and he wanted to do something of his own. There was Jeana there, she didn't have a job, and they wanted to do something on their own.

"So he quit RAF. Jeana never worked there. He came to me and said, 'Burt, you're my brother and you're going to design an aerobatic airplane for me and I'll sell kits. It'll be the biggest program in the world and I'll sell hundreds of them. Make lots of money.'

"And I said, 'The hell you will! First of all, I don't do an aerobatic airplane for those reasons [liability, danger to pilots]. And I don't have time anyway. Why should I design a plane to compete with my outfit? And, anyway—to hell with you.'"

"I essentially told him that 'I will not do that.' And he said, 'Well what do I do now?' All up in arms. So I said, 'Why don't you do the world flight unrefueled, it's possible now.' He'd done record flights in my airplanes while he'd worked for me, you know.

"The funny thing about it, is when I told him that, I had done only some cursory calculations, to prove to myself that it might be possible, I didn't know for sure. I was encouraging him to do it. And this was the famous Mojave Inn lunch, and whatever, and he was begging me at that lunch to build him an aerobatic plane. And the subject of that lunch was to tell him, 'No, I'm not going to do an aerobatic airplane for you.'"

"But I did tell him, though, that if he would go out and do world flight nonrefueled I would design the airplane for him under a certain agreement that I'd be the concept designer. He'd have to get a lot more design work done because I didn't have the time, Hell, I was working on the *Starship*! I was building a new company, SCALED Composites, we're talking February '81. I hadn't built the company yet, but very shortly thereafter did, I was working on the *Starship* design.

"So I made an agreement with him that he pay me 3 percent now, 5 percent after the world flight, of any money that you make on this. That was not very much. 'And I will design it for you. But you're going to have to do everything else. I don't have time for it.'

"OK, fine. We wrote up an agreement and signed it. And I spent sometime over the next couple of months, is all, detailing out a conceptual preliminary design for the thing, in which I came from this ugly flying-wing kind of thing to the *Voyager* configuration, essentially the one that flew. I did this over the next few weeks and came up with Model 76 and that was it. And I said to Dick, 'I think this will do the job and I'm more confident now that it will.' And so Jeana made a nice little isometric sketch of it. I made no more calculations then, I didn't have the time!

"So then Dick went off, with this plan to go out and get big corporations to sponsor it. He thought he'd have the fuselage built one place, the other parts other places, and SCALED Composites was going to bid on it. He was going to get all these big pieces done, not have to do the work on it himself, then bring them together, and 'I'll do my own flight test program, not Burt's. I'll do my own development.'

"And that was the only agreement I had with him. See I didn't charge him very much, this 3 percent-5 percent was not very much. The rest of the design and calculation work would have to be done by others. I was the conceptual designer, I would show them the way, but then obviously they would have to do it. Because I told him I couldn't spend much time with him.

"But it did need the inspiration, the design had to be right for it to work, and I would set all the ground rules for it. So that's all he needed, 'Good, my brother's behind me anyway.' So they went off with this big business plan, got some brochures printed up. And

196

they went out on the road, spending Jeana's money, see Dick didn't have anything. He got his divorce. And they went through, I don't know, twelve, fifteen thousand dollars of Jeana's money, went through all of it.

"They came to me every couple of weeks, for a hotel or so, just another day would do it. They didn't tell it in the book but there was this editor, he was the guy who was talked about in the book. Anyway, I went to a couple of these meetings with Dick and Jeana, I had a feeling that there was not much chance of getting money up front. All they had was this paper sketch. But Dick was sure that he was going to do it.

"Finally, he came up with a offer from—a Japanese video company—and the deal was, well it didn't seem enough money, though I thought it was enough. He really wasn't going to have to buy the engines and avionics. But Dick thought he would. And Dick said, 'Well, I've had to buy everything so far!'"

"And the deal was that the company would pay in increments, just to keep ahead of the cash flow. But he had to guarantee that the airplane would be built in eleven months, or something. To go around the world in another four months. This was so that this major world feat would be done in time, so that their new miniature video camera could be named —or rather that the airplane could be named after the video camera. And they could use the success of this historic and interesting feat to promote their new video camera.

"That was the plan, okay? They paid him on success. He wouldn't get paid everything if it the flight weren't successful, and he wouldn't get paid anything if the airplane didn't fly, and a few milestones like that. And I said, 'Dick! This is *not* a good deal! You've got to get somebody who'll take the risk, give you the money up front. Furthermore, I don't even want to work on the thing if it's a Japanese deal. Because it'll be a big Japanese advertisement. The Smithsonian won't even hang the airplane if it's got their big ad on it. The hell with it.'"

Not that there is anything wrong with the Japanese. They are marvelous at design and manufacture. But this was a project that Burt Rutan saw as being uniquely an American one.

"And he says, 'It's all I've got. And I'm broke.' He didn't like it either, but it was all he had.

"Now here's the thing that wasn't told in the *Voyager* book, and you'll see *why* it wasn't told in the book. Dick and Jeana are down in the doldrums, their money is all gone. He's there twisting my arm to change this, to take this Japanese thing and go with it. His money is all gone. He can't eat next month unless he does it.

"So I said, 'Listen Dick, it's stupid, there's only one way to do this thing and it's like I've done all my airplanes in the past. I don't go out and put on a tie and go out and sell something that doesn't fly, yet. I go out and *do it*, first; fly it.'

"And he looked at me as if to ask where I was going to get the million dollars to and I told him it wouldn't take a million dollars. 'Where are you going to get the engines?'

"'I've got the engines.'

"And I laid the whole program out. I would build the airplane, in what's called Phase One. And the ground rules were, and I had my own family involved in this, my mother and father would let Dick and Jeana stay in their house for nothing. They would specifically put food in the refrigerator, this was a part of the whole plan.

"My mom [Irene Rutan] would start the Voyager VIP Club. Dick and Jeana would work their *butts* off building it. I would hire other people, so that we would have a team. And I would pay all expenses, I would develop the airplane. My overhead, I would stop the next project I was planning, in order to do this. I would try to get the thing done in a year, although who knows how long it's going to take. And, I'd flight test it under my budget. I'd supply the engines, and Dick thought this was crazy because I couldn't afford to do it, but I knew I could.

"And when I got it to the point in flight tests where I could tell exactly by flight test results, exactly the engines that would be needed in order for it to go around the world, then I would be done with my responsibilities. Phase One would be done.

"By flying it, measuring accurately, I could then specify very accurately what engines it would need to go around the world. I could fly it initially though on a couple of junker engines that I already had. Engines from VariEzes. OK?

"Now, Phase Two was Dick's. And the problem was that he would no longer be an entrepreneur during Phase One, he'd be working for his brother again, so it was tough for him to swallow. But I had to call the ground rules because I meant Rutan Aircraft Factory. Phase Two, he would go out and get the engines that were called for, the expensive ones, though I knew he wouldn't have to pay for them [they would be donated], the world flight requirements, the recorders, the satellite, all the avionics, the navigational gear, autopilot.

"He would be responsible for developing the new airplane as it related to the new engines. I would fly it 'bare bones,' I wouldn't put any money into it. But the thinking is, once I had it flying at the end of my phase, and he had a picture of it flying. You know the picture on the poster, the most popular poster? That airplane, at that point , was in Phase One. Dick didn't have anything to do managing or anything at that point. So that's what he didn't want to say anything about in the book.

"He would do Phase Two, including the world flight, and because we thought that Phase One and Phase Two were roughly of equal cost, responsibilities, it was very equitable that they were. But he pointed out that the navigational gear would cost $300,000, and the engines would cost $100,000. But it didn't matter. It didn't matter to me. I wanted it to be done. And the idea was that any money coming in on *Voyager* we would split 50-50. A totally different contract from my designer one.

"So what happened was, when you got money off from giving a talk on *Voyager*, sold a tee-shirt, I'd get my 3 percent as the designer, and then we'd split the rest of the money, 50-50. OK? So, now isn't that a good deal at that time, to him. Boy, it sure is. Because, 'It's all I've got.'

"And the neat thing about the deal was that it wouldn't be painted with Japanese letters and there wouldn't be anybody as boss but us. So that's what happened. And that's the story that should have been in the *Voyager* book. But Dick and Jeana are very up tight about the fact that they worked for a couple of years for the younger brother, and he called all the shots. And they worded around that story in the book.

"You know I didn't read the book at all until it was in covers. And you know the most fascinating thing about it? The writer, the ghost writer's name is on it; Pat never talked to me. Pat never talked to me! Never talked to Melvill at RAF. Strange!

"Well anyway, that was the plan. What happened was we took twenty months instead of twelve months. Dick was just beside himself, it was taking so long. But they got in there and they worked hard. I hadn't, even counting my overhead, $190,000 in that airplane. Now that's because $90,000 of the carbon fiber was donated. See I had the clout in the industry. You see Dick would go out to these guys and they didn't know who he was. But I was Burt Rutan who did things with the *Starship*, the *VariEze*, the *Long-EZ* and so on, so I had all the materials donated.

"Almost all the materials were donated. I paid Bruce Evans, I paid him $24,000 a year, and he worked not 2,000 hours a year but twice that. He's a super guy. He's working on the *Pond Racer* now. But Dick, during that phase, he liked to think of it as his project still. Because you know, he worked a lot more hand to hand with Bruce Evans, so to him Bruce Evans was his guy, you know. They gave Bruce good recognition in the book, he was treated well, and he deserved every bit of it.

"And we fought a lot, on things. Dick wanted it gold-plated. Just incredible. But I knew what it would take to fly around the world and it was an enormous job for me to educate those around me. Bruce was much easier to educate on it than Dick was, on what it really takes to go around the world unrefueled. They *worked*; it took 20 months. Dick very much wanted to have his project for his own. And in September of '84, I turned it over to him for Phase Two.

"Now, it turned out that the appeal of the plane flying, the photographs, and the airplane went to Oshkosh '84, and Dick got with Peter Riva and got the dollar signs in his eyes. This thing could be worth millions, he thought. My God! I've got to give half of it to Burt! That bothered him more than anything else.

"But we said, 'But wait a minute, Dick. What do you mean, we're not worth it. What would you have had if we hadn't built your airplane for you. My God, you'd have nothing. You'd be out —

"It's not unusual, a little normal sibling rivalry. He wanted to do something on his own. Halfway between the time he took over, very late in '84, he was planning that summer he would do it. He'd lined up these promo guys in these big lucrative things. And it just bothered the hell out of him that he would have to give half the money from this thing to his brother. He just couldn't appreciate that maybe he deserved it.

"So he came to Rutan Aircraft Factory and said, 'Listen, we just want our own identity, Jeana and I. We want it to be our project. We want to buy off the contract.'

"I thought, the downside of this, well Dick's got million-dollar deals lined up, the books and all, but that wasn't the important thing to me. To me was the *Voyager* was just one thing, and that was the technical accomplishment. I can make money other ways. Dick had scraped a lot more than I had, certainly since '78, when he got out of the service. I didn't pay him very well! And he had really scraped during the building, he didn't have any income. I bought him lunch.

"So he just didn't want to share, if it was going to be a really successful thing, he didn't want to share it with his brother. He was divorced from me, now had his own project. Indeed, he was calling his own shots.

I asked Burt: "How did you find time to do *Voyager*?"

"While the thing was being built at RAF, it was primarily an evening project for me. About five or six o'clock I'd go over there and work with Bruce on what was to be built that day and design what was to be done. And Bruce would come over and bother me once or twice a day, but no, it wasn't that I sat there full-time designing the *Voyager*. There were only 24 drawings on it, not counting the loft, computer drawings, in fact a lot of it on scraps and pieces of paper that got thrown away!

"But *Voyager* was a very simple airplane. At any rate, it probably wouldn't have happened if it wasn't for Bruce Evans. A super guy, a lot of stick-to-itiveness. He knew how important it was for it to be light. It had to be strong enough and safe enough, yet light.

"But Dick wanted his own identity. He asked me what it would take to buy out of this contract so that, 'We can call it all ours.' Here it was early 1986 with the world flight planned in early September. The only reason I'd even considered *Voyager* was as my means of repairing this thing with my brother. The Christmas before that, we had ended up yelling at each other on Christmas Day, and my sister was here, and all the family was together. And so I said, to myself, if I do this thing and it's all his, then we won't ever have to yell at each other again. I won't have to audit his books to see if he's giving me half, and so forth.

"My reward was to be the success technically, not the money that would come in off the airplane. I can make money building other airplanes. My reward is the recognition and so forth, that would help. I figured out the direct cost. It came to $186,000. OK? So I told them $186,000. I thought that he'd yell about it and say I hadn't paid this or that. There were other factors involved, too, that I wasn't charging for—I didn't do another homebuilt while involved in *Voyager* as I'd planned. But anyway, I thought it would be another big fight with my brother.

"But he laughed and he came back and he says, 'OK. Sign here.' He could only pay me half then. He paid me interest, though. But he went out and borrowed, a lot of it from our folks! He paid me and he paid them interest. If he went out and signed up a million-dollar deal to do a book, or something, it would be all his.

"Then he joined up with Peter Riva. They are suing each other. "Riva and Dick—well, it just didn't work.

"But at any rate, RAF got paid cash, half of it then, and it was after the flight that Jeana came in with the rest of the money. They were making $20,000 a talk. So it was real easy for them to pay off. They brought in a lot of money from *Voyager*.

"And, after the flight Jeana also came to George and Irene Rutan with a check not only for the $40,000 they had borrowed, but another $10,000 'interest.'

"By the time it slowed down, it wasn't that lucrative. My only agreement was at that time the 3 percent thing, which made very good money. The problem is that Dick had dealt with a divorce at that time, in fact two divorces, for he and Jeana split up several weeks before the *Voyager* flight. So he's had to split things with her and with his ex-wife, with Peter Riva, and give me my 3 percent. He had to pay the guy that books the talks, and he had a deal with lawyers. And by the time you spread things out that much, you really don't have much there for you. He does drive a nice car.

"Dick wants to be a millionaire as much as any guy. But he realizes now that he can't, though. [Author's note: A good market has developed for Dick's talks on the *Voyager* and on his theories of human motivation.] At any rate, he's leaning on me for anything he does in the future, the *Pond Racer* and others. At any rate, that's the story of the *Voyager*, how it was financed. That's the whole story.

"But it's an interesting story, dealing with a family. Here a family putting him up, then lending him money so that he could pay me off. And it was the best way for us to do it though. If we'd kept that contract, every time Dick made a talk, we'd be in making sure we got our half. All the Rutan Aircraft Factory people, which is just Mike and Sally Melvill now, and myself, we'd be fighting with Dick and Jeana. It's just awful and you don't do that.

I commented: "It's amazing, you know, but the Rutan family really built and financed the *Voyager*."

"An interesting thing," Burt said, "was that it was my RAF company behind it that made it possible, too, and the money from RAF profits that came from homebuilders. I didn't go out and borrow money to build *Voyager*, I didn't go out and get a sponsor. 'I'll put your name on it if you give me money.' What I did was go out and say, 'Give me materials.' There's a sticker on it that says 'Hercules.' People are my friends. Everybody I went to for *Voyager* came through. I didn't bring in a dime of income, on the project, until well after it was flying and turned over to my brother, not a dime.

Burt acknowledged the generosity of those who donated engines, materials, radios, and the hundreds of people who sent in donations. EAA pushed the flight and was enormously helpful in getting it put across. Dick and Jeana had been magnificent. The volunteers who came to work on the plane, to help get it tested, to man the communications trailer during the flight—these, too, he said, were amazing, amazing."

When it is mentioned to him that his brother has received the lion's share of media attention and publicity, for flying the plane that he created, Burt shrugs it off with a grin. "Who remembers who built Lindbergh's plane, anyway?"

CHAPTER 39

AFTER VOYAGER, LIFE GOES ON AT MOJAVE

1987

After the enormous effort of *Voyager* was done, once the tremendous achievement of the flight had been launched, followed and flown—life went on at Mojave.

On February 27, Mike Melvill made the first test flight of a new Rutan design, the Model 144, the CM-44, *California Microwave*. This was built by Composites Prototypes, a small division of SCALED Composites, in the old RAF, Building 13, for California Microwave, Inc.

The prototype was loosely based on the *Long-EZ* design but larger, with an over 30-foot wingspan and a 210-horsepower turbo-charged Lycoming engine, the T10-360. It is a manned/unmanned reconnaissance aircraft.

Announced in the April 1987 *Canard Pusher* as "Burt's latest design, the Model 144 (CM44UAV) was built in what used to be RAF, and made its first flight on February 27, 1987, with Mike Melvill at the controls. The aircraft is currently in flight test and will be delivered to the customer, California Microwave, in the next few weeks."

Back at Oshkosh

Meanwhile, in the EAA Air Adventure Museum at Oshkosh, workers had been busy building a mockup of the *Voyager* and a display. On Friday afternoon, May 6, 1988, a dedication ceremony was held. The exhibit was formally unveiled to the public with Burt, Dick and Jeana there.

The exhibit had been prepared with the cooperation and assistance of Burt and Dick Rutan, and Jeana Yeager. It has an audio-visual of the original concept of the flight, which shows the long days of construction, various flight tests to prove systems. There is an exciting audio-visual of the big flight itself!

The mock up of the small cabin area brings home the courage and endurance that Jeana and Dick had to have for their flight. There is as a part of the exhibit, a post-flight section of crew/designer's recognition. The major sponsor of the exhibit was the BF Goodrich Company's Aerospace and Defense Division.

The Collier Trophy—May 15, 1987

The National Aeronautic Association (NAA) awarded the Collier Trophy for 1986 to the entire Voyager team.

The citation reads: "To Jeana L. Yeager, Richard G. Rutan, Elbert L. Rutan and the team of volunteers for the ingenious design and development of the Voyager aircraft and their skillful execution of the first non-stop, non-refueled flight around the world."

The Collier Trophy was established in 1911 and the first recipient was Glenn Curtiss. It is awarded annually by the NAA, administrator of the trophy, for the greatest achievement in aeronautics or astronautics in America, demonstrated by actual use in the previous year.

Presentation of the trophy was made on May 15, 1987, at the Shoreham Hotel in Washington, D.C. at the annual Robert J. Collier Trophy Dinner, hosted by the National Aviation Club.

In its press release on the 1986 Collier Award, NAA lauded EAA, stating: "*Voyager* also represents a culminating achievement for the Experimental Aircraft Association and the homebuilder movement. *The Rutan brothers and Jeana have been closely associated with Paul Poberezny and EAA over the years; they have gained much from this association and have contributed much to homebuilding, now recognized as one of the most promising fields of U.S. aviation.*" [Author's italics]

Lightning Strike!

On May 23, Dick Kreidel in his *Long-EZ* had a strange experience [that he told about three months later]. It was one he hoped never to repeat, but he reported it fully in the Rutan Aircraft Factory *Canard Pusher* newsletter, hoping to help other pilots avoid his predicament.

Kreidel had left New Orleans Lake Front Airport going IFR to El Paso, Texas at 9:30 a.m. He had obtained a thorough weather briefing but the weather forecast "didn't work out." He flew into heavy rain and began to pick up ice. Air Traffic Control controllers worked with him, trying to find a route out of the severe weather system developing around him.

Even so, diverting northward, hoping for better clearance from a line of thunderstorms, he began to receive electrical shocks in the cockpit when an eerie blue glow developed on the airplane and in the cockpit. His electrical instruments went haywire and he could hear nothing but static over his headset.

"I saw a bright flash way ahead of me that seemed to go from left to right that really lit up the cloud I was in; I assumed that it was cloud to cloud lightning and that I was definitely in deep grease! ... I was so scared that I was sure that this would be the way it would all end and my wife, Kay, would really be pissed!

"I smelled a thick sweet odor, got one good shock from the microphone and then there was a tremendous flash of light, an incredibly loud 'crack'—I felt it in my bones and chest as opposed to hearing it."

When Kreidel could see again, he was delighted to find that he was still alive. He could hear and could transmit again. He followed ATC directions and was vectored clear of the storms. Even so, the plane was heavy with ice and Kreidel realized he was in no mental state to fly a complex IFR approach at an alternate airport. He elected to climb clear and go on to El Paso, normal IFR, where he landed four hours later. On the ground, looking at his small airplane, damage was found to be several dark patches on the wing and winglet leading edges where only the glass skin remained! The plane had definitely experienced a lightning strike, though fortunately of mild intensity. A more severe strike could have burned a hole in the aircraft, melted control cables and fused electronics.

Kreidel praised his airplane but advised pilots not to attempt to fly difficult IFR weather with embedded thunderstorms. He was delighted to be able to return to his wife and his California home in Yorba Linda.

1987 Sun 'n Fun

EZ Races started by Dick Rutan in 1981 were flown at this year's EAA Florida Fly-in. As always, homebuilders enjoyed themselves with seminars, dinners and intense exchanges of knowledge and experiences. The Florida weather was superb.

With the long and arduous *Voyager* project completed, it was a year in which the homebuilders could celebrate. Certainly their devotion (some call it eccentric) to designing and building aircraft had been more than vindicated.

Around the World in Long-EZs

John Koch and Ed Roman, in their *Long-EZs*, arrived in Sacramento, California in June 1987, thereby completing their amazing around-the-world flights.

In 1986 they had left Spokane, Washington and flew across the United States, from the Atlantic to Europe. From there they crossed to Egypt, India, and Australia which involved extensive cross-country, trans-oceanic flights. After visiting Australia, they went to Port Morseby, Papua, New Guinea. There officials grounded them.They were not allowed to fly the 400 miles of water that they had just flown. After a few days, however, they were released.

Crossing very rough areas, many uncharted, they traversed New Guinea on to Biak, then to Menado in the Celebes, to Manila in the Philippines. From here they went to the island of Truk, southeast to Guam and back to Truk. Then they crossed vast stretches of water and a few islands to get to Hawaii. Before their final tremendous stretch of water flying, the two visited several of the beautiful islands of the Hawaiian chain.

From Hawaii they flew to Oakland and Sacramento. This was the longest leg of the demanding trip. One plane arrived with 20 gallons of gasoline and the other with 15 gallons left.

The planes were equipped with auxiliary gasoline tanks, of course, or Loran. Asked if they would do it again, the pilots said, "You bet!" One reservation was Taiwan. They would skip that stop, if they did it again, they said. For overnight parking and fuel they were charged $1,560.

It was an amazing and successful flight, a tribute to the pilots and their aircraft.

The Return of the Voyager

Back in California, the *Voyager* was loaded with care at Mojave Airport and trucked in for the Oshkosh '87 Convention, after the world flight. Homebuilders could see this ultimate homebuilt aircraft, on static display, for the last time before it went to the Smithsonian. They could enjoy looking at it as one of the rewards for their support in spirit and in funds. The volunteers could see the results of their generous contributions to the project. Needless to say, Jeana, Dick and Burt were wined and dined, sincerely admired. The EAAers were builders and pilots who could appreciate the achievement of *Voyager*.

"This is where it all started," Dick told the EAA crowds. He, Burt and Jeana were featured July 31, 1987 through August 3 at the EAA's Theater in the Woods and in forums, too.

So all week at Oshkosh 1987, there it was, the display of the historic *Voyager*, an opportunity for fellow EAAers to honor its designer, Burt Rutan, and its pilots, Dick Rutan and Jeana Yeager. EAA rolled out the red carpet for the people who had done the modern equivalent of Lindberg's flight.

A Merger—Tonya and Burt

It was in 1987 Tonya Simone finally agreed to merge her life with Burt Rutan's. They lived together in Burt's Palmdale house. It was there, two years later, that I met Tonya.

Before Burt arrived to talk with us, March 1, 1989, I talked with Tonya. She is not tall and is very tiny. In fact she appeared, at first glance, almost like a child dressed up in her mother's grown-up clothes. Her voice is light and rather unformed. She was eager to be cordial but was not at ease. Interviews are situations, of course, that can be rather tricky. What will the writer do with the information you give her? Writers of biographies are, after all, looking deep into lives.

Tonya is quite a bit younger than Burt, and was a little defensive about it in that 1989 interview. She told us early on in the conversation that she was thirty.

She is interested in horses and rides in dressage training and shows. Tonya has taken part in several equestrian events. She hires a well trained horse and has a coach to show her the finer points of the art.

She was raised in nearby Lancaster, California, and has a college degree. Her parents live there. She was interested in real estate but found that it interfered with her taking trips with Burt, so instead she went to work for her mother's business.

When Burt came in, it seemed to me that he was genuinely fond of her, gentle. He is more aware of her, sensitive toward her, than he is of most people, or so it seemed in the few hours spent with them.

In a March 1989 interview with Patricia Storch, she was to comment on the relationship between Burt and Tonya. "Obviously I know him well. Tonya's perfect for him. Not only is she perfect, but he's been happier, longer, in this relationship than any other one."

I related to Patricia that Burt's mother had commented that all his beautiful ladies seemed to leave him.

Pat hesitated tactfully and then said, "Well that might seem to be the case, but I'll tell you what, this situation he's in right now, I've told him, 'You'd better marry this girl.' "

"They met about three years ago?" I asked. "Maybe Burt's been with strong women and wants someone more passive?"

"Well Tonya gives that impression of being the little girl [type] and all, but that's just an impression," said Pat. "She has a college degree and she's very smart. And she's also very independent. Burt had to fight a long time to get her to live with him. But I think because she has that image, she appeals to Burt, and whatever she's doing, it's working. Because, you know, your coworkers can tell if you're happy or not and he really is happy and I'm glad for him."

Irene Counts Her RAF Planes

1987 was memorable and satisfying in many ways. For example, "Mom" Rutan was hard pressed to count all the Rutan designs flown into the 1987 Oshkosh Convention. Volunteers helped, but even so, with 50 *VariEzes*, 79 *Long-EZs*, 3 *Defiants*, 3 *VariViggens* and 7 "spin-off" planes registered, even more were seen but failed to register with Mrs. Rutan. As was usual now, Rutan designs outnumbered others by far.

Voyager's Final Home—The National Air & Space Museum

After the EAA Convention, *Voyager* was taken to Washington, D.C. "*Voyager*...The Final Journey," was the title of an article by EAA writer Jack Cox, which gave the entire story of the trip from California to Oshkosh, Wisconsin, to Washington, D.C. Bruce Evans, *Voyager's* crew chief, accompanied his demanding but beloved airplane on the journey.

This turned out to be an adventure in itself. Great care had been taken not to cut the aircraft apart but to leave it in the same condition as it had been during the flight. Yet, when the *Voyager* got to Washington in September, the Smithsonian display team had to cut it apart to get it into the museum and mount it by October.

On first anniversary of the *Voyager* flight, December 14, 1987 (its takeoff)—ceremonies formally installed the *Voyager* as an National Air and Space Museum exhibit. This, Michele Gardner Behrens told me, was a grand reunion for the *Voyager* team of designer, pilots and volunteers. "I'll never forget it." She remembers. "We were walking there in Washington, D. C. and went into the museum. There it was. It looked beautiful. We just stood and looked and looked, we really couldn't speak. Then some little boy said, 'Hey, aren't you—?' and we were able to laugh and relax."

This, Michele says, was one of the rather few times that they could all be together again. They could tell their stories of the flight to each other, share their experiences. It was, "simply a great time."

Exactly one year after that early morning takeoff at Edwards, Dick on December 14, 1987, hosted a breakfast for several hundred very important people (Voyager's Impressive People), at the Grand Hyatt in Washington, D.C., located not far from the Air and Space Museum. Dick, Jeana, and Burt spoke to the crowd. "Mom" and "Pop" Rutan were called upon to speak, remembering that tense morning a year ago.

In the evening, Teledyne Continental hosted a party right under the *Voyager* in the museum. About 500 people were there with the *Voyager* suspended above their heads, battered wingtips, oil stains intact. Champagne flowed, a band played, delectable food was passed around. The VIPs, Jeana Yeager and the Rutan family celebrated together. Following this party, many in the group hailed a taxi and rode through the rain to the Hyatt for a late "family" dinner.

You can still see *Voyager* there today. It "flies" in the lobby of the Independence Avenue entrance to the National Air and Space Museum. There is a continuous video presentation and labeled charts and other displays explaining the achievement of the around-the-world flight. It is one of the museum's most popular displays. People appreciate this American miracle of courage and invention.

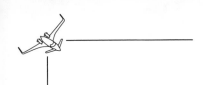

CHAPTER 40

THE BEECH STARSHIP

While the overwhelming presence of the *Voyager* project was ongoing, Burt was also deeply involved in the development of the *Starship* and in his work at Beech Aircraft Company. As mentioned before, one of SCALED Composite's early projects was the *Starship*, the 85 percent scale flying prototype for Beech Aircraft.

Burt also had his usual dozens of other projects going as well—the consultant work that supported his homebuilders, running SCALED Composites, hiring people to carry out design and building work. His personal life certainly had its ups and downs. Yet somehow he kept on going.

The story of the *Starship* is told here in its own space rather than scattered through the years of its design and development. It is both the remarkable story of a beautiful aircraft design and its remarkable designer.

The Starship Concept

Beech Aircraft places the origin of the concept of the Starship in 1979. Company engineers were asked to submit a successor to the Beech *King Air*. They were told that a large and comfortable cabin, even larger than that in the *King Air*, was wanted. Also, the design was to be powered by turbo-prop engines.

A dozen promising designs, three of these canard, pusher-engine designs, were selected from those submitted by the engineers. Preliminary Design 330, dated January 30, 1980, looks quite a lot like the present *Starship*. It had a swept main wing, "tip sail" vertical fins at the wingtips, and a canard below the forward fuselage. This also looked very much like some of Burt Rutan's work.

During 1980-81 the attention of Beech Aircraft executives was focused on the merger of Beech with Raytheon. Raytheon bought out Beech and by 1982 a change in management in the top echelons had taken place. President Brainerd Holmes was now chairman of the Beech board. Holmes, an active pilot and aircraft owner, felt that new designs were needed to shake general aviation out of its stagnation.

Aircraft design had languished for years. One important reason was the expense and extended hassle of proving a new design and obtaining from FAA a type certificate to make and sell it.

Holmes urged the development of a radical new design. He looked over the concepts that Beech engineers had suggested. The new design that he and others agreed upon, it turned out, would be essentially based on the concept of the PD 330. A plan was also agreed upon that the new aircraft would not be made of metal, but of composite materials.

By this time, Burt Rutan and others had brought the design and building of aircraft made of composites into being and to a high level of performance. Burt commented later that the big aircraft companies, with all their millions of dollars worth of equipment and research personnel, had not dared to do what he and his fellow homebuilders had done—learn to work with composites!

About this time Linden Blue was chosen to be president of Beech. He had a wealth of aviation experience, as former president and general manager of Gates Learjet and later, chief executive officer of Lear Fan. Blue knew about composite construction; about building sleek, fast aircraft; and he was familiar with new pusher engine designs.

Burt was sought by Beech to refine and perfect the PD 330 design because of his experience and success with composite materials and his innovative work with canard configurations. Canard design is not simply a matter of placing the small forward wing on the aircraft. It involves complex and critical matters of stall performance, weight and balance, and the interplay of flaps and the canard, with shifts of the center of gravity of aircraft during various flight situations. For example, when the flaps are lowered for landings. Not all canard designs were as successful as Burt's.

Also, Rutan holds the patent for the variable-sweep canard. This device proved to be a vital part of the success of the eventual *Starship* design.

For these reasons, Beech contracted with Rutan to build a proof-of-concept scale model of the *Starship*, 85 percent of full size.

At Mojave, excitement swept over Burt and the small staff of SCALED Composites. One of the world's oldest and most prestigious aircraft companies was looking to Rutan and his crew in recognition of their achievements and talents to perfect a totally new aircraft design! It was a tremendous windfall.

With typical "can do" energy, the men and women went to work. Using foam-core fiberglass and their composites "know-how," the team created the aircraft swiftly. Frankly, no one else in the world seemed to have the unique ability, energy and team of dedicated workers, to carry out this remarkable assignment.

Before the aviation world knew what was happening, (Beech and SCALED Composites kept the work under wraps) the *Starship* was shown off at the annual convention of the National Business Aircraft Association, September 1983, in Dallas, Texas. The actual *Starship* design was announced and the then proof-of-concept (POC) aircraft flew low over Love Field. A mockup was unveiled on the ground for conventioneers to see. The crowd was rocked back on its heels by this beautiful and unique new design.

[An odd footnote to this event is that the mock-up, built by a display company, cost Beech more than SCALED Composites had charged for building the flying POC aircraft!]

Beech President Linden Blue told the crowd of corporation aircraft owners, pilots and newsmen that the aircraft would be available for delivery in just two years. Delivery by 1985? It seemed a tall order to develop, test and prove out such a new design with such new materials in such a short time. Yet the magic of the design, its futuristic looks, captured the imagination of the aviation world.

New words swirled about the convention floor, "computer design," "canards," "composites!"

To make the dream of such a short pregnancy possible, Beech executives set to work to find suppliers who would be able to build pieces of the aircraft. Manufacturers of

209

composite goods agreed that they could provide a wing, fuselage, and other components. Linden Blue left Beech and Max Bleck assumed the presidency of Beech Aircraft.

Yet even this intelligent idea had its problems. The prototype was built of materials that would not necessarily be in the final version of the plane. Beech had to pioneer new techniques in composite construction. The construction material selected for the primary airframe was carbon-fiber epoxy over a honeycomb Nomex core. About $310 million later, the techniques were perfected.

Now Beech had to tackle FAA's complex and demanding certification procedures. Added conditions were made a part of the certification because of the new materials used in the Starship. And, little was known about lightning protection, for example. Since the composite materials were nonconductive, aluminum mesh was embedded in the top layer of the aircraft's composite skin. All large metal parts of the aircraft were bonded together to form a grounding plane.

At the time the *Starship* was being built, composite materials and the labor involved were much more expensive than conventional aluminum building materials and labor. It is hoped that later the costs will decrease substantially.

Difficulties by the score were overcome by Beech workers. With a thrill of excitement, the first full-sized prototype was rolled out and flown on February 15, 1986. It was no sooner back on the ground amid miles of smiles than work on improvements and changes commenced.

This formal roll-out was in contrast to the earlier one in Mojave. "Back when the Beech people saw the prototype model being light-heartedly rolled out—they panicked!" "Pop" Rutan says. The "carefree," or rather the freedom of the Mojave is in interesting contrast to the corporate life, which is so much more conservative.

A second full-size *Starship* flew a few months later and in June 1987 a still more refined version, a third, full-size prototype flew.

In 1983 Beech Aircraft had announced its altered plans for the *Starship*. "Certification of Beech Aircraft Corp. Starship 1 expected at end of 1987 but delayed, pending completion of required 150 hours of function and reliability tests and crew complement determination, (whether to have one or two pilots) by FAA." Beech estimates "certification to be granted in the first quarter 1988. Deliveries are expected to begin at the end of 1988."

Storm Clouds

But in 1987 this beautiful period of inventiveness and almost unlimited resources ended for Rutan.

The *Starship* project turned out to be very costly and demanding of Beech. It also generated reams of excellent publicity and attention for the company. The aircraft itself was compared with the Italian-made *Avanti*. The *Avanti*, a twin-turboprop aircraft is faster and is, like the *Starship*, a beautiful plane. A design similar to the *Avanti* was, ironically, one that was originally considered by Beech Aircraft.

Storm clouds gathered at Beech for Rutan. Max Bleck, Beech's new chief executive officer, fired John Roncz, the talented aerodynamicist and computation expert. Roncz was a close friend and had long worked with Rutan. Rutan was furious. He is said to have stalked into Bleck's office and demanded that Roncz be reinstated. Burt's mother, Irene, remarks that with Burt loyalty is two-way. Burt's workers have his loyalty and job security.

Further events boded ill for Rutan at Beech. CEO Bleck stopped work on all research prototype projects and saved only one, the *Tuna*. Bleck left the *Tuna* on the schedule as a minor project for research.

Bleck, it was soon understood, would like to divest Beech of the SCALED Composites Company. In November 1988, Burt took him up on the offer to sell and bought SCALED Composites back.

Burt Rutan is, above all, a designer. He is not deeply interested in manufacturing or supporting a customer base to manufactured items, so buying SCALED back gave him a place to design and build prototypes and try out new design ideas.

Pin-stripe Ambitions?

"Good businessman?" Burt remarked. "Well at one time, I had a thought that I could move up the pinstripe ladder, be a vice-president of Beech, a president of Raytheon, someday, whatever. Well I was on the board of directors, married to a daughter of a Beechcraft vice-president. Boy, I'd have to learn to get into the country club deal, and hey, look at all those neat perks they have.

"But when I went into that environment a little bit, and I bought a pin-striped suit, and I traveled first class a couple of trips. I sat in these board meetings and I realized some of the *garbage* they deal with. The decisions they make, and the time that that's wasted, I said, I'll get peptic ulcers and hate myself doing this. I'd rather wear my Levi's and stay back in Mojave, and develop airplanes, and not play golf.

"And I tell you I got turned off by that. I tell you, I was a director at Beechcraft, that's an $800-million company. And I was a vice-president of Beechcraft, but to me though, the more important things were that I sat on the scientific advisory board of the Air Force. And I was able to go up and brief an armed forces advisory council, and that I had interesting business at the Pentagon, and had the freedom to go out and develop airplanes. These things were more important to me.

"I got so turned off by listening to these things [at Beech], the guys they pay the most, the things they deal with, and what work they really do. These guys are smart, don't think for a minute that big vice-presidents and directors are not smart, they're brilliant. But they make for themselves an environment where they can make decisions, decisions that are to them very important, but I could see that the decisions they were making were things that were really affecting what I thought should be done.

"But then I could see something awful going on. I'll generalize and say this applies to many corporations. They were going after next quarter's profits. Not looking five or ten years down the road. They were looking at better profits for next year. That never

Burt Rutan in his pin-striped suit.
Photo courtesy Beech Aircraft Corporation.

happened in the general aviation companies when the founders were there. It never happened at Beechcraft when Walter Beech was there; or when Cessna and Bill Lear and Piper were operating. But, they weren't necessarily profitable. Each one of the companies went bankrupt at one time or another, but struggled back. Nowadays, if a company isn't profitable, they go in and fire everybody and don't develop any new products for next year. Or, they sell the company.

"Raytheon has Beech. But anyway, this kind of *garbage*, I said, 'Listen, life's too short to spend any time with this at all.'

"So, I retreated back to my Mojave shop and my work. I'd go back there for meetings. So at any rate it was clear that I was a lot happier back here doing what I am, with (a smile to Tonya) my gal, than messing around trying to learn to play golf and going to board meetings. So I had kinda considered that during parts of 1985, but those aren't my aspirations. I'd rather develop software.

In July 1988, EAA's magazine, *Sport Aviation*, announced that the *Starship* was certificated, on June 14. It was only the second all-composite aircraft design to receive the government's official blessing. The first was the Windecker *Eagle*, certificated 19 years before on Dec. 18, 1969.

An increased FAA certification complexity of requirements had to be met. "Now that the barrier is broken we can expect to see a lot more all-composite designs in the future. The *Starship* is also the first pure canard configuration ever certified by the FAA (The *Wren 460*, is not a pure canard but aerodynamically is a three-surface airplane)."

Beech announced at the Oshkosh '88 convention in a video presentation that first two years of the *Starship* production were sold out.

"Beechcraft's avant-garde business turbo-prop, the *Starship*," reported AOPA's magazine, *Pilot*, had been awarded an FAA type certificate in June [1988]. This had been a lengthy certification process. FAA, and much of the manufacturing industry, was unfamiliar with the use of exotic composite materials and the unusual configuration of the aircraft." At any rate, the $3.667-million *Starship* was approved under Part 23 of the FARs.

Due to the maximum takeoff weight of approximately 14,000 pounds, more than the 12,500-pound limit for single-pilot operations, the plane would, FAA decreed, require a two-pilot crew. Naturally, to make the aircraft more attractive to buyers, Beech decided to work on getting single-pilot certification. The plane just didn't seem to require two pilots to fly it. By May 1990, single-pilot approval was granted by the FAA. Though normally the ship will be flown by a two-pilot crew.

Beech announced that the company would also acquire certification of the pneumatic-boot deicing system and an autopilot after the original type certificate was approved. The company saw comparatively little more flight testing to do before these systems could be approved by FAA.

Pressure increased on Beech Aircraft when its competitor, the single-pilot Piaggio *Avanti* was certified, except for icing, in May 1990.

The first production unit was supposed to be delivered late in 1988, but Beech decided that this first aircraft would be used as a company demonstrator and the next airplane off the line would be the first customer unit. Delivery was anticipated for mid-1989.

And, true to Beech's plan, in June 1989, the AOPA *Pilot* reported that the first *production Starship* had recently been flown at Beech Aircraft's Wichita Factory Airport. The plane, serial number NC-4, was be used for demonstration flights for its first few hours, and then delivered in June 1989.

By then the certification of the new airplane's autopilot system was nearly complete. Testing for flight into icing conditions had received 95 percent approval. The aircraft was beautiful. It was a powder blue due to a filler/primer coat over its composite exterior when it rolled out of the factory. It would be given a second primer coat and a final finish before it is turned over to the customer, the first to own a *Starship*. But certification of de-icing and autopilot took time.

J. Mac McClellan, prominent aviation writer, described the plane in the March 1989 issue of *Flying* magazine: "The unique business turboprop sports a swept wing with nine-foot-tall winglets (Beech calls them tip sails) that replace the conventional vertical stabilizer, and a variable-sweep canard. Twin Pratt & Whitney PT6As power the airplane. These spin metal, five-bladed pusher props. The aircraft is constructed almost entirely out of carbon fiber—reinforced honeycomb with a thin aluminum mesh under the skin to provide lightening protection. The *Starship* will also feature a Collins Avionics "all glass" cockpit, utilizing 14 cathode-ray tubes to display attitude, navigation, and engine performance information."

The original goals for the *Starship* design were for a 348-knot top cruise speed aircraft, with a maximum range of slightly over 2,000 nautical miles. New FAA requirements added weight and took up room in the plane. Even so, the aircraft as it was certificated in June 1988, came very close to these specifications. It has a top speed of 336 knots and a maximum range of nearly 1,700 miles. Beech is continuing to improve the aircraft as it moves into production, so these numbers may change.

Pilots who have flown the plane report that it is a delight to fly, "but does feel a bit different." The plane has a certified ceiling of 41,000 feet. It is, of course, pressurized.

It was late in December 1989 that the BF Goodrich de-icing system and the turboprop's Collins APS-85 autopilot were approved by FAA. Beech still hopes to obtain FAA approval of single-pilot operation for the ship. Certainly the safe operation of the *King Air* is similar and may well demonstrate to FAA that this is a quite viable option. The cockpit workload is being analyzed with this single-pilot approval in mind [approved May 1990].

The development time turned out to be not two years, as announced, but five years. Even so, this is a remarkably short time in which to bring to certification and production such a complex new business machine. It promises to be all that so many Beech aircraft have been for many years, fast, comfortable and safe. It has a magic, futuristic look—the Beech *Starship*.

[Out in the Mojave Desert, the *Starship* proof of concept 85 percent scale model sat on the ramp of SCALED Composites' hangar, awaiting its fate.

Beech Aircraft company executives wanted to scrap it. They preferred that the public have in mind the larger, finished version of the *Starship*. Burt, however, was protective of his beautiful little POC aircraft. Several museums have requested permission to install the aircraft in their collections. Burt sees the POC aircraft as an important one, historically speaking. He threatens to call a press conference to watch if the Beech people decide to destroy it.]

The development of the beautiful and efficient aircraft, the *Starship*, has been long for Beech. Yet the company fought through the complex process of bringing this design through the certification hurdles. As announced in the April 1990 edition of *Flying*, the aircraft has cleared all of its major certification tests and that customer deliveries should begin immediately. It was to be September 1990, however, before deliveries began.

To insure a good safety record, all *Starship* captains must earn a type rating. This is similar to the requirements of those who buy Learjets and other business aircraft. Factory training is given to enhance efficiency and safety.

According to company information, 40 of the nearly $4,000,000 aircraft have been sold. By the end of 1990, over 10 of these aircraft are expected to be in service.

Max Bleck went on from Beech to become president of the Raytheon Company (which owns Beech).

1990 Starship Arrival

Two of the largest flying magazines in the country, *Flying* and the *AOPA Pilot*, assessed the Beech *Starship* in their October issues. Both publications featured stunning photographs of the plane on their covers.

"Flying the *Starship*," by J. Mac McClellan of *Flying*, told of a radical composite pusher aircraft that flies like a larger aircraft with excellent cabin comfort, great stability and superb high-tech avionics.

After seven years of development, Beech Aircraft Corporation has come through with a beautiful and able airplane, McClellan says. This time for development is not really that exceptional for an all-new turbine aircraft.

He liked the roomy, "whisper quiet," cockpit and the excellent visibility, although he warned pilots that they had better not forget the 54-foot-wide wing behind them as they taxi. There was, he said, almost no vibration. Certainly, he commented, the all-glass panel in the cockpit is the most advanced of any turboprop aircraft. He liked the placement of the engine throttles and the conventional engine controls.

A plus for operators of the *Starship* will be the electronic engine-instrument-crew-advisory system which displays all checklists, engine instrumentation readings and warnings. In fact, the ship has a complete warning system to detect a variety of possible problems and advise the pilot.

Several times, pilots upon first flying the plane comment upon its exceptional stability and what Richard L. Collins of the *AOPA Pilot* calls the "non-event" of the stall. Pilots report that flying the plane down the instrument landing system approach should be a snap

The beautiful Beech *Starship.*
Photo courtesy Beech Aircraft Corporation.

216

due to the approach angle and the *Starship's* stability. This stable operation helps the plane fly comfortably through air turbulence.

Pilots report that the aircraft cannot be used on the smallest of airstrips, yet the takeoff and landing distances make use of those paved airports with over 4,000-foot runways. The length of runway needed varies, naturally, with the elevation of the field, the load in the plane and air temperature.

Certified to 41,000 feet the airplane is, of course, pressurized. The aircraft is air conditioned. The icing prevention and de-icing equipment is automatic. The forward sweep angle of the wing and flap extension is automatically synchronized.

Beech advises that the cruising speed of the aircraft is 335 knots at 22,000 feet. Again, cruising speed will vary in any aircraft due to variations in altitude, loading and temperature. With a 45-minute reserve of fuel, the plane has a 4.12-hour range.

The *Starship* has been approved for single-pilot operation but since it weighs more than 12,500 pounds for takeoff, its pilots need a type rating to fly it. Also, to operate the plane as a single pilot, you are required to take a single-pilot type rating check ride to qualify.

McClellan admired the fact that virtually all of the complex systems on the *Starship* are standard equipment. It comes complete with the futuristic cockpit instrumentation and radios. The only two options are a stereo entertainment system and an air-to-ground telephone. It is ready to fly away when you buy it. Customers can choose the interior materials and the colors they prefer.

The price tag of $4,100,000 is quite a reasonable price for a beautifully equipped aircraft with (maximum) seating of 11 persons.

Richard L. Collins, of *AOPA Pilot*, called the plane "magic" and something not from this century, but the next! True, he agreed, no new airplane is quite perfect to begin with, there is work to be done yet on cabin air conditioning and sound levels, but Beech is well equipped to handle these "tweaks."

The *Starship*, says Collins, is perfect in "sizzle!" After nearly 40 years of flying, the pilot-writer had found a next-generation airplane. He liked the way the plane flew, its takeoff and climb, its fantastic resistance to stalling. He, like others, commented on its amazing stability.

He had wondered if there would ever be a turboprop that would go over 300 knots and found that the *Starship* does 300 knots and more.

Beech Aircraft invested enormous amounts of money in developing the *Starship*, but Collins notes that not only will the company recoup from aircraft sales, but in other ways, too. For example, with its new advanced composite technology it can bid now on C-17 landing gear doors and other items in the years ahead.

Collins remarked on the exceptionally thorough testing done by Beech and the FAA on the new plane.

It is, Collins said, possibly the most needed airplane ever built, a bold entry into the next generation of aircraft for general aviation.

CHAPTER 41

THE "MOJAVE YACHT CLUB"

1988

Far from the Mojave Desert, Burt Rutan looked out over miles of open water. Furthermore, it was water arranged in steep peaks and valleys. Aboard a sailing yacht, he watched the vessel tug at the wind, lean over and heave across these watery mountains with a will, throwing up clouds of spray in the process.

What was the aircraft designer doing aboard a yacht? This was almost the first time he had been to sea. Burt admits that he knows little of sailing, but sails have many similarities to airfoil designs, and he had been called in to build a new kind of sail.

"How much does this thing weigh?" he asked.

"Oh around 70,000 pounds."

"And how fast is it going now?"

"About eight knots, Burt."

"*Eight* knots!!" You could see him comparing this ponderous vessel with sleek airplanes that weighed under a thousand pounds and cruised at around 200 knots.

"Ah hah. Eight knots, amazing."

Burt Rutan was involved in fabrication and design assistance work for the Sail America team, headed by veteran sailboat racer Dennis Conner.

The history of the America's Cup yacht race is a long one. The oldest surviving yacht club in the United States is the New York Yacht Club, founded in 1844. Its America's Cup is the top prize of international yacht racing.

Back in 1851 the schooner-yacht *America* was built in New York City for a group of yachting enthusiasts, members of the New York Yacht Club. She was 101-feet long. The yacht was sailed to England where a challenge was issued to the Royal Yacht Squadron. The *America* won what was known as "the 100-guinea cup," in a race around the Isle of Wight in 1851, against 17 British yachts.

The cup became known as the America's Cup after it was deeded to the New York Yacht Club by its original owners in 1857 to be an international challenge trophy. It was successfully defended from 1870 to 1983—132 years.

Yachts owned by Americans traditionally would practice in Long Island Sound and then in the summer move to Newport. There they would compete with other Americans for the right to be the one to defend the Cup. Then, in September, the American contender would race the boat or boats that came from abroad.

In 1983, the unthinkable happened—the *Australia II* won, unveiling a winged keel (keel "wings" weighted with lead) designed by Aussie Ben Lexcen.

So, in 1987 the competitors would be racing for the trophy in Australian waters. At Fremantle, Australia, twenty-six 12-meter boats under the flags of seven nations were ready. It took 360 races that summer to select a challenger to meet the defender. On February 5, 1987, the *Stars and Stripes*, captained by Dennis Conner, retrieved the Cup for America by winning over the *Kookaburra III*.

The Cup had been lost by the Americans to the Australians in 1983 because of that Australian innovation, the winged keel. This then forced serious contenders to move into high-tech, computer-aided, very expensive yachts. Commercial sponsorship entered the contest, as syndicates were formed to raise the millions of dollars now needed.

It is ironic to note that in 1983 Dennis Conner protested that the "peculiar keel" was illegal, since heeled over it would draw more than the nine feet allowed. Yet he and others were to be forced into innovations as futuristic and more. And again ironically, during the 1987 Cup races, Conner challenged the legality of the Kiwi contender, the first fiberglass 12-meter ever approved for the Cup.

At any rate, Conner was in the United States, happy at having won back the America's Cup. Around on the other side of the world in New Zealand, however, Michael Fay, read the rules of the America's Cup and learned that he could challenge Conner's team. He promptly challenged the holder of the Cup to a rematch. Justice Carmen Ciparick, of the New York Supreme Court, which oversees the deed of gift that sets out guidelines for the competition, upheld New Zealand's rogue challenge. This gave the Americans little time to design and build a boat to defend the America's Cup trophy.

This is what sent Conner and his Sail America team to Burt Rutan. He needed help in the design and construction of an innovative new kind of sail that Conner wanted for the Sail America racing yacht, *Stars and Stripes*. Rutan, when asked how big an oven would need to be to cure the proposed sail (made of composite materials), showed that he was aware of the legal battles involved in the America's Cup races by replying wryly, "Oh long enough for about 12 lawyers!"

When asked (six months after the September 1988 race) what the America's Cup was like and if it was fun, Burt replied, "It was fascinating."

The design is a controversial issue, with us going in and being known as the designers of it when we'd never done boats before." We were talking to Rutan in his living room in Palmdale, California. At this point his small blue parrot, "Winglet," fluttered about and flipped over. "Oh poor Winglet," Burt laughed as he rescued the little bird.

"The reason we got into it was because of this company that makes composite materials—Thermoplastic Materials. They wanted very much to get their materials in the next America's Cup race. So they worked with Dennis Conner. They realized that if it was going to be done in time for the challenge it would have to be done in a shop like ours. It couldn't be done in an aircraft manufacturer's place or a boat shop. Actually, the reason Michael Fay, the New Zealander, put money into the challenge was because he didn't think we could build the sail fast enough. He was so confident that he showed up in a slow boat!

"OK, at any rate, the Sail America people were brought over by these composites manufacturers to us. It really sort of backfired on the manufacturer, however, for we looked at their requirements and said, 'Yeah, we can do that.' But we needed room-temperature curing materials and couldn't use these high-temperature materials. So we essentially shot down these people who made the introduction!

"But I wasn't sure that they [the Sail America team] were really serious. Why would they come to us who had never done a boat before? Here's what happened. They were in an enormous panic. Conner had lost the America's Cup once and if he would ever do this again, this would be death, worse than death, the humiliation. So they were absolutely livid to make the best boat possible. They had decided to build two catamarans, one with a soft sail, and one with a hard rig, because computer programs and some experience had shown that the hard rig was better.

"Now the interesting thing was that they had about twelve designers scattered about all over the country, which was a horrible thing to do. But the good news about it was that not too many of them knew much about a hard sail. The only ones that did worked together were Dr. Duncan MacLane and Dave Hubbard.

"They had designed the *Patient Lady* series, which were 35-foot, small, hard sails. They were the designers of the hard sail catamaran rig. And they were coming to us so that we would build the structures. They were going to build them out of plywood. They didn't know much about composites. They knew enough about composites, however, to know that it could be built of composites. They knew that we'd built the *Voyager*, and all these airplanes, and that we could build fast.

"Now what's the interesting lesson that we learned on this thing was, we think we do things pretty fast, but what's interesting is, if they had brought this thing to us earlier, told us, 'Look, here's what it's got to do. Here's how complex it is. Here are the loads. Here's how big it is.' And if they'd said, 'You design it, tool it, build it, load it, deliver it.'—We'd have said, 'It will take eight or nine or ten months.' And hey, that would still have been phenomenally fast, for a job like this usually takes longer than that. But right up front they said, 'You've only got 13 weeks!'

"Instead of just saying 'Hah, hah, hah, you should have a clown suit on to say that,' we got patriotic and wanted to be a part of the America's Cup. We stuck our necks out and said, 'Yes sir, it can be done.'

"Now, as far as who designed it. I flew back there and looked at their *Patient Lady* series of boats. I said, 'Well I don't know, I wouldn't do it this way. What airfoils did you use?'"

" 'We got them out of this book.'"

" 'No, no, no,' I told them, 'You've got to design them to the exact application, like you do in airplane design. Listen, I've got the best guy in the country, John Roncz, the guy I work with, and we should get him in on it. So they went to John Roncz, in just a day or two. So he did the airfoils, the aerodynamic configuration of it, working with Dave Hubbard.

"I don't want to shoot down Dave Hubbard's role in this, for he was the designer, but John Roncz is the guy who went to the computer and did the calculations and showed that it needed to be triple-slotted, and he also refined the plan form, the shape of it, and I designed the tip of it and so forth. So really the detailed aerodynamic design refinement of the basic concept of the hard sail for the America's Cup, was a John Roncz/Burt Rutan job.

"We helped them with it, we helped refine it. They were the designers of it [Dave Hubbard and Duncan MacLane]. We didn't have any experience with hard rig catamarans. We asked a lot of questions, ' My God why do you do this?' I would have done it differently if I'd begun the design from scratch, but you don't do that when you've got that kind of schedule."

What was it that they built?

Burt had to clear a long, long area in his shop at the famous Hangar 78, the home of his company, SCALED Composites. In just a little more than ten weeks, Rutan and his men, working in plus-100-degree temperatures, translated the engineering drawings into a wing mast. It was one never seen before on the water.

It had three movable elements. These together formed an airfoil. The spar was to stand 85 feet above the deck of the *Stars and Stripes* catamaran. At the base, the three-part sail was 23 feet across. It tapered to just four feet at the top.

The forward part of the rig was the thickest. It was molded from carbon fiber and Divinycel core, into a shape designed to pick up the lightest of breezes, and deliver them without stalling, over the narrow middle element, the "elevator." The air moves on past the slot to the longer after section. Pilots would call this aerodynamic arrangement of units, the wing mast, a "Fowler Flap." [The Fowler Flap is used on short takeoff and landing, STOL, aircraft, that need plenty of lift and low stalling speeds.]

The molded leading edge merges back into ribs covered with heat-shrunk-on mylar. This gives the hard sail tremendous lightness and strength. For heavy loads had to be assumed under certain circumstances. Not only would winds impose loads, but in the event of a knockdown or a capsizing, the sail had to withstand the punishment, or break away in a planned way.

The top 18 feet of the wing mast was designed to break away in the case of a capsize. Otherwise it could act as a lever to break the mast. Watertight bulkheads make the top part buoyant, for easy recovery if broken off. Further, the top part of the sail can be removed for strong winds, if desired.

From deck level, each of the wing elements can be controlled separately. Also, the aft element can be twisted as much as 30 degrees at the top with the lower sections not twisted.

To build this huge thing with its long mast and cure it properly was a task that required composite materials know-how. Burt was challenged and interested by the job.

"At any rate," Burt said, leaning back in his Mojave Desert living room, "we did all the structural design of this thing, built the tooling in only 11 days. Sure enough we built this thing under schedule, and *made money* on the schedule incentive. Unbelievable.

"Now the hard rig was considered a high risk thing. It may break down. There are all these flaps and they have to twist. It'll probably break down because it's complex. It's huge, there's this enormous thing that has to camber. It's just got to be heavier. Wrong.

"First of all we delivered first. They found that the way Duncan and Dave designed the lower controls that camber and twist of this thing, would set itself up, move back and forth and could be sailed with just three winches on each side. This meant it could be sailed with fewer people, it didn't have to have as many sails on it, and because of the less people and winches and hardware that wasn't needed, that it was lighter.

"Then they took the hard rig out and sailed it a couple of hours and came back and everything worked, first time. The soft rig, when it was delivered later, went out and promptly broke down. They couldn't get the sail up. One time the mast fell over. They had a lot of problems with it."

Newspaper stories and magazine articles in September 1988 declaimed, "Dennis Conner the present holder of the America's Cup, having won it back for the United States from Australia last year, is defending with a catamaran, against a contender from New Zealand with a huge sailing yacht!"

Reporters announced, "Conner is sailing a radical design for the race, a 60-foot, 6,000-pound catamaran with a 118-foot tall sail which is light and looks fragile, the *Stars and Stripes*. He has a crew of nine. The New Zealand boat is a 132-foot monohull, 12 meter design with mast twice as high as Conner's. It has a crew of 40.

"While the catamaran is thought to be much faster, Conner says that this is not the entire race, that it has to be sailed and that equipment and judgment must not fail."

The use of the catamaran and the hard sail came in for much controversy. The question is, is this indeed a sailing yacht? Or, should the definition of a yacht mean that the boat has to be a monohull? Justice Carmen Ciparick decided to wait to see the outcome of the race before ruling on the legitimacy of the U.S. entry.

Burt recalled the race: "We'd designed the sail to sail in Long Beach winds of 12 to 15 knots. Then they moved the course down to San Diego with lighter winds there. Once the Sail America people tried both out they found that the soft rig would win, they could put up this enormous sail, and particularly downwind, they could sail faster than the hard sail.

"Well we felt that we were doomed. But they had some money, so we got together and said, 'Listen, let's design a rig for the San Diego winds.' We had eight weeks. The race was to be the third of September. In eight weeks we built one that was 30 percent bigger, 108 feet tall, but Conner had been racing a soft rig. He wasn't a hard rig guy. He had his mind made up. He thought the hard sail couldn't win.

"As soon as we got this new sail done, we took it down to San Diego, and they took it out. Dr. MacLane took the hard rig out and Dennis sailed the soft rig. The hard sail won. Conner said, 'Well, we didn't have all our sails up, the spinnaker, the foresail, and so forth.' So the next day he put the extra sails on, and the hard rig beat him again!

"In 11 races in a row in 11 days, the hard rig won every one of them, by big margins. Interesting thing, Conner during those eleven days never allowed himself to go over on the hard rig, never went over on the hard rig during those days. So he had very little experience in it.

"Two weeks before the race he decided that the hard rig was it, no question. The news media may not have known this. He went out and worked with the hard rig. Even in the light winds of the race, which was supposed to favor the Kiwi's boat, the hard sail's extra area wasn't really needed. The Kiwi boat just wasn't any good."

Burt was asked "Where were you during the race?"

"Wasn't it boring?" he asked as he looked over at Tonya Simone, his friend. She smiled and nodded. "It was awful." Burt went on: "We were on one of those VIP chase boats, and half the people were sleeping."

Tonya said, "The TV commentators were there, and on commercial breaks they'd turn to each other and say, 'When is this going to be *over*?'" Watching the America's Cup race has been likened to watching grass grow.

The race began September 7, 1988 at San Diego, California, with 20 miles to go upwind and 20 miles to go downwind.

The San Diego Yacht Club officiated over these America's Cup races. There were to be three races with the boat winning two out of three to be declared the trophy winner. Conner's 6,000-pound, state-of-the-art catamaran easily won, 2-0, over the challenging 132-foot, 83,000-pound, monohull keelboat, the *New Zealand*. The "Kiwi" boat team was led by Michael Fay, of the Mercury Bay Boat Club, based in Auckland, New Zealand.

Later, talking with Burt about the America's Cup adventure, he said, "Our sailing experience was certainly limited. The first time we sailed we were on a boat that Dennis had won with for a Japanese commercial spot. We spent four hours out there and never saw more than seven knots. And that was absolutely the most awful thing. It was a little bit of fun with all these things winching around and things to pull on, but then I wondered when we were going to get on the step and get going. Oh it's horrible. Maybe in 30 knots of wind it would be fun.

"It was miserable. A sail should go into the wind, not away from the wind. Everyone laughs at me for this. Our other experience in sailing was on the hard rig.

"At any rate, the performance that we did in building that thing and successfully testing it and the fact that it held up without any problem was good.

"David Hubbard deserves the credit for designing that boat, we were very pleased to have a part in refining it. I don't think that any place in the country could have built it in that time. We put up a sign in the Mojave Desert at the Mojave Airport in our shop that said, 'Mojave Yacht Club.'"

"So it was, for us, a passing thing to do. And it was interesting to meet these people. Though Dennis when he's drunk is not real gentle. But I love his books and I admire his drive and dedication. He just doesn't give up."

The Outcome

In a March 28, 1989 ruling, Judge Carmen Beauchamp Ciparick ordered Dennis Conner and the San Diego Yacht Club to forfeit the cup to New Zealander Michael Fay's Mercury Bay Boating Club. The reason was that the defense in a catamaran in September 1988 was: "An unsporting and illegal mismatch." The last living signer of the Deed of Gift, George Schuyler, was cited as amending the Deed in the late 1800s to ensure fair competition. "A match means one party contending with another party upon equal terms as regards the task to be accomplished," he wrote.

Fay, upon learning of the court decision, announced that he was ready to host a multinational regatta in April 1991 off Auckland.

April 3, 1989, however, saw the San Diego Yacht Club board voting to appeal the court order to forfeit the prize to New Zealand. This promised to delay the next regatta until 1992, possibly 1993.

In 1989, a court decision came down in mid-September, reversing the lower court decision and awarding the trophy to the American team.

San Diego plans to host races in 1992 featuring a new class of 75-foot boats.

Before the next regatta, yachtsmen may well want to decide on more explicit rules for competing yachts. Several nations have signed up to compete for the Cup. One thing is certain, ocean racing will never be the same!

CHAPTER 42

WORLDWIDE PILOTS FLY RUTAN DESIGNS

1988

"No," Burt wrote in early 1988, "I'm not selling plans at RAF again. There is so much interesting work going on at SCALED Composites, I am just lending builder support through RAF as long as I can. The money for this comes from the funds that built up at RAF when it was actively selling plans." More funds are donated to RAF by Burt that are earned from some of his speaking engagements.

Rutan promised his builders that he would be on hand at future Oshkosh EAA conventions and other gatherings.

"Right now," he wrote in the January 1988 *Canard Pusher*, "I am still very busily and happily employed at SCALED Composites in Mojave, California, next door to the old RAF building and together with a bunch of engineers and builders (a staff that includes many of our old homebuilt aircraft buddies), working heartily away at some very interesting airplane development projects." He went on to say that he intended to continue this work for the foreseeable future, "as it is one that is being done in a very creative environment and involves some very interesting projects such as the design and fabrication of the wing for the wing-masted catamaran for the America's Cup challenge race this fall."

As Burt changed his operation at Mojave Airport, he kept the builders of Rutan designs advised. He felt it important to warn them that the homebuilder, not RAF, was the manufacturer of the aircraft built by the homebuilder. "If you sell your project, or even just your plans, you are ethically responsible to provide builder support and to pass on safety information."

This concept is not a familiar one to many of us. But, legally, manufacturers are under strict liability. There is a responsibility that has no end, really, at this writing, for the product. No matter how many owners have the aircraft, the manufacturer still has considerable liability exposure.

For this reason, Rutan refuses to sell the aircraft he makes and instead, donates them to museums for static displays when their usefulness is over. In this way the historic aircraft are preserved but the RAF or SCALED liability expires.

The Advanced Technology Tactical Transport (AT-3)

In January 1988, SCALED Composites reported that the first flight of the AT-3 had been made at Mojave Airport on December 29, 1987. The pilot was chief test pilot, Fitz Fulton, a former NASA test pilot and a pilot who had flown the NASA 747 with the shuttle spacecraft aboard.

The Advanced Technology Tactical Transport (AT 3) aircraft is a 62 percent scale, proof-of-concept, twin-engined turboprop. It was designed to operate STOL (short-landings and takeoff) from rough runways and to fill the void between the large C-130 transports and helicopters. The full scale AT-3 goals include a low altitude, unrefueled range of 2,400 nautical miles with a cruise speed of 326 knots. This would be while carrying a payload of 14 troops plus 5,000 pounds of cargo. A maximum gross take-off weight is estimated to be in the 50,000-pound range.

As the *Los Angeles Times* in an article dated January 23, 1988 put it, a unique double-winged experimental aircraft built with Pentagon funding was unveiled in Mojave, California. The photographs accompanying the article show a smiling Rutan in front of his AT-3. The plane at this time had two wings, one located several feet behind another. Also, there was a large single tail.

The reporter speaks of Rutan as "acclaimed aircraft designer" who gained fame as the designer of the *Voyager*. The AT-3, the writer says, was built under a $2.5-million contract from the Defense Advanced Research Projects Agency, a Pentagon office. Military planners see the plane as fulfilling a variety of missions. It could ferry troops up to 1,200 miles, land on a short, rough strip and return without refueling.

At this time, SCALED Composites was still a subsidiary of Beech Aircraft Company. It had been acquired by Beech in 1985. Lockheed's Georgia division were on hand to witness the public flying demonstration of the proof of concept AT-3 at Mojave Airport. Lockheed and Beech explained that they had an agreement to explore the possibilities of such a transport and to exchange technological data.

New technology included the AT-3's fiberglass, carbon fiber and poly-vinyl chloride foam construction; the two sets of wings that allow the plane to carry both its payload and ample fuel. One innovation that intrigued onlookers was the unusual flap mechanism in which electrically operated flaps are used only seconds before takeoff. This avoids drag during the take-off roll and reduces takeoff distance needed.

A number of Air Force officials were on hand, not because they were involved in the project, but because, "... everything Rutan does is very interesting," as Brig. Gen. Charles A. May, Jr., said. "Rutan does things that take unconventional principles and put them in the air."

Rutan had been secretly working on the aircraft with only four engineers and around ten shop people at SCALED. At the unpretentious Mojave Airport hangar, he had said little about the project until this Wednesday. Rutan said, "It's more convenient for us not to discuss it. The more time you spend talking, the less you get done. We don't have a public relations department."

The plane was built, Rutan revealed, with "absolutely no wind tunnel documentation on this aircraft before the first flight. We consider this our wind tunnel model."

The AT-3 was built for only $2.5 million by not having extensive custom tooling and by holding down engineering expenses before the production of this 62 percent scale, flying prototype. "It was an unusual way of doing things," Rutan explained, "but it is the right way of doing them and it is the way SCALED Composites does business."

What would now happen with the At-3 project? Burt was asked. He said that SCALED would now test fly the plane for scores of flights in the months ahead, to explore its full capabilities and flying characteristics. Lockheed and Beech would evaluate the flight test program to see if they could develop a derivative plane that could fill a void in military transport.

"Hospitality Club"

On the morning of New Year's Day 1988, 40 futuristic looking aircraft arrived at the Chino Airport in California.

The *EZs* flew in to honor George and Irene Rutan for their 50th wedding anniversary. The older couple's faces beamed at the group gathered at Flo's Cafe. Hosting the event was the International VariEZE and Composite Hospitality Club. Irene and George had been active in the Club's many fly-ins and had acted as IVCHC Historian.

Burt had been consulted in 1978 by Don Shupe and his wife, Bernadette, who had built their own Rutan plane, about forming a hospitality organization. Burt agreed that this was a good idea and helped them get it started with notices in the RAF newsletters. The club was founded in 1979 by the Shupes to promote travel and support for builders and pilots of composite aircraft. A spokesman reports that, "club members have frequent lapses of sanity and take on the task of hosting a fly-in. They have complete freedom to do this when and where they please!"

The club boasts with justifiable pride that no matter where you fly in the world, if you need a friend there will be an IVCHC member not far away.

The Catbird Flies

Now Burt had time to finish his *Catbird* design, which had been set aside for the development of the *Voyager* and the *Starship*. His goal was to design a high-performance, single-engine, five-place plane like no other in existence. The aircraft is a turbocharged, pressurized three-surface design. On January 14 the plane was test flown by Mike Melvill. Mike had conducted taxi and lift-off test the previous day. Now with Burt and Doug Shane flying a *Duchess* chase plane, Mike swung the new plane into the wind at Mojave Airport. Three runway flights were done to be sure that the pitch trim was satisfactory.

Finally, at the end of the runway, Mike pushed up the power and the plane began to roll. The *Catbird* rotated at 50 knots and lifted off at 60 knots. The climb to 8,000 feet was smooth with all the tufts glued to the wings behaving as they should—showing that the airflow was as Burt had predicted. Mike reported to the chase plane that the flying qualities were excellent, engine temperatures "in the green."

An hour later, for the large crowd of SCALED Composites and Composite Prototype employees assembled on the ramp, Mike brought the *Catbird* down for a couple of low passes. Then he lowered the gear and set the new plane gently down on the runway.

Pilots later reported the plane was a delight to fly. The pilot in the *Catbird* sits forward with two passengers to either side who are facing rearward, two other passengers are located farther back and face forward.

Burt flew his *Catbird* to "the races" on July 2, at Jackpot, Nevada. On the way he checked out the aircraft's systems, going to 17,500 feet for the flight.

Over 75 RAF-type and composite aircraft arrived for the event. At a bistro, called appropriately for that desert area, "Cactus Pete's," the homebuilders, 150 strong, stoked their food away cheerfully.

Later, on July 25, Burt entered an efficiency race at Santa Rosa Airport. Loaded with five people and ample gasoline (63 gallons), the *Catbird* lifted off in about 1,500 feet. In spite of one brief navigational slip, the estimates of fuel used and time required were accurate. The *Catbird* pilot and crew split the prize money five ways.

Burt had done what he set out to do: design a unique, personal aircraft.

Mike Melvill in South Africa

After 16 years, Mike Melvill returned to South Africa on a month's vacation to see his mother and sister and visit old friends. With Mike away for one month, Burt only occasionally available to RAF, builder support was passed along to others.

Meanwhile, in Africa, Mike hadn't forgotten airplanes. He joined up with a group of *EZ* builders. "Flying over the countryside where I was born was quite an experience," Mike reported in the *Canard Pusher* in the spring of 1988. "It is a very beautiful place."

Along with his family, Mike was wined and dined (well it was a bar-be-que) and showed *Voyager* videos and slides to repay his generous flying hosts.

After he got back to Mojave, Mike was swept up in helping to get the *Catbird* ready for efficiency races and for the annual EAA Convention.

Happy Birthday, Burt!

But first, by noon on June 18, there were over 80 Rutan designed flying machines on the Mojave Airport ramp outside the SCALED Composites hangar. On a homely note, the homebuilders flying in brought dishes of food to contribute to the buffet.

In great spirits, Burt spent hours on the ramp by his new *Catbird* explaining its features to an appreciative circle of pilots. He gave the pilots a tour of most of the projects under way in the SCALED Composites hangar.

Sally Melvill, Joan Richey (bookkeeper, friend, builder and former FBO) and others

The Rutan *Triumph*.
Photo courtesy SCALED Composites.

organized the event. By the end of the day over 90 planes had been counted—more Rutan aircraft than attended Oshkosh! The birthday party was becoming a bi-annual tradition.

Tonya Simone was celebrating not only Burt's birthday but her first solo flight made the day before the party. First solo is a special event and one a pilot never forgets.

Celebrating the Fourth of July

There was another summer celebration, a 4th of July Fly-in. This was the sixth annual fly-in at Jackpot, Nevada. This and previous ones were organized by Shirl and Diane Dickey. Burt called it one of the highlights of his year. And no wonder, there were airplanes, pilots, pretty girls, flying contests, an inviting swimming pool, and a picnic. Best of all, there were talks and friendships of the people gathered there.

This Fly-in was only one of dozens of such enthusiastic events across the nation during the year. The freedom of Americans to fly almost everywhere, and the availability of flying to most enthusiasts was commented on by visitors to Mojave Airport, Ivan and Judith Shaw, from England, who came in 1988 to live in California.

Small Business Jet Aircraft—First Flight, A Triumph

In a first flight for two Williams jet engines, and for Burt Rutan's small business jet plane, Fitz Fulton, ex-NASA test pilot now working for SCALED, took off July 12, 1988, from Mojave Airport. Mike Melvill flew his *Long-EZ* to serve as the first-flight chase plane. Mike chased the mini-jet and reported that the flight test was a most successful one.

Whereas most aircraft designs are flown with much pre-flight publicity and anticipation, this unusual "mini jet" plane was test flown successfully with little fanfare out in the Mojave Desert. One paragraph in the RAF newsletter mentioned the first flight. The plane was later to be named the *Triumph*.

Once flown, it went "under wraps" as Rutan liked to do with some of his work, while he experimented with it. Some of his proof-of-concept airplanes spend years in gestation before being brought into the full light of aviation publicity.

While bringing out new designs in 1988, Burt was busy with the fabrication of the American team catamaran hard sail, getting the AT-3 Advanced Technology Turboprop Transport ready for the EAA Convention and planning his talks there.

Oshkosh '88

The Rutan popularity was never higher at the EAA Convention that summer. It is hard to imagine the impact that this cheerful, uninhibited young designer has had on the homebuilt community. Over 140 Rutan designed aircraft were gathered in Oshkosh that year.

Burt flew his *Catbird* to Oshkosh, Mike and Sally flew in their *Long-EZ*; Fitz Fulton, SCALED test pilot, flew the *AT3* in. With all these Rutan aircraft at the convention, only one mishap occurred. The *Catbird* had a minor prop strike there. This, in a typical practical homebuilder way, Burt repaired with a hacksaw and a file.

Looking Back on '88

A year full of activity and for Burt a happy year. He and Tonya were together, planning a new house, busy with scores of activities and trips.

Reports were coming in from all over the world of the successful operation of his Rutan aircraft. *Long-EZs* had flown around the world; from Alaska to South America; to the Bahamas; from Sweden to Leningrad and Russia. Australians, English, French and South Africans were flying his designs. An amazing list of achievements as 1988 ended.

CHAPTER 43

PROCUREMENT INNOVATIONS:
RUTAN REVISES PENTAGON THINKING

"How do you get away from all that Pentagon procurement paperwork?" I asked Burt Rutan.

During an evening interview in 1989, Burt and I talked about how he bypasses the cumbersome and costly proposals, drawings, and bids that usually bog down the development of new military designs.

"Well, we've done the SMUT (Special Mission Utility Transport) program for DARPA (Defense Advanced Research Agency)." He stopped to tell his huge green parrot "Starship," "You're going to have to go to bed, you are a beast. A prehistoric beast!" He handed the parrot over to Tonya, who bore the bird away on a slender arm to another room.

"We dealt with the technical people," he resumed, "and not with the contracts people first. I told the people at DARPA, 'The way we do work is, if we have to keep a separate tool crib for government work, if I have to change my bookkeeping procedures, forget it. Listen, the way we do it, we look at the results. We look at what you want, why you are doing it in the first place. We clearly define the goals. Then we write the specs (specifications) that tells how we are going to go about the goals.' And then we say to the customer, 'Look, it's going to cost two million dollars.' And then we tell them, 'How we spend your money getting there is none of your business.'

"'I need flexibility to change my mind, not have to negotiate with someone at every step. But in a program that will take maybe two years, I don't have the money to carry it.' So in order to get paid, I defined some common sense milestones which are clearly, easily definable technical milestones, which are easily visible. For example, 'tooling for the fuselage is complete; or the airplane has passed this proof-load test; or, we've made a first flight.' And I say, 'At these points, you can send a child in here to see that I've done it.' And then I put my hand out at these points and say, 'Give me 10 percent.' That's it, simple. Take it or leave it.

"And they said, 'Yeah, I think we can do this. So they got us started on letter of authorization, while they were spending months to write this contract up. And the money was washed through the Navy and complicated, DARPA doesn't write their own contracts. As it was passed on to different agencies of our federal government, we ran into these people who said, 'No, we can't do that.' And we were saying, 'Yeah we can. And it's the *only* thing we're goin' to do.'

"'No, no, no. This is a government contract for research over one hundred thousand dollars, we have to come in and audit you.'

"Why do you have to do that?"

" 'To make sure you don't make excess profits, according to this set of regulations here.'

"'I'm developing an assault transport man, I'm tooling it, designing it, static load testing it, flying it, recording it—I'm doing this whole smear for two million dollars and you're worried I'm going to be making excess profits from it?'

"'My God, go to Boeing if you want. You're looking at 200 million. OK?'

"'Listen, it's partly because of all these stupid things you're asking me to do that you are going next door and paying 20 times as much. OK?' And then I said, 'I'm a patriotic American. I'm also a taxpayer. I hate your regulations. Get the hell out of my office!'

"'If you want it bad enough you'll find a way to do it.'

"'No, No, we can't do that,' they said, 'We have to audit to be sure your man-hour rate is OK.'

"'And I said, 'Why do you have to do that? You're not counting my man hours' I says, 'You know I read in the paper that you've discovered that some major airframe manufacturer has spent government money on building a dog kennel for the vice-president's wife's dog. And you know what? It's okay if I spend some money on a dog kennel for the lady's dog, as long as I give you your product. You shouldn't want to know about that. If I do, it comes out of my profits. I'm not structuring this thing so that I can put my dog in a kennel. So it's none of your business.'

"And then, at a point in this thing when it just became impossible, 'You just don't understand, Mr. Rutan, you can't do business this way .'"

"And I said, 'Okay, good we'll make money elsewhere." And we let their airplane gather dust. 'Stop work on it,' I told my people. 'Stop work! If you're not going to pay us, we'll work for someone who'll pay us.'"

"And Boy! Didn't it hit the fan then!

"We let the airplane sit for weeks, five or six weeks, and [paper] work that would have taken them another year or two, probably, got done in five or six weeks and they discovered a way of doing this thing. And we completed that program for DARPA and we never once had anyone look at our books. And when I tell that to Boeing, or one of my other customers, they say, 'My God, is that still possible to do?' Or, 'Are you out of another century or something?'"

"'Well, what's happened?' I thought at the time. Well, I'll be a bad guy, blackballed from ever doing any government work, *instead* I get a call from Robert Costello, who is the acquisitions czar at the Pentagon, over all the Services, who says, 'Listen,' (first of all, he flew out here in a business jet and was supposed to stay a half an hour and ended up staying three, having lunch with us) 'DARPA tells us that there is this way of doing something without wasting time, in just five or six weeks.'

"We ended up telling him how we do things. To him it was almost unbelievable. But to me it was nothing, just the way things used to get done before government regulations screwed it up. 'Listen,' he said, 'I want you to come back and talk to the Armed Forces Policy Council at the Pentagon.' And I said, 'Oh I am just too damned busy right now. I can't take the time to take a day to travel back and forth.' He says, 'But I think it's important for the Policy Council to hear this.'

"'Well, OK.' But I just hated to leave. So I said, 'Listen, can I do it when I'm in Washington for this other customer?'

"And he said, 'Yeah, that will be fine.'

"I had my secretary call Costello's office to find out who is on this Armed Forces Policy Council. It turns out it's the Secretary of Defense, Chairman of the Joint Chiefs of Staff, Costello (that acquisitions czar), Chief of Staff of the Air Force, Chief of Staff of the Army, Chief of Staff of the Marines, Secretary of the Air Force, Secretary of the Army, Secretary of Defense. Everybody but Ronnie Reagan.

"They had the meeting in a huge room, all these Secretaries and important people. When they get a presentation, it's slick, four-color presentation with View Graphics equipment, you know.

"So I said, 'Gentlemen, I don't own a View-Graph machine because I think it's a Communist plot. The biggest aerospace process now is to produce View-Graphs, and they produce them by the hundreds of thousands. And what this means is, when you have these machines, someone is going to shine them on the wall and you're going to have a hundred people sitting around, looking at that, wasting your time.'

"So I says, 'First of all I don't like these things. So I'll show you a little film clip here. I'll talk about what we do with our airplanes and discuss what we do in developing aircraft and how we feel about contracts. And how we weren't able to develop aircraft (doing it their way) at a reasonable cost.'

"There was this guy there, quiet, didn't say much, he kind of leaned up in his chair and he said, 'Bob [Costello], I want you to describe thoroughly just what Rutan has on this contract, and put it in your acquisitions handbook as an example of what ought to be done on these small contracts.' The quiet man turned out to be a top official.

"And Costello was smiling, of course, for this was what he wanted him to say. Costello said, 'Yessir, I'm already doing it.'

"Here I thought I'd be blackballed, thrown out, never do any government work, and instead I've been asked to do those things. The first time that the major, all the top, acquisitions people from all the services *ever* got together in one place was last year (1988). They never see each other, all the services have separate acquisitions departments and all are different. The first time Bob Costello brought all of these guys together for a several-day seminar, he let me go in to talk!

"David Packard was there, whom I respect, he's the founder of Hewlett-Packard, and the Packard Report on Acquisitions is really neat . It was written four or five years ago. Costello sent me around to talk to the Space Division, sent me to talk to all these different people and I go in there and say, 'Listen, this is what's wrong, fire all the lawyers, and so forth.' And the things I mentioned were so absurd. At first they sort of rolled their eyes back. Then these guys think, 'My God, he's right!' But then they sort of pooh-pooh it, and say, we can't do it because of no audit.

"It was a lot of fun. That's what we did about the acquisitions process. We sort of put our foot down. We lost our shirts doing fixed-price things on some contracts. Incredibly, if you don't ask enough money, these guys don't take you seriously. We've been making a lot of news as an innovator in acquisitions. There are the published proceedings of that acquisitions seminar somewhere. Imagine, the Secretary of Defense, David Packard and myself! What a group!

"I hope Costello's going to survive the new administration and carry out some of these common sense practices."

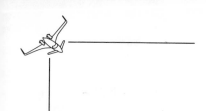

CHAPTER 44

DESERT DREAM HOUSE

Burt Plans His House—1988

For years Rutan has been thinking about housing. When the energy crisis of the 1970s spawned fields full of electricity-generating windmills in the Mojave Desert, Burt was thinking up ways to make homes more comfortable with less investment in energy. Today he lives in just such an energy-efficient, and attractive, home.

In 1988 Burt began to seriously plan "his ultimate house." His parents told this writer that he has chosen a site in the desert sand, near Mojave Airport. This will greatly facilitate his route to work. Living in Palmdale in 1988 is different from years past when traffic was light. Now Palmdale is expanding and the traffic is thickening.

This will be the first house he had ever built just for himself. As you might expect from this pioneering aeronautical designer, it will be more than unusual, it will be a fantasy made real. In his Palmdale home in 1988 Burt had rooms full of computers. There in his new home, he planned a specially-built room for computers.

His house would be energy efficient. The first floor walls to be "bermed," banked with sand, embedding the house in the ground, clerestory windows are designed to flood the house with light.

Building the House—1989

When his parents were interviewed in 1989, Burt had bought several sandy acres in Mojave, not far from the airport. He originally hoped to move in March 1989, but as with most new houses, much less such an original design as this one, there were weeks of delays.

In the amazing and original house, fantasies are made real. Both comfort and pleasure are assured, by spas, a jacuzzi, a water bed, provisions for oversize television screens.

Talking with Patricia Storch, a friend and employee of SCALED Composites, we discussed Rutan's new house. "His main idea is to be energy efficient.To do that the less glass you have the better it is. It is a lot lighter than I thought it would be. It's a real unusual house."

Looking at the house you see a domed, pyramidal structure. It has only a few windows, those required for fire escape reasons. There is a window in the computer room, glass beside the one doorway. The door itself is made of heavy glass. There is a row of clerestory windows and the peak of the house is a clear plastic dome. In the (huge) attached garage there are no windows. A clear plastic dome at the peak of the garage, however, admits light.

The garage has large, solid doors leading outside for vehicles and aircraft. One door from the garage leads into the house.

While talking with Patricia Storch, I mentioned that at the shop that day [at SCALED Composites, Mojave Airport] I had seen the tail of the military plane prototype simply sawed off and left it in a corner. Burt had decided to better fulfill the military needs, to take off the single tail and replace it with a pod, located between two booms which extended back from the engines. To do this, he simply sawed off the original tail, and stood it in the corner.

He jokingly said that he'd place it on his new house, looking as though a plane had plunged into the house. I said to this, "Yes that will really drive Civil Air Patrol crazy!! [I am a CAP pilot.]

He did, it turns out, take the sawed-off tail section out to his house and installed it near the drive, nose-down, as though half a plane were driven into the sand. It is safe to say that no one else has a mail box stand like this one.

Living in a Dream

The house was featured in the November 1989 issue of *Popular Science* and labeled, "Stealth House?" The writer, Jim Schefter, called it a "stark pyramid" in the Mojave Desert, and "the ultimate energy-efficient house."

Once bermed with earth, the house has indeed fulfilled Rutan's expectations. The air temperature varies hardly at all from night to day and the air is kept moist by an attractive but mysterious water wheel in the great living room. While talking with Rutan the wheel at unexpected intervals emitted slurps and gurgles.

There are back-up provisions for air conditioning and there is a wood-burning stove that can be used. Burt has found the house needs little cooling nor heating.

Typically, Burt used computers to help design the home. He turned on his Macintosh II and, using Versacad software, tried several floor plans until he arrived at one he liked. If he hadn't been an aircraft designer, he told Jim Schefter, he might have become an architect. In his practical way, however, Burt realized that he needed two essential people to plan his dream house. He hired two men from Bear Valley, an architect, David Cassil and a building contractor, Douglas Stone.

When the plans were brought back to him, his specifications were more than answered. Rutan takes credit only for planning an insulated structure with a pit for thermal storage. Cassil's design was hexagonal in shape with an attached garage which was also hexagonal. He showed Burt how the heat rising in the pyramidal structures could be vented outside in the summertime and used by recirculation in colder weather. They decided to drop the idea of a thermal storage pit.

The entrance faces south and has glass to admit light into the structure. To make the house brighter, mirrors are used to imitate the effect of more windows, repeating views of the nearby Tehachapi Mountains, caught by a single window on the second floor.

As a true technocrat, Burt has installed security systems and wired up the house for optimum computer use, modem, telephone lines, and cable television. He has a satellite dish and has provisions for computerizing the temperature controls. The two huge

Burt's pyramids being built, 1990.
Author photo.

skylights that let light into the house are seated on fiberglass-foam structures, made at Rutan's aircraft shop.

In California, even in the desert, houses are expensive. Rutan's home cost, even with all the innovations and additions, only around $350,000.

But all is not high tech. His friend, Tonya, has added touches here and there, brightening and softening the interior. Her office provides her with room to work on her projects. In Burt's long computer room, Burt's two parrots, "Starship" and "Winglet," are adjusting to their new home.

It's a house that might be unsettling to some. There are strange angles, not only to the house and garage itself, but to the pool table Burt designed, the beautiful dining room table and the chandelier above it. These are also Rutan inventions.

On the second level is a loft that projects out over the living room with a large spa, library and bath. This area can also serve as a guest room. Tonya's office is on this level.

I know that not everyone would want a house like this, Burt admits. But, "It's the last house I'll ever build," he told Schefter, "and I like it."

Interview Over Obstacles

When you drive up Rutan Road in February in the dark, it's hard to see. There are no streetlights out here in the desert. The stars are white, hard and brilliant in the black sky that caps the Mojave. The wind is still blowing. Bits of snow spit at the windshield and a long-eared rabbit runs across the road.

Next the soft bulk of the house looms up, red sparks are belching from the double chimney, whirling away on the cold desert wind. Sure enough, there is the back half of an airplane (removed from the *At-3*) nosed into the sand with a mailbox in its belly. When you pull up, fumbling for switches and seat belt in the unfamiliar rental car, you can see right into the house through the glass doorway.

You enter a foyer with steps down and steps up, doors off to the right and left. In front of you and down, is the dining area with its futuristic lucite dining room table. The thought crosses your mind that an unwary visitor could be stabbed by the angles of the table, but that didn't happen. One looks up and there is a most unusual and attractive lighting fixture over the table, echoing its unusual shape.

Farther along you step up into the domed living room area. It's surprisingly cozy. There's a television corner with sofas and a coffee table, a bar, a wood stove cheerily consuming its logs. Off to the right is the kitchen area and a breakfast bar. It all looks like fun and like state-of-the-art living. Everywhere are mirrors, metal, clear Lucite, warm rugs, easy furniture.

Tonya wasn't home yet and Burt apologized for heating up and eating his dinner at the same time we were talking. He was also busy with his household bills which he had been paying while watching the great oversized television screen overhead in the corner. He turned the set off. This had been the only time he could give for an interview. The next day was out. "No, no," He'd said earlier, "That's Valentine's Day and Tonya will be mad at me if I glitch that up!"

As I seized the opportunity to fill in some gaps in his early personal life, I felt a pang of remorse at interrogating the man about his first, second and third marriages, as he tried to eat his dinner after a pressure-cooker day at work. Gamely Burt did his best to give me answers. This is the unapproachable, curt designer? He was more than courteous under obviously trying circumstances.

Leaving Burt and Tonya later, with sincere thanks, I pointed my rental car toward Palmdale. What a monotonous ride. The sagebrush, like gray smoke, streamed back on both sides of the highway. The long straight road was hypnotic, unreeling beneath the wheels. No wonder Burt had hated the drive back and forth between Mojave and Palmdale each day. It was an hour lost to this time-driven man. Also, once you get used to the country, you probably no longer notice in daytime the purple and tan mountains, the curious cloud formations and the bowl of the sky. At night there is even less to see.

It's a unique land out here. Some people, as strong as the country is hard, prosper. There's a ranch outside Mojave. Its owner rents cattle, horses and ranch vehicles to motion picture companies. At the airports brown, energetic people work with their aircraft. Everywhere you look you see rock, tan soil, dry gullies and grey bushes. Few trees survive. Even the housing developments seem to crouch. Houses are close together, feature overhanging eves to shield the windows from the sun and fences to try to break the almost never ending desert winds.

Yet, there is something about the desert, an attraction, a feeling of adventure there, I mused. And, it's interesting, too, I thought, that Burt, who loves to fly, loves his freedom, and resists demands and constrictions on his life—yet is comfortable with the idea of building a cave-like structure to live in.

CHAPTER **45**

THE POND RACER

The *Pond Racer* is to be a totally new, "unlimited" class, air racer. Dick Rutan, looking for new challenges, is looking to air racing. He has flown fighters, flown distance records and made the historic *Voyager* flight. Now he hopes to get a plane that will beat the powerful, souped-up WW II fighters that for over 20 years have won the unlimited races.

Bob Pond, industrialist, pilot, aircraft collector, is backing the design of this revolutionary new air racing machine.

Burt Rutan's SCALED Composites has contracted with Pond to do the preliminary design study. Rutan is to think up a machine that will be the fastest propeller-driven, reciprocating-engine airplane in the world.

John Roncz, Burt announced, has designed "all the curved surfaces"—all the flying surfaces and propellers.

United States Air Races—Background

Air racing began early on, as far back as 1909 with the James Gordon Bennett Cup. In 1913 The Schneider Trophy Races began.

Looking back at the 1930s National Air Races we find that, with one exception, (1936 when a French Caudron C-460 factory-built airplane swept the honors), the fastest unlimited category racing planes *were all homebuilt!*

For instance, Roscoe Turner won the 1938 Thompson Trophy Race, at 283.4 mph, in his Laird-Turner *Meteor*. Again the following year Turner won. Racing speeds were approaching 300 mph. Air racing then stopped due to World War II and was not resumed until 1946 when the war was over.

By the 1946 races, it was more practical for air racing owners and pilots to use surplus fighter aircraft than to homebuild new designs. From 1946-49 all of the races were won with surplus fighters, usually radically stripped down and souped up. The big engines rose in power to over 3,400 horsepower. They burned exotic fuels and were fantastic performers, flown by some of the nation's top pilots.

Unlimited category races were held in Cleveland, Ohio, 1946 to 1949. Later, in Reno, Nevada, unlimited air races began in 1964 and continue to the present. The late Bill Stead revived air racing in Nevada. Reno's Unlimited Championship Race is 73.77 miles long. This is eight laps around a 9.222-mile, eight-pylon course, at around 5,000 feet MSL.

The fastest closed-course speeds yet run were those of Steve Hinton flying his *Tsunami*, at 462.218 mph; and of Lyle Shelton in his *Bearcat*, qualifying at 474.622. As these speeds demonstrate, the planes are being pushed closer and closer to the supersonic area. Supersonic speed at sea level is around 760 mph. The speed varies due to changes in temperature, air density and humidity. Tests have shown that parts of aircraft "go supersonic" ahead of the rest of the aircraft. Also, propeller tip speeds run into the supersonic range with subsequent problems (proplems?) that need to be solved.

The only competitive homebuilt since 1939 is acknowledged to be John Sandberg's *Tsunami*.

September 14-17, were the dates for the 1989 Reno Air Races. This was the 26th consecutive year that the Reno Air Races had been held. Daily crowds are now nearing 50,000 people.

Pond Racer Talk at Oshkosh 1988

Forum Tent Four was packed. Burt Rutan, designer; his brother Dick Rutan, pilot and promoter of this project; Bob Pond, pilot, aircraft collector, businessman and financial backer of the project; and several important members of Burt Rutan's SCALED Composites Aircraft Company, were due to arrive.

An appreciative murmur rose from the pilots and designers gathered there when a gleaming white model of the new *Pond Racer* design was brought in. Dick Rutan, his face shining with enjoyment, greeted his fellow pilots warmly, introduced his brother and Pond, and began to tell the crowd about the radical new design in air racing.

SCALED Composites is developing a prototype and is at the same time tooling up in order to be able to produce more racers. "By next spring or summer the plane will be in the air. The aerodynamics are done," Burt Rutan told them, "Tooling is in progress." Then Burt brought his brother and Bob Pond forward.

Bob Pond, a burly, energetic-looking man told the crowd that, the "why" for the racer was that he remembers the old days of air racing when pilots and designers were developing new systems every year. After World War II, this lapsed because there were so many pursuit planes available with huge engines and high speeds. These are wearing out and have about reached their peak, Pond inferred.

Pond told the people that after a Navy stint in the 1970s he became interested in these powerful World War II planes. He liked the *Bearcats* and later in the 1970s sponsored one racing *Mustang* and then another. By the mid-1980s, however, he realized that the supply of World War II planes was dwindling and that there were really no radical new advances being made in the technology of going faster, flying efficiently, flying more maneuverably.

Pond, at this time, was looking for a better way to develop aviation via air racing with spin offs for all aviation in efficiency, cost availability and safety. It was then that he met Dick Rutan who was looking for wider horizons in air racing. Dick, an experienced military and record-breaking pilot of *Voyager* fame, wanted a plane that would expand air racing and also have spin offs that would be helpful to general aviation. [General aviation is everything that is not airline nor military.] "Let me tell you a little something about why I'm doing this," Dick told me recently. "Why aviation's on it butt! Even a lawyer can't afford a new plane anymore. There's just been a tremendous lack of vision in aviation manufacturing. Old technology, really old airplanes, not an improved product.

242

"Who pays for R & D? In the automotive industry racing cars become billboards. The races are sponsored with the millions of dollars by large companies, selling sodas, tennis shoes, soap, beer, tampons and hamburgers. These races research better crash survival, better engines, automation steering and so forth.

"Now in aviation, air racing wasn't promoted. We need to build air racing up, get exposure, sell the sides of the planes as billboards. These R & D funds created by the competition of men and machines, will bleed down and save general aviation. You go to air races to see new things, speed, danger—not old airplanes. We want to revitalize general aviation.

The objection, the interviewer remarked, is that air racing instills the idea of flying as being dangerous. To this Dick replied, "Bull! What would Indianapolis be if they didn't have an occasional crash? We want to revitalize racing by promoting new planes to compete with the *Pond Racer*. More technology to aviation. I want to do something for my country.

"Manufacturers today are caught up in what I call the aluminum mentality. The future lies in carbon fiber materials. The inertia is holding us back. The people in power are aluminum airplane builders. And there's no reason we have airplanes that spin today. No reason today for structural failure. That should be a part of our aviation past, not our aviation future. Aluminum is just not very strong. So far the FAA lets standards be set within the limits of aluminum."

Set Back

In February 1989 the powerplants planned for the *Pond Racer* were two 1,000-horsepower Nissan auto engines, being developed by John Knepp of Electromotive.

By July 1989, EAA's *Sport Aviation* reported that the *Pond Racer*, as of June 6, was being prepared by SCALED Composites technicians for load testing. The accompanying photograph showed a small, sleek, composite-dark-gray aircraft. Structurally complete, the airframe was painted the next week. By August EAA's *Sport Aviation* showed photographs of the *Pond Racer* in its fresh paint with a mock-up cowling and spinner taped in place on the port nacelle.

Yes, the airframe was ready, Burt Rutan and his team had done their part. The question was, would the whole package be ready for the September 1989 Reno Air Races? Then came a devastating blow: a subcontractor unexpectedly withdrew from the project causing a delay in the modification, design and delivery of the engine/gearbox packages. By September it was announced that the engines would just not be available for the plane. It would not fly in the Reno '89 Races.

This was heartbreaking for Dick Rutan and for Pond.

The races went on without the Rutan entry. Lyle Shelton qualified for the 1989 Unlimited race at a speed of over 467 mph. He was flying his highly modified Grumman *Bearcat*, powered by a Wright R-3350 engine. He was to win the race itself with an 8-lap average speed of 450.91 mph.

Shelton, in the summer of 1989, had set a new world's speed record for propeller driven, piston engined aircraft under National Aeronautical Association supervision in the Grumman with a speed of over 528 mph.

John Sandburg had high hopes for Reno in 1989 as well, but at the last moment as he qualified at a blazing 462 mph, in his *Tsunami*, his engine "blew." These racing engines can self destruct, for they are designed to produce tremendous power for the race itself. Often, to ferry a plane to the site of a race, other engines are installed. Then, at the race location, mechanics with complete mobile workshops pluck the ferry engines off and install the racing engine. George Rutan says that the design could be made trailerable and so avoid this ferry problem. Builders and pilots, however, often talk about trailering airplanes, yet they don't seem to really enjoy doing that.

Reno is the scene of triumphs and heartbreaks and most of all excitement. Money is not the attraction. The largest cash prize awarded is the $40,000 one for Unlimited category winners. This does not begin to pay for the cost of preparing a plane to enter the races. The incentive for the racing seems to be for the fun of it. Competition is fierce in the air, but on the ground the owners and pilots are friends.

Dick Rutan in 1990

Talking with Dick Rutan at the Mojave Airport in February 1990 I asked if the plane would be, well frankly, dangerous due to its great horsepower and relatively light weight. "The airplane is heavy!" Dick forcefully asserted. "It's made of almost solid carbon fiber. Five times stronger than steel. We're working on speeds right up to the speed of sound."

"Well how about the tight turns at those speeds?"

The G loads on the pilot at Reno are around four to six Gs. It was difficult to voice the point to this lean and fit pilot across from the interviewer but he was after all reaching middle age. "How will you deal with the G forces, a G-suit?"

"No problem, I have a pure heart. I've been flying airplanes in a high-G environment all my life. Getting older? No, just takes a little longer to heal, that's all. The problem isn't really the G loads, it's how long the load is imposed on the pilot. You can withstand a lot of Gs briefly. You develop the physical ability to withstand G loads. Now I can take Gs, but can't withstand them as long.

Riding out to Edwards Air Force Base to visit NASA's Ames Flight Research Facility with Irene Rutan, we had an opportunity to talk about Dick and air racing. Deftly guiding her car down the long road across the flat Mojave, she said, "I am not going to let myself *think* about anything happening to Dick. He's a wonderful pilot. He's survived military combat flying. It's like the *Voyager* trip. I knew that it might crash, but I also knew that if anybody could do it Dick and Jeana could do it. I just refuse to think of Dick failing or getting hurt. I just won't do it." We mutually turned our conversation away from death and disaster.

"There's the chapel where Dick and Geri were married," she pointed over to the left.

As of 1990, Dick and his brother are awaiting the power packages for the racing airplane. Waiting in the SCALED Composites hangar, to make its unique mark on air racing, is the iron-gray *Pond Racer*.

1991 Plans

The goal is now to begin racing the airplane during the 1991 season, Dick Rutan told EAA's *Sport Aviation* writers in October 1990. Unlimited racing is on the increase with at least five of the unlimited air races planned for 1991. Those at Salina, Kansas; Denver, Colorado; and at Reno, Nevada are set. Under consideration now are races that may be located in Florida and in Sherman, Texas.

The Nissan engines were delayed due to the development of the gearboxes which is holding up delivery of the engine/propeller packages. Once the engines are delivered to the Mojave Airport they will be placed on test stands with all of the hoses, radiators and other accessories in place. In this way, with the engines set up just as they will be on the Pond Racer, thorough tests can be run by Dick Rutan's Voyager Aircraft Company. This testing should assist in working out most of the "bugs" in the engine and installation before the powerful powerplants are installed on the airframe.

CHAPTER 46

1989 AND INTO THE 1990s—PROJECTS IN HAND

On a March 1989 evening, before he moved to his American pyramid near Mojave, Burt talked to me and my friend, Susan, in his home in Palmdale, California. It is a spacious, modern house with a huge fireplace in a family room, open to the kitchen and to the right of the entrance area. To the left as we had entered the front door, was a formal living room, obviously almost never used.

As he talks, Burt sticks to the narrative, tending to pass over or brush away interruptions, remarks, even some questions. He definitely focusses. He wants to be gentle and polite, but feels the pressure of his life and its absorbing work. He took time out for this interview, time that he could ill afford, to be courteous and helpful plus to please his parents, possibly. But, he's not wasting the hours. If he spends time on this, he wants to accomplish it, get it done and get some points across clearly.

He asked that a tape recorder be used. "It's so easy to be misquoted." As the interview began, he was affectionately talking to his great green parrot, the four-year old *Starship*. Asked if he had had time to eat supper, Burt said that he'd had a sandwich bought in Mojave. He wanted to be on time for the interview but was embroiled in traffic tie-up on the freeway.

His companion, Tonya Simone, courteously offered us a drink, a snack, but water was the chosen tipple. This was going to be an intense session. Time was short.

"So I suppose you do want to cover the growing up as a toy airplane maker—deal? As well as what I'm doing now? In what order?"

"Well yes, I really want to know that, but I also want to know, 'What drives Burt Rutan?'"

"That's a hard question for anybody. I guess I just have an inner drive, a feeling that there's just not enough time to do interesting things. I've probably got a month or two of vacation time built up, but I'd rather be at work catching up, getting interesting things done than taking a vacation.

"John Roncz, my aerodynamicist who does airfoils and so on, and I, took a trip and we went on this 10-day cruise. This was before Tonya and I met," he looked over and smiled at her, "and oddly enough she was supposed to be going on this same cruise, but we didn't know each other.

"Anyway John Roncz and I went on this cruise, very interesting, it started at Puerto Rico and St. Thomas and went on down to Venezuela, through the Panama Canal and so forth on this gorgeous boat. And we took a computer along, picking up an extension cord we needed at St. Thomas. John wired the thing up and we developed some new software and analyzed some designs. It was a place where no telephone bells would ring and yet I could also be creative.

"Now that's the kind of environment I'm trying to build now. I hate this drive back and forth [from Mojave to Palmdale]. My third wife absolutely hated Mojave, and insisted we move down here [Palmdale] in this big fancy house here. I won't be able to reproduce this house in Mojave but, I'm building a very unusual house and Pop will probably take you by there whether you want to or not. Anyway, when the environment works and I can get something done, that's when I'm happiest. [I found it interesting that Burt has his ex-wives organized in an orderly way, "My third..."!]

"Right now for example I have 67 employees. And that's not many people when I tell you what we're doing.

"We're developing a new business jet about which you've probably read, the *Triumph*. I started doing it for Beechcraft and when Beechcraft changed management they didn't want the design so, as a speculation, I bought it from them."

The Triumph

Rutan was speaking of his full-scale, proof-of-concept light twin, the *Triumph*.

The *Triumph* of 1989 and 1990 grew from Burt's design ideas when he was a vice-president of Beech Aircraft. In October 1984, SCALED Composites, then owned by Beech and under Burt's direction, began to develop a cabin-class twin aircraft to challenge the very successful Cessna 400-series. Rutan was advised to create an aircraft that could take either turbofan or turboprop engines. This resulted in the design having a tall landing gear to accommodate possible propeller engines. It gives the airplane an elegant look.

When Beech Aircraft decided in 1988 to cancel the jet project and to divest itself of Rutan's SCALED Composites Company, it included the partially completed jet in the deal. Rutan took his company back and attracted the backing of Wyman-Gordon, a Worcester, Massachusetts aircraft forgings manufacturer. Wyman-Gordon, which employs former Beech CEO James Walsh, acquired SCALED and Burt's direction of the research and development center.

The plane was known at SCALED as the *Rutan Jet* and later as the *Tuna* (since "cabin twin" has the same initials as the popular Los Angeles disc jockey Charlie Tuna). Eventually the plane was named, the *Triumph*.

Burt realized that the aircraft could handle a new turbine (turbojet) engine, with 1,800 pounds of thrust, and was being developed by the Williams International Company.

The engine, the FJ44 has been under design by the Williams Company since 1983, according to the president and founder of the company, Dr. Sam Williams. His company has designed and made 30 separate types of small turbine engine and manufactured over 9,000 of them for a variety of military applications. He emphasized, however, that the new FJ44 was not derived from a cruise-missile engine but from the beginning was planned for aircraft use. Dr. Williams is linking his company with the venerable Rolls Company of England to share engineering and manufacturing capabilities and to avail Williams engines of Rolls' worldwide service network.

The plane was first flown, a full-scale, proof-of-concept light twin, using two FJ44 engines, before September 1988. Then late in 1989 it made its debut at the National Business Aircraft Association Convention in Atlanta.

Burt's idea is to develop and test the *Triumph* to the point that it would require reduced certification time. Then he hopes that it can be sold to a manufacturer for certification and production. The advantage of a turbojet engine over a turbofan is that the former is less expensive and less thirsty.

By the time the plane was shown to aviation experts and writers in 1990, it had evolved into a stable aircraft with an amazingly short takeoff distance and a phenomenal climb. It sports the Rutan trademark, a forward canard wing, a sophisticated main wing with the engines mounted atop and at the back of the wing, and a raked back T-tail and rudder combination. The cabin in its POC configuration could accommodate six to eight people. The plane is primarily built of composites.

Aviation writers in the summer of 1990 were enthusiastic over its handling characteristics and stability. They were amazed at the few hundred feet needed for takeoff. The plane can use a 1,500-foot runway.

The aircraft can climb to altitude at nearly 5,000 feet per minute. Maximum operating altitude is presently 41,000 feet. The plane is 10 percent slower than the 25-year-old design, Lear 23, yet it uses only half the fuel. The *Triumph* is a 400-knot aircraft, yet its takeoff, stall and landing speeds are low.

Landing was no problem by 1990, but in earlier stages the sleek, light, business jet did not seem to want to come down at all. By adding trailing-edge air brakes and thrust antenuators, the airplane was cured of its wish to float forever. Most pilots, aviation writers agreed, would have little trouble flying this docile and nimble airplane.

"Will you set it up for a production airplane?"

"We'll see. Possibly. We haven't finished the testing on it yet.

"We're also developing a close-air-support airplane, a little mud-fighter.

This is Burt's *Ares*, acronym for Agile Responsive Effective Support, a light attack aircraft.

The Ares

Will the Pentagon buy a new fighter that is versatile, inexpensive, simple and reliable? That is the question that Burt addressed with his design, the *Ares*.

The "Agile Responsive Effective Support," about the size of a P-51 aircraft is named for the Greek god of war. It harks back to the Swedish fighter, the *Viggen*. That plane was the one that inspired Burt at the beginning of his career as a designer of homebuilt aircraft to design and build the *VariViggen*. The Ares has some similarities to those designs.

Without wind tunnel testing, the aircraft was shaped from Burt's concept, refined through the use of sophisticated computer programs and built by Burt's fiberglass and graphite, plastic foam and epoxy composite combination of materials. It has the Rutan canard forward of the main wing. It sports twin fins mounted on short booms at the rear of the aircraft. Overall, it has a sleek, futuristic and balanced appearance.

What is it for? Burt sees it as useful as an agile, close support fighter. Or reconnaissance, border patrol, drug-runner attack plane, ground attack, forward air control or for weapons training.

It can operate from roads or rough fields. It carries a 25mm cannon mounted on the right side of the aircraft. The cannon can fire 1,200 bullets a minute.

It also generates enough smoke to choke off and stop a jet engine. To prevent this, Burt mounted the single Pratt & Whitney of Canada JT15D-5 engine (that can assert 2,900 pounds of thrust) asymmetrically. The engine is mounted aft, on the left side of the aircraft and has a curved tail pipe. The engine is off-center and canted a little to one side.

The entire airplane is slightly asymmetrical to compensate for forces exerted when the cannon fires and for the forces of the jet engine.

With a gross weight of only 6,500 pounds (and this includes over a ton of fuel), the plane is amazingly maneuverable. It has a tight turning radius, lively takeoff and climb.

The flying prototype was shown to an appreciative audience of aviation writers, military men and industry executive on February 26, 1990 at Mojave Airport.

Wall Street Journal writer John J. Fialka wrote a May 29, 1990 article entitled "Rutan Has Tough Time Making Simple Idea Fly With Pentagon That Likes Things Big, Expensive." [Don't Pentagon officials remember that it was a civilian Cessna that landed in Red Square, Moscow in May of 1987?]

Burt proposes this $2 million, 400-knot (at 12,000 feet), combat plane but the Air Force says it doesn't need such an airplane. The Army is also turning a deaf ear to his proposals. There is the added complication that the Air Force has agreed not to oppose the Army's acquisition of helicopter gunships but would oppose the Army's purchase of armed airplanes.

Even so, using his own funds at SCALED, Burt built the plane to show that it could be done. It also demonstrates simplicity of systems, greatly reduced costs, reliability and the ability to be maintained in the field.

So far the services have not accepted Burt's offer to let the military test the plane in simulated combat situations for $3,500 an hour. Apparently the services can't seem to take any sum seriously if it is in thousands of dollars. The military mind seems set into budgets of millions and billions of dollars.

The Rutan *Ares*, 1990.
Photo courtesy SCALED Composites.

"We're also developing an assault transport, which we call the Special Mission Utility Transport [SMUT], but DARPA didn't like the acronym, but that's what we call it. [DARPA stands for Defense Advanced Research Agency. It is not tied to any one military service.]

"That's three. And we're doing the *Pond Racer* very ambitious program, tremendous, very risky, that's four.

"And we're building major components, the wings, tail surfaces, inside structures of the *Pegasus* launch vehicle, which is our space program.

Pegasus

Burt was describing the first all-new space load launcher since the Space Shuttle:

"It was Orbital Sciences Corporation scientist, Antonio Elias, who came up with the idea for *Pegasus* in 1987. It is about the size (49.2 feet long) of the X-15 rocket planes of 1960s fame but will operate without a pilot. The missile is designed to be fastened under the wing of a converted NASA B-52 bomber. The 40,000-pound rocket can carry up to a 900-pound payload.

"It was announced formally in August of 1989 with a roll-out ceremony at Edwards Air Force Base, California. Over four hundred government space officials, news reporters, aerospace industry executives, military officers and others attended. *Pegasus* was rolled out of NASA's Ames-Dryden Flight Research Facility at Edwards.

"The white winged rocket is a first of its kind, a winged, workhorse. It is named for the winged horse of Greek mythology, and developed by Orbital Sciences Corporation with the Hercules Aerospace Company. They came to Burt Rutan and SCALED Composites to get parts of the missile built.

"Later, [April 5, 1990] the prototype *Pegasus* was to be carried out over the Pacific under the wing of the B-52. The shackle attachment made of steel gave trouble until Burt came up with a strong shackle made of materials stronger than steel that worked. Carried high by the B-52, the missile was then launched successfully, carrying a Navy communications relay satellite into orbit.

"By being carried high above most of the earth's air the three-part rocket does not have to expend fuel escaping the atmosphere. Launched offshore of Monterey, California, it flew like an airplane at speeds approaching Mach 8 until, at 200,000 feet, it shed its wings and tail fins with the first rocket stage. It then shot upwards like a conventional rocket.

"The rocket can put satellites into orbit at a cost of $6 million to $8 million per launch. NASA charges $110 million to launch a satellite from the space shuttle and has shut down its commercial space on the shuttle in recent years. The rocket will

---

make placing certain satellites much cheaper and will also make space research cheaper.

"True, the Space Shuttle can carry 50 times as much and most present satellites are too big for the *Pegasus*. Still, the rocket is an important step in making satellite placing and space research less costly.

"The first customer for the *Pegasus* project was the Pentagon's Defense Advanced Research Projects Agency which contracted for six flights. The ability to launch a number of small satellites into space could come in handy in periods of crisis.

"Commercial customers are to be served by launches from aircraft taking off from a civil airport using modified Lockheed L-1011s or Boeing 747's. This may be Mojave Airport. Several civil customers are signed up.

"And we're doing some work on several studies; and we're building blivets that get deployed off of military airplanes.

"Well, you know crash recorders crash with the airplane and if they go into the water they may never be found. We're doing this for a customer and we can't tell you who it is because of the competitive environment.

"We're designing currently, in addition to those six, three different airplanes. Not building but designing them, and we'll see if the customer likes the design, then we may build them.

"And tomorrow, we're signing the final papers [March 2, 1989] to sell my company, the majority of the stock and we—well, I just *scamper*. And I don't have enough time to get things done, I've been working Saturdays and Sundays, which I don't like to do."

I asked him, "But isn't this what you like? Working to capacity?"

"Not really, nobody works good for a long period of time like that, I'd really like to take that vacation we'd planned. Tonya and I did get away to Santa Fe and took skiing lessons, went skiing, so that was neat. But, if you look at this number of projects and the number of people doing them, My God, it's just an incredible job.

"A lot of people noticed that when we built the *Starship*, I did all the aerodynamics myself and we had three or four people help me on the drawings, before we built it. A three-month time period is all. And then, with four engineers, nine shop people, with a total company of eighteen, everyone included, we built the *Starship* [the 85 percent scale flying model] in nine months.

"And we had here a complex airplane, twin turbo-prop engines, variable speed props, retractable gear, new concept, new high lift system, new all composite structure, and yet as we fly the first 100 hours on flying that airplane, that airplane was so reliable that when we added up our records of that first 100 hours, which are usually the worst, we had—the military likes to keep records of the maintenance man hours per flight hours, there are the normal records you keep you know, the routine checking everything, and then there's the unscheduled maintenance you know,—and the unscheduled maintenance on that airplane during the first 100 hours was less than three tenths of and hour per flight hour. Now normally on a military airplane they try to get down to something like .25 or .30 on production airplanes. And here we went through 100 hours, in thirty days, and we hardly worked on the airplane, just a couple of little things. It was an unbelievable record.

"Even after they had all our experience, how long it took the customer to get to the stalls was interesting.

"Always we've had this phenomenal success. I don't believe you can find a company that has developed twenty-two airplanes with this record. Why? Because we are all going to fly in it, or our best friend is. It's not done with paperwork, stacks of quality control. Review boards, or all this horse shit that they call flight safety. Flight safety is an attitude. You keep your eyes open."

"Is it a matter of dedicated people, Burt? An instinct for what will work? You seem to be successful in canards, for example, when other designers couldn't get them to work right."

"An instinct? Canards. Well people ask me why don't you find any birds with canard wings. Well you know Darwin said in his *Evolution of Species* that it's the survival of the fittest, so birds haven't quite yet evolved into canard wings, but when they do, all the standard birds will die out within 10 years!

"John Roncz is going to put one on Starship here one day." The parrot climbed across his master and sipped from his glass of Bailey's. "You're going to have to go to bed, Boy," said Burt.

I laughed, "There's just nothing worse than a drunken parrot, Burt." He smiled and nodded.

"Tonya and I have turned down an all-expense paid trip to South Africa, Hawaii, just because it's been too hectic. Fortunately, we're going to Hawaii soon. I'm not really a workaholic. The real problem is, you just cannot, when you're doing creative work, work that requires that lightbulbs come on, the stuff I'm real good at—you're never satisfied with someone else's work in that area. I'm talking limited areas, you know, a lot of the work I can't do, work that's absolutely necessary, but a lot of the work that relates to coming up with structure, design concepts, aerodynamics, it's really hard to find someone to do that. And that's confusing to me because that's the easy part, that's simple. People say, how do you do that! My God, getting out of bed this morning, that was harder.

"Someone has to be the leader, I guess. If two designers were at work, they'd come up with two different airplanes?

"A lot of design by committee these days. So much absolutely horrible work going on out there. Some of these military programs—the design is just dreadful. I can see how it happens because it's really tough in a big company to be creative. Everything has to happen by evolution because they won't take risks."

A Year Later

Back in the Mojave Desert in February 1990, I found Burt living up to his predictions and more. He was so busy that the only way I could get an interview was for me to come by his American Pyramid in the desert during the evening.

At the office he had been busy planning a rollout of the new *Ares*, the "mud fighter," he had mentioned the year before in the next few days. It is a turbo-fan powered, light attack aircraft. Set for February 26, 1990, this rollout was a great success with the aviation press impressed by the amazing concept.

The *Ares* carries what Burt calls "the blood and thunder department," a General Electric 25mm GAU-12/U cannon, 220 rounds of ammunition, a selection of missiles, and fuel to fly 1400 nautical miles. A maximum cruise speed of 400 knots is anticipated.

All of this is packed into a sturdy but light airframe only 28.6 feet in length with a wingspan of 35 feet.

Rutan's aim [pardon the pun] with this cannon-firing aircraft is to provide a *low cost*, low complexity, highly maneuverable, attack aircraft by using modern materials and innovative engineering.

Rutan developed this amazing plane, a SCALED Composites, Inc. press release states, "on a speculative basis using company research and development funds." The Army would be a logical customer but right now the Army is purchasing only helicopters.

In the SCALED Composites hangar earlier that day, this writer saw the *Triumph* gleaming under the lights. Rutan's planes have a sleek and elegant look and this one was no exception. There is a resemblance to the Rutan *Catbird* design. It had just come down from being test flown by Mike Melvill. Mike was beaming with delight at the way the airplane had performed.

The *Triumph*, Model 143, can be set up to seat six people, at present size, with a crew of two. It has a 1,600 mm range and can approach Mach .7, go 400 knots at 35,000 feet. One of the design's advantages is its excellent fuel economy. Less than 40 feet long, with a wing span of 48 feet, this turbofan business jet is another of Rutan's speculative ventures. Once testing is completed and he is satisfied that it is certifiable, he may sell the design to a manufacturer for production.

[As of March 1990, the FJ44s had been removed, and further test plans had not been revealed.]

Bede Reunion

Even with all this activity, another project was under wraps—the "Bede Reunion." With no reporters invited, Jim Bede and those who have worked for him assembled for a weekend reunion and party. Burt had notified around 50 people, provided refreshments and planned to show them his current projects.

Among the 1990 projects, the *Pond Racer*, expected to fly at Mach .7 stands, awaiting its engines, in the SCALED Composites hangar. The plane is all graphite for strength. It has a "wet wing" entirely full of fuel from wing tip to root and from the leading edge to the controls. Special materials were needed for these wings since the engines will be burning methanol. Methanol eats into epoxies.

Will Burt fly this airplane himself? He says probably not. If so, it will be only the second of his designs that he has not flown. He did not fly the *Voyager* and he says of the *Pond Racer* that it is a high-risk, very high performance aircraft that will touch down on landing at 110 knots. SCALED Composites will do the test program but Rutan may not personally fly the aircraft.

RAF Monitoring Builders

As builders notify Mike Melvill at RAF of their successes (and "glitches") the *Canard Pusher* still serves to keep builders of the Rutan designs up-to-date on news. *CP* reported early in 1989, for example that "There are now at least 15 *Defiants* flying that we know of. All of the builder/pilots who have reported to us are pleased ...." One *Defiant* was licensed in England.

The self-launching *Solitaire* was completed by a number of builders and the first design the *VariViggen* continues to be built.

A couple of scary reports were given, one of a bird strike and one of a canopy latch not being fastened. Both pilots after a horrendous amount of noise and personal stress, managed to return for a landing without injury. The *CP*, using capital letters and under-lines, congratulated these pilots and stressed the fact that both continued to fly the airplane and kept their heads. This is not easy to do, one commented, when the air is roaring past and your wife is sitting there with a decapitated duck in her lap.

Rutan Aircraft Factory—Lotus Suit

Back in 1982 RAF contracted with Colin Chapman of Lotus Cars, Ltd. to design and build a microlight aircraft. So, a proof of concept aircraft was built and basic flight testing was done. No problems were found with stall characteristics.

In England another company built a similar but heavier version and had problems with it, including poor spin recovery characteristics. Testing should have continued with the English company equipping the aircraft with safety spin recovery parachute, the April *CP* notes, but instead the company decided to sue RAF for several millions of dollars.

Around the Outback!

On a happier note was the account of a circuit of Australia, the "Aviation Event of the Decade," a newspaper called it. It was a race around Australia which was a part of that commonwealth's Bicentennial. General Electric sponsored the event.

One hundred and five competitors began the handicap race, among them several Rutan designed *Long-EZs* and *VariEzes*. These "unusual tail-first homemade airplanes," came through among the leaders of the pack, a creditable showing! *Long-EZ 84*, piloted by Magna Liset, came in third. In Perth, someone observed that Liset was a lucky chap. A friend of his replied, "Yeah mate, and the harder he works, the luckier he gets."

Oshkosh 1989

The top event of the year at Oshkosh, Wisconsin, came around again. Burt Rutan was scheduled to speak four times, sharing the honors at one of these seminars (on the *Pond Racer*) with his brother, Dick.

Burt and Tonya flew to the EAA Convention in his *Catbird*, skirting some dirty weather on the way. On the way they flew at 17,500 feet, and Burt had the opportunity to enjoy his Doug Spear AP-1 autopilot tracking the Northstar Loran.

"Mom" Rutan's curly head was seen as she and her helpers counted 99 *EZs, Defiants* and *Viggens*. "Pop" Rutan towered above the crowd and talked with his many friends who look forward to seeing him there each year.

The big news of this year's convention was the presence of Russian designers, planes and pilots, and the chance to talk with them at last.

Most Fun!

Bob Woodall, a builder from Maryland, wrote to RAF: "With the possible exception of the *P-51*, my *EZ* is the most fun of anything I have ever flown in 46 years of flying—including 25 years in the military. On second thought, my *EZ* is the most fun."

"No," said *Solitaire* builder/pilot Don Wemple, "our sailplane is the most fun to fly. Some of you who follow sailplanes know that the *Solitaire* won the Sailplane Design of the Year from the Soaring Society of America in 1982. Burt and company actually designed and completed the prototype in that one, single year, a miracle that we have come to expect from RAF, but certainly found nowhere else in all of aviation. The thought of an inexpensive, relatively easily built, self-launching sailplane, excited the imaginations of a lot of us .... It, like all of Burt's designs is incomparable!"

Another builder/pilot, David Domeier, wrote in the *Canard Pusher* that he was retiring his still-flying *Long-EZ* by donating it to the St. Louis Aviation Museum. There alongside other aviation classics of McDonnell-Douglas fame, it will long be admired by museum goers.

"I very much appreciate that Burt Rutan shared his genius for about 10 years with the grass roots pilots of the world. I, for one, will never forget the day the *Long-EZ* plans arrived, and the day I first flew the airplane .... Thanks to him and each of you at RAF."

SCALED Model Starship's Demise

It hurt when Beech Aircraft refused to let the SCALED model, proof-of-concept flying model be donated to a museum. No, the company insisted. We want the public to see the full-sized, gleaming, sophisticated and finished aircraft. So they sent a team out to Mojave, repossessed the beautiful little aircraft and cut it up.

Reporters were invited there, but not many wrote it up. Maybe it is sentimental to feel sadness at this event, but the people at SCALED Composites and RAF were shocked. They don't like to talk about it.

"The Next One"

And so 1989 melted into 1990, the round of activities the same, but never the same. There were designs to rework and improve. There were the familiar faces to greet for Rutan. And, always new designs, new people to meet, new places to see. Each year brings its successes and its sad times. Living on the edge, reaching out for new ideas for flying and for living—we hold our breath and watch it—the complex life of Burt Rutan, our all-American, aeronautical genius.

Asked which is his favorite airplane he smiles and says, "That's easy. My favorite is the next one."

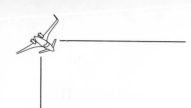

CHAPTER 47

RUTAN INNOVATIONS

Burt Rutan has not, in many cases, been the first to think up innovations, but he has used innovations creatively and has added to and combined them. Often, too, he was the first to use design theories and innovations in an actual aircraft. He certainly pioneered ways of using composite materials that have revolutionized the aircraft industry.

The Wright brothers used the canard, for example. Their first powered, controllable aircraft had canards, wing-like control surfaces that were located forward of the pilot. After a time, aircraft designers placed the engine in the front of the aircraft and located the control surfaces at the back end of a long fuselage and discarded the canard. This was because designers chose tractor (puller) engines rather than pusher engines.

At the Rutan shops the canard is sometimes jokingly referred to as a "sparrow strainer." Rutan has a patent on a variable sweep short wing or canard.

When Rutan was so successful with his canard-equipped designs, other aircraft designers attempted to copy his work. For a time, however, it seemed that he was the only designer who could really make the canard safe and workable.

For example, "Pug" Piper, joined with George Mead, a former member of the Rutan Aircraft Factory team, to build a single-engine aircraft with a canard. This, Piper believed, would challenge the market formerly occupied by the Piper *Cherokee*, a popular single-engine trainer and personal aircraft. Sadly, the aircraft crashed on a test flight and Meade was killed. It seemed the canard aerodynamics were not arranged properly. The geometry of the canard configurations must be carefully worked out and well understood to be safely used.

John Roncz has worked out how the Glasgow University airfoil canard used on Rutan designs actually flies. He put the numbers involved through his computer and came up with the "answer" that a portion of the airfoil was actually stalled at all angles of attack. He found, after much study, that it flies not really like a proper wing but rather by what Roncz calls "wake body effect." This is in part a function of the airfoil's shape and in part the *VariEze* application with its small chord.

This is a mistaken belief that "Rutan aircraft are stallproof because the canard stalls first." Burt corrects this idea: "People say that the forward wing, canard, stalls first and drops the nose of the airplane at the stall. But that's not what happens," he says.

"What achieves the natural stall-limiting is that the elevator is also on the canard. The canard stalls first, but when you lose lift on the elevator surface, you also lose the elevator ability to *drive* the airplane to a higher angle of attack. So the airplane doesn't drop when you reach stall speed, it just stays there."

The use of the winglet was a first for Rutan. It was developed by Dr. Richard Whitcomb, NASA aerodynamicist. Following Rutan's successful use of winglets, these are now on several production aircraft, including the "Longhorn" Learjet 31, the Gulfstream IV, Cessna RAM-modified 414A, the *Jetcruzer* prototype built by Advanced

Aerodynamics and Structures Company, the Beech *Starship*, and King Air 350. Winglets are in every modern designer's bag of tricks today.

How do they work? Winglets convert some of the wingtip vortices energy into a forward force. Beech Aircraft calls them "tipsails," an appropriate choice of words, for the winglets are like a sail tacking into the angled airflow sweeping inboard and over from the wingtip as it goes through the air. Lift is angled a little forward from a line across the span and a fractional thrust forward is achieved.

This thrust, coming from the energy usually lost in the tip vortices, essentially reduces the induced drag. There are some penalties and trade-offs associated with using winglets, so designers have to choose whether or not to use them, and how to use them.

Elevons, a combination of ailerons and elevator used on early VariEze canards for pitch and roll control, have been used on other aircraft. combined controls have also been used on other aircraft. Combined controls have also been used on other airplanes, such as the V-tailed Beechcraft *Bonanza*, which combined the functions of rudder and elevator. In the Engineering Research Corporation (ERCO) *Ercoupe*, the rudder and ailerons were simply tied together so the pilot needed no rudder pedals but just moved the control wheel left or right. Burt has found ways of placing control surfaces in innovative positions. He is not tied to the conventional placement of rudders, elevators and ailerons.

Perhaps Rutan's greatest contribution to modern aircraft design is his use of composite materials. Burt gives credit for his new construction techniques to Fred Jiran, who operates a glider repair facility at Mojave Airport. But it was Burt who pioneered ways of building with composites that demanded no expensive set-ups or ovens. Burt found ways that amateur homebuilders, and indeed aircraft manufacturers, could build strong, light aircraft with simple tools and without cumbersome molds and machinery.

Today, using composite construction, wings and control surfaces can be built with complex cross sections never before achieved. Composites can flow into beautiful and effective shapes.

Today's batlike Northrop B2 *Stealth* Bombers (half a billion dollars each) is a built-of-composites airplane.

He planned for a while to market his Car-Top Test Rig but eventually decided against it. He used his test rig effectively to test control characteristics and stability from the 1960s into the 1970s.

Three-surface lifting airfoils are used by Rutan is several new configurations.

Vortilons are devices used by Rutan to direct airflow across a wing. Vortilons keep the airflow "attached" to the wing in ways that increase control effectiveness.

Rutan Technology Affecting Civil and Military Aircraft

In 1987, writers in EAA's *Sport Aviation* were saying, "Increasingly, homebuilt aircraft technology is finding its way into commercial and military aviation. The latest: leading edge vortilons on the Gulfstream G-IV Biz Jet ...just like those designed by John

Roncz for *Long-Ezs* ... and the California *Microwave CM-44* manned/unmanned intelligence vehicle, a spin-off of the *Long-Ez*, designed of course, by Burt Rutan and built by SCALED Composites."

The Lear 55C has slightly raked, wingtip fins (Tip sail fins). It also has boundary-layer energizers called "shark's teeth." These used on the Starship are called "starteeth."

Lear 55C price is $6,475,000, complete. It is ceiling certified at 51,000 feet. Max cruise speed is 458 kts.; Normal cruise, 440 kts.

In his newsletter to his builders, Burt commented that Bill Lear had gotten a set of *VariEze* plans in mid 1976. Then in 1977 Lear announced that he planned to produce an all-composite airplane. The new models of the Lear jet will use Whitcomb winglets.

Also in the Oct. 1977 newsletter, Burt noted that the USAF was planning to test winglets in 1978 on the KC-135 tanker aircraft.

Curtiss *Ascender XP55*, a plane plagued by bad stall characteristics, Burt commented, that if it had been modified to a loaded, high lift, high aspect-ratio canard configuration, it would have had excellent stall characteristics! This news came from a NASA study and new research planned to investigate the improved stall/spin characteristics offered by the loaded canard concept, a concept that Burt Rutan used so well.

A Mojave "Mole" from Russia?

Early in June 1989, Burt Rutan was surprised and amused to see in the June 5 edition of *Aviation Week & Space Technology* photos of Russia's new *Sukhoi Su-84* airplane. It was a three surface, four-place, all-composite general aviation aircraft with a very strong resemblance to his *Catbird* design! Also, the Russian Sukhoi Design Bureau was showing off the new Su-80, a three-surface, eight-place, twin engine utility/passenger airplane that is very much like the Rutan *AT-3* shown at Oshkosh 1988. It even has a twin tail like the one just recently installed at Mojave on Burt's light transport!

At the 1989 EAA Convention in Oshkosh, a Russian contingent of pilots accepted Burt's invitation to take part in one of his seminars. They told about their designs and told the crowd that, frankly, some of these were copies of Rutan concepts.

"Discovery" Very Like a Rutan Design

The *Discovery*, a new plane, a two-place, three-surface, all-composite aircraft, flew in the spring of 1989 to some California fly-ins. The plane shows a strong input of Rutan design features: the three-surfaces, the pusher engine, the composite construction, even the kneeling-when-parked Rutan innovation.

The *Jetcruzer* is a very Rutan-look-alike 200 mph airplane with winglets. Advanced Aerodynamacist Structures, Inc., has announced that the production version of the 450 horsepower, six-place, pusher-engine turboprop is nearly complete. It is an all-composite, swept-wing, canard design. Sound familiar?

Forward-swept Wings

The National Aeronautics and Space Administration (NASA) showed off its gruman X-29 high performance research airplane to the EAA's 1990 Convention.

Thousands of pilots, builders and designers admired its unique forward-swept wings. Many realized that Burt Rutan's work had laid the foundation for materials used in this aircraft.

The forward-sweep of the wings is made possible by the use of high-strength composite materials. Metal wing structures would be damaged at high speeds by divergent forces. Composite wings can be designed in such a way that as the speed comes up they "wash out" instead of "washing in." This design technology is called aeroelastic tailoring.

CHAPTER 48

COMPARISON WITH WRIGHT BROTHERS

Burt Rutan ranks right alongside the Wright brothers, according to aviation writer, Andy Lennon [*Canard: A Revolution in Flight*]. This is due to Rutan's overall contribution to aircraft design as well as for his dedication to the "canard" concept.

A niece of Wilbur Wright remembered that: "When he had something on his mind, he would cut himself off from everyone. At times he was unaware of what was going on around him."

In a December 1987 interview in Washington, D.C. with Burt's parents and sister, Nell said: "When Burt gets an idea he goes away, and even if there is a lively party in progress, he might just as well be off by himself. He can concentrate so on his thoughts that he doesn't even hear you at first when you speak to him." Both Irene and Nell Rutan affirmed this.

Burt's relationship with his brother, Dick, seems somewhat similar. The Wrights were able to work for long periods of time peaceably together, the Rutan brothers cannot. Yet the Rutan brothers care for each other. The gifted designer Wilbur Wright, on sending Orville up in the first powered aircraft for his first flight in it (Wilbur had made one just before then), Wilbur gripped his brother's hand in a way that a bystander noted as being encouraging yet fearful and caring.

The same relation existed when Burt saw his brother enter the *Voyager* for its hazardous takeoff and around-the-world flight. The tensions between them were pushed aside.

The caring is there, the mutual trust, the family love.

Mobile Test Rig

Rutan tested his early designs, and some of the later ones, on a test rig mounted atop a car.

Wilbur Wright, too, mounted a testing device to test air flow and lift, on a bicycle wheel mounted on a metal framework over the front wheel of a bicycle. He then rode on days when the wind was calm around his hometown of Dayton, Ohio, to test various airfoils [aerofoils they were called then].

The ability to adopt and adapt earlier work by others is similar. Wilbur Wright did not, for example, think up the idea of a wind tunnel originally. [This had been an invention made in 1870 by Francis Wenham, with other members of the British Aeronautical Society. Wenham made a wooden, 18-inch-square box to text wing sections.] It remained to Wilbur Wright, however, in 1901, to make practical use of the idea. He rigged up a wind tunnel and used a fan to blow air through it and then systematically measured lift with various airfoils.

Composites

In a like manner, Rutan is known as the aircraft composites guru of the 20th Century. Actually, he has adapted and improved upon their use, not originated the idea. According to an article in *Sport Aviation*, it was 20 years ago that Ken Rand fired the imagination of thousands with his low cost KR-1, an overgrown model airplane, really, with the first truly composite airframe.

He built a basic wood box structure to carry loads and added to it with plastic foam and a fiberglass skin to give it shape. Today the idea has progressed to a company making replicas (look-alikes) of military aircraft, War Aircraft Replicas, Inc. (WAR), of Santa Paula, CA. Also, at Burt has commented, sailplanes were using composites and plastic materials.

Burt, in adopting the composite idea, adapted it so that he also used new composites for loadbearing members, spars, fuselages and wings. He found a new way to combine fiberglass and foam so that homebuilders could master the techniques.

Rutan, a trained engineer, looks around him and in new ways adapts some old ideas with new applications.

Canard

Many early gliding experiments had been flown with a tail surface behind the wing to give the wing stability. The Wright brothers used lifting surfaces ahead of the wings, these could be flexed by the pilot for longitudinal control—the canard had been invented.

By 1909 the canard was replaced for the most part, even by the Wrights, by a tail in the rear horizontal surfaces. Interestingly, writer Andy Lennon in his book, *Canard: A Revolution in Flight*, speculates that the reason the tail controls were favored was that they were easier to stall and spin! While useful in airshow work, this is not a desirable characteristic in civil aircraft.

Yes, the lifting canard had been used by the Wright brothers, located forward of the main wings. Burt Rutan is famed for his reviving the use of the canard and his ingenious applications of canards in various designs.

The Wrights' elevator had a three-square-foot area and looked like a small wing located out ahead of the glider. It acted not only to control up and down rotation of the nose, but as an added lifting surface.

Like the Wrights, Burt Rutan analyzes the work of others. He uses some notions, discards others, adds his own.

Both Engineers

Burt Rutan is a college-trained, and self-trained, engineer.

Few of us realize how much of an engineer Wilbur Wright was. We get the impression that he was a tinkerer, an inspired experimenter, a bicycle repairman—yet he was much more than that—for he studied, used scientific method, computed tables and used mathematical formula—in short, he was a self-educated scientist.

Secrets

Like the Wrights, Burt Rutan can keep a secret. It is necessary for him to do so, for his work is on the leading edge of aircraft development and he needs to keep his own counsel. He needs to conserve his time. He also enjoys the times when he can invite aviation writers to Mojave for a dramatic "roll out" of a new airplane.

Relationship with News Media

The Wrights were strictly secretive and non-communicative. At times they could relay news to the media, but often chose to avoid publicity.

Rutan is not like the Wrights in his relationship with writers. He is much more outgoing and is an excellent communicator. Once a plane is rolled out, he writes articles, holds seminars and shares his enthusiasm with writers/pilots/builders. He is eminently quotable.

Practical craftsman-designers - Both Homebuilders!

The Wrights were "homebuilders." Burt Rutan is a "homebuilder."

And, like the Wrights, Rutan cuts through red tape, reams of drawings, and simply designs and builds. Like the Wrights, Burt is a "can-do" man. The cost of the planes he builds is much less than that of one worked up via long committee meetings, submitted drawings and computer workups. He does use all these techniques at times, but in a most streamlined fashion.

In 1989 Rutan was finding it difficult, however, to schedule and order his work. He is taking on so many new projects, has so many responsibilities and so many people working with him who need direction. Also, those employing him often want face-to-face conferences.

When the Army was dickering with the Wrights in the early 1900s, they asked for detailed drawings of the *Wright Flyer*. The Wrights had no such drawings! At the same time Professor Samuel Langley, head of the Smithsonian Institution, and others were spending thousands of dollars in attempts to build a powered heavier-than-air machine that would fly, all of the Wrights' developmental costs, over a period of several years, totaled less than $5,000.

Problem Solver

Burt seems to like to find a problem and then design answers to the problem....range...speed....short haul capability...economy. Irene Rutan said, "About five years ago, in 1982, I realized we had a genius on our hands; really. Burt has tunnel vision,

264

everything is blocked out. It makes me mad at him, 'Hey, I'm your mother! Listen!' but he doesn't hear when that brain focusses on an idea. Tunnel vision. And at the end of that tunnel is a little airplane!"

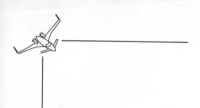

CHAPTER 49

THE FUTURE

Rutan's Future Concepts:
The Look of Tomorrow's Airplane

The airplane of the future should look attractive, as cars are made handsome, to appeal to the customer, Burt Rutan says. The plane should be fun to fly and have built-in safety features that let you enjoy using it.

Rutan is thinking with interest about planes that could be built by robot. Possibly, large parts could be simply molded, fastened together. Planes could thus be built using fewer individual parts. Possible. Yes.

Tomorrow's airplane should have good visibility, with symmetrical visual cues that make positioning it easy for level flight, for takeoff and landings.

It doesn't really matter, Burt says, what the general configurations are.

New Cockpit Display System

The big change, the big shift in "mind-set" for airplane makers, Rutan asserts, is in the new cockpit that is needed. "Today's cockpit is an absolute disaster," declares Rutan. As always unafraid to breast the wave of innovation, Rutan urges that information needed to fly the airplane be superimposed on the windshield or perhaps on a transparent screen in front of the pilot that represents the outside world such as mountains, geodetic features, runways. "You could steer with visual information. You don't have to go to a panel full of hieroglyphics when you fly into low visibility, as you must now."

Navigation?

How would you navigate this smart bird? Easy, Rutan asserts, you would just "fly through hoops," on the screen. These could be powered by Loran, and assisted by other sources when needed. Your airplane nose would be a shaded elliptical area, perhaps, with an arrow showing your proposed track to a runway, for example. If there are three hoops on the screen then you have three miles to go. You just fly through this tunnel of hoops. It couldn't be easier.

But wouldn't the technology be formidable? Does it exist? Yes, Rutan says—and he should know being on the technological leading edge of aircraft design out there in his Mojave think tank. Cars now have "heads-up" displays. We have the technology, he says. What we need is someone willing to make it work.

Why should a guy, or gal, have to duck their heads down in bad weather, to figure out a bunch of needles and numbers just when a pilot needs to think about a lot of other things,

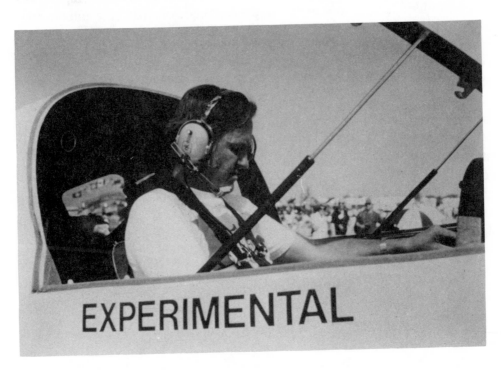

Burt Rutan would like to see cockpit instrumentation changed and improved.
Photo courtesy the Experimental Aircraft Association.

flying the airplane, talking to controllers, navigating in to a safe landing? Why not "see" where you're going and follow the arrows?

Also, if you have to learn all these intricate dials and hieroglyphics to fly safely, it's going to keep many out of the air who would like to fly, to buy airplanes and to use them. If cockpits could be made simpler, more people would see flying as possible.

We are, Burt says, using today an Air Traffic Control System originally developed in the late 1950s, after the collision of two airliners over the Grand Canyon. A controller on the ground radios us and tells us which way to turn. We then look at a bunch of needles and try to figure out how to turn the correct way. If you are wrong, you die. the technology to avoid this risk is available now! It's now even that expensive.

Controlling Tomorrow's Aircraft

An even more startling concept, in view of the great conservatism of pilots, manufacturers and the FAA, is Burt's insistence that today's mechanical systems could be discarded in favor of attitude controls. That is, if a pilot holds the stick centered, or releases it, then the plane flies straight and level. If you hold the control stick over to the right a certain number of degrees, then you get the right bank you want.

An autothrottle would also be good, says Burt, his enthusiasm showing. This is easy to do. You wouldn't have to look at the airspeed or angle of attack, the autothrottle would set that for you. You'd be limited so that you wouldn't overstress your airplane, stall or spin. You could program in flying qualities, too. Want stability? Want maneuverability? Flip a switch.

He knows that pilots don't like to let go of the direct control of their airplane, but he feels certain that this new concept lies ahead. There is also the objection that computers can't be programmed to foresee every situation. But, Rutan insists that the technology is here. "Look at radio-controlled airplanes," he says. These have programmable non-linearity in controls, rudder/aileron interconnect, mixing—a long set of amazing integrated flight control capabilities. "And the whole system costs just $300!"

Rutan doesn't see retrofitting airplanes for this, but designing for attitude control, autothrottle, from the start of the design. It would even be cheaper to do this, he says. A lot of back-up systems and redundancies could be built in. Airplanes for general aviation tomorrow could be just like today's military and airline aircraft in control design.

Why Aren't We Doing This?

A lot of people think that you get the terrific technology at the top-money level: the military and the airlines. Then these people think the technology will trickle down to general aviation. Forget it. That's the wrong way to do it, according to Rutan.

The Apple computer (that later grew into the MacIntosh) didn't start that way, Burt reminds us. It began in a man's garage. That's where the creative person can come up with innovations. [That is the way Burt has come up with most of his new ideas.]

268

Or Loran, it didn't "trickle down." It became popular in general aviation aircraft because companies were making low-cost Lorans for boats. With a Loran in your panel, you can dial up your position very easily, learn where the nearest airport is and how far away it is.

Asked about "fly-by-wire," he had also worked out ideas on this.

The Fly-By-Wire Concept—A Forecast

"Speaking of fly-by-wire, this really would transport passengers more safely," Burt says. "But again, the lawyers decide whether or not new ideas can be tried out!" exclaimed Burt at a seminar at the EAA Oshkosh Convention in August 1988.

Fly-by-wire is a system which replaces the conventional stick (control wheel) and rudder with a series of computers and miles of electronic cables. Pilots control the plane with "side-sticks" similar to the single levers used in video games. This control indicates what the pilot wants the plane to do. Preset computers then give instructions to the motors which actually move the controls. The computers are programmed to stay within the flight envelope, the safe flying range, of the aircraft's performance. Is it possible to program for every possible contingency?

Bernard Leroldier, a leading French aircraft engineer, who is with the firm Dassault-Breguet, builders of business jets, says about fly-by-wire: "It's the optimum way to design a new airplane, but the costs are too great for a business jet at this time. A fly-by-wire airplane is actually controlled by computers that convert pilot control inputs into airplane control-surface movements. The computer can make an unruly-but-efficient airplane fly like a dream."

The F-16 fighter and Dassault's new *Rafale* are using fly-by-wire, as is the new *Airbus A320*.

Some authorities disagree with Dassault. "With fly-by-wire, stability and controllability can be sacrificed in favor of maneuverability and efficiency because the computers can easily fly a plane that humans find unflyable. Right now, however, conventional controls are ahead with, at most, some electronic stability enhancement. Fly-by-wire just can't return enough performance to justify its incredibly high development costs.

"I tell you something," Burt says, "if we get told all these things by lawyers so that we won't take risks—there'll be no more fun flying in this country!"

The tent in which Burt spoke was jammed to the walls, with people leaning in, crouching outside. It was about 100 degrees and "super hot." Yet all of us hung on his words. His manner is direct and unassuming. You could feel his sincerity and his interest in his work. The rapport between the designer and the homebuilders/pilots gathered there was intense.

"Lawyers are against progress, calling it risky, they automatically disapprove. So we have to spend development time not really inventing, but testing to avoid liability."

Rutan argues that fly-by-wire airplanes, if designed from their inception for this, would actually cost less.

Len Morgan, aviation writer, has this to say about more automation in flight. He comments that while properly flying a large transport today, with the precision that airline flying requires, needs intense focus. But monitoring its dependable automated flight is "child's play." The only danger arising from this is complacency.

Today's airplanes have been made reliable to a degree not dreamed of in the past, being virtually foolproof. Slowly but surely, too, these airline aircraft have been made almost completely automatic. They can be programmed to fly without a pilot's input—save for the programming and the monitoring. The computer can fly the plane more economically and with greater precision that can a human pilot.

"Now comes fly-by-wire," Morgan says. "Clearly the wave of the future." He goes on to explain that the pilot does not move the flight controls or the power settings manually. There are, in fact, no mechanical linkages between the cockpit, the controls and the engines.

By moving his (or her) control stick and thrust levers controlling the power, the pilot signals computers that actually work hydraulic boosters and fuel controller devices.

What makes pilots uneasy (at least until they prove for themselves that the systems do indeed work) is surrendering their judgment for that of the black boxes. These won't allow the pilot to exceed the limits of the engines and airframe. The computers remember the limits. Can all these factors and combinations of factors be programmed in?

It began with the introduction of the autopilot 30 years ago. The accident rate for airlines has declined, yet pilot-error accidents have stayed about the same. Some experts say that the way to solve human error problems is to get humans out of the cockpit! But then this might create a whole new set of errors.

An Airbus A-320 crash in June 1988 at the Paris Air Show was attributed to a combination of human error and computer constraints. In 1981 an Air New Zealand DC-10 blundered into a mountain in Antarctica, its navigational system incorrectly programmed. In 1983 a Korean Air Lines 747 was shot down having wandered into Soviet air space. This could have been another case of navigational error being set into the aircraft's systems.

One factor in today's airline flying is that of long hours in the cockpit, droning along on automatic pilot. Pilots get tired. They go from time zone to time zone with disrupted sleep patterns. Alertness sometimes suffers. Fortunately, airline pilots are dedicated and skilled and work constantly to overcome these factors.

Human error has created new technology. There are now four-color video maps. Some training programs now emphasize a "turn-it-off" phase in which pilots are encouraged to turn off the computers, when the pilot believes it necessary. Training can also help to keep manual flying skills at peak levels.

In several airplanes, the highly automatic Boeing 767 and 757, which went into service in the middle 1970s, the flight engineer is gone. A computer monitors systems. The same is true of the McDonnell Douglas 80 and the new MD-11. The futuristic control panel of Boeing's jumbo jet 747-400 "looks more like a video game than an airplane," comments *Washington Post* writer Laura Parker. The new Airbus A-320, a medium-range, jetliner going into airline service, is a tremendously technically advanced airplane.

These are called "glass cockpits" and likened to "watching TV with the radio on." Cathode-ray tubes (CRTs) date back to the beginning of airborne weather radar receivers. The new high-resolution CRTs coming into service make old instrumentation look antique. These are used on the four-place Mooney airplanes and on the Boeing 747-400. The all-electric Beech *Starship* panel was designed to make the operation of a *Starship* as convenient for the pilot as possible. The Gulfstream G-IV is another glass cockpit set up to give the pilot information he can "see" rather than have to interpret from several instruments. The claim is that such presentations are simpler and less complex, with less numerous instruments.

It would seem that the day of the pushbutton pilot is at hand. Rutan holds that this will make flying more accessible, less expensive and safer. Eerie, but better.

Freedom

Burt decries the conservative, evolutionary approach to aircraft design. "We need creative design," he says. "You try something and then analyze it to see if something's there. We need to provide an environment for creativity, bring innovative people together, bounce ideas around. We have to be free to take risks. "We need to maintain our freedom to stick our butts on the line in order to achieve things that are really worthwhile."

Our bureaucracy, design by committee can stifle, stop creativity and original applications. We need to advertise for solutions, stage competitions, for example, for the National Aerospace Plane being discussed by NASA.

Changes in aircraft design need to be revolutionary, not evolutionary. "I have a feeling that I've just begun in this airplane design thing," says Burt.

EPILOGUE

The desert wind blows across the Mojave Desert as it has for centuries and will for centuries to come. Windmills in Tehachapi Pass sigh and whirl. Across the morning sky a jet hurtles over Edwards Air Force Base. Its sound reaches the desert floor like a giant's prolonged inhalation. A small plane, gleaming white, with wings of a new design lifts off the Mojave Airport. A long-eared rabbit pauses to listen. It is 1991.

Over in Palmdale, Irene and George ("Mom" and "Pop") Rutan are back from a trip to Russia. George looks at his just-completed 50-foot cinder block wall by the house. Irene tells me when I telephone, that Burt and Dick were honored in December 1990 by their Dinuba High School and inducted into the California Public Education Hall of Fame by the state School Boards Foundation.

She tells me that George is just celebrating his 75th birthday. They have been over to visit their newest grandchild, Eli, born in June 1990 to Burt's daughter Dawn. Eli joins Lindy, nearly four and Whitney, almost five.

Patricia Storch is now Mrs. Rick Aldrich and is engrossed in her work as Treasurer at Scaled Composites. She and Rick have been a team for over five years now. They live in the Tehachapi Mountains in a house "with a 360-degree view," where deer graze on their property and snow lingers at the 6,000-foot elevation.

Pat tells me that many people work for Burt because of the creative atmosphere, the exciting projects at Scaled. (In early years the pay was low but bolstered by bonuses when possible. Now it is up to industry standards.)

"And it's true Vera, airplanes will never be the same since Burt's impact on the industry. As he continues on—well!" And around the United States around 15,000 aircraft are registered in testimoney to the strength of the homebuilt movement that Burt has so profoundly affected . "A lot of people envy him, but they are not willing to do the work, to dare to try certain things."

Also living the Tehachapis are Sally and Mike Melvill in their recently-built home. Their sons with their families live nearby, enjoying life in the mountains.

On another mountain, beside an airstrip, the Rutan family vacation home waits for their regular holiday family gatherings. It was there that Nell came up with a name for Burt's plane the *VariEze.*

Life patterns have shifted. Judy remarried years ago and Carolyn is married again. Bruce Evans works for Dick's Pond Racer team and is often over at the Scaled shop. "Bruce is a wonderful man." Patricia Aldrich tells me.

Nell Rutan is looking around her attractive new home in Palmdale. She drives into Los Angeles each day, continuing to work for American Airlines. She is glad to be able to see her brothers and her parents more often. Pop was over the other day and planted a tree for her. Yes, she decides, the San Francisco furniture doesn't fit, it has to go.

On Mojave Airport, down the flight line from Scaled Composites, Dick Rutan is working with Bruce Evans, his crew chief, testing two V6 Nissan engines on the Pond

The Mojave Desert, everything old, everything new!
Author photos.

Racer. Taxi tests have been made. John Knepp of Electromotive is getting 1,000 hp apiece out of the 3.2-liter methanol-fueled engines.

Burt did the design; John Roncz did the airfoil and propeller designs. Hartzell four-bladed propellers have been cut and squared off at the ends to try to keep them subsonic. In fact, possible supersonic flight is a concern for the airplane. To beat Lyle Shelton's 528 mph F8F Bearcat speed, will require bringing the plane perilously near transonic speed. Here in the Mojave Desert the story of air racing opens another chapter.

Dick does a lot of public speaking now, about motivation and focus, and about the Voyager flight. The telephone rings and his agent lists another engagement. But he pauses to talk with me over coffee and tells me with pride that both his daughters have married jet pilots. Then he is off again to catch a plane.

Out in Wisconsin, Tom Poberezny is now President of the Experimental Aircraft Association. His father, Paul, has retired after 37 active and productive EAA years. Paul is invited everywhere to speak and to receive awards for his achievements.

Over by the Pacific, Jeana Yeager works to form a museum which will feature the Voyager flight. She hopes to interest young people in the sciences and in aerospace careers. She, too, is sought for appearances but now has some time to devote to her horses and to travel. In 1990 she spent time in South Africa.

Will a movie about the Voyager flight materialize? She has seen a script for one. So there is a possible movie in the future that will tell the Voyager story in fictionalized form.

Out in Indiana, John Roncz is happy that in 1990 he settled a lawsuit with Beech Aircraft by accepting $2.2 million. (His contract with them was cancelled with three years remaining.) John has completed a series of breezy articles for EAA's *Sport Aviation* magazine that make up what is virtually an aircraft designer's basic handbook.

Over in Kansas, Beech Aircraft is delivering production Starships. The beautiful airplane sells for around four million dollars. The National Society of Professional Engineers awarded Beech their 1991 New Product Award for the Starship. The Society has over 75,000 members. It made the award in recognition of Beech's tremendous achievement in manufacturing and certificating the innovative, all-composite, tandem-wing business turboprop. It is the first of its kind to be certificated.

Early in 1991 Burt is jubilant as a three million dollar lawsuit filed against him is decided. Years ago he built and tested a design and prototype aircraft for the then Lotus group. Another English firm, Aviation Composites Co., Ltd., took over the company and built a second prototype. Jurors decided at the trial in U.S. District Court in Fresno, California, that the design of the second airplane, the Mercury, was so changed that it was not the same one designed and tested by Burt, so he was found not responsible for its faults.

Burt is comfortable in his new home, his pyramid, in the desert where he lives with his friend Tonya. I smilingly asked him one evening early in 1990, how he felt about being a grandfather for the third time. He looked momentarily puzzled and then grinned, "I guess I don't think about it! I"m just glad that Dawn is happy. And you know, it's good to see my son Jeff more now, too. Dawn and Jeff are both super people. They've done really well."

Burt Rutan while the *Voyager* flight was in progress.
Photo courtesy the Experimental Aircraft Association.

Outside the Mojave Desert continually sighs in the wind. It is the graveyard of many dreams, the birthplace of many others. There are abandoned shacks, dry ponds, empty corrals. Sometimes if it were not for the mesquite you would think you were on the moon. This makes all the more valiant the little houses, the fluttering real estate flags and the struggling trees. It's a dry place, a frightening place. You need daring and courage to work and live here.

What is Burt up to now?

Before Thanksgiving of 1990 he earned his helicopter rating. Is there a helicopter design to come?

We know that he is busy with Larry Newman and Newman's crew to develop a gondola for a proof-of-concept balloon. It will be a pressurized gondola made of composite materials. Newman hopes to take the novel two-part, Project Earthwinds' balloon around the world in the fall of 1991.

The aviation press reports that the ARES has been fitted with a General Electric GAU-12 25mm cannon and is being flight tested with the new armament.

Whether he is skiing at Aspen, or sitting quietly in his Mojave Desert pyramid, we know Burt is thinking, and there is more to come in the Burt Rutan story.

He's probably not thinking about the past. You don't when you are as busy with as many projects as he is these days. Your mind reaches out instead to new wings, the next interesting fly-in, the next EAA Convention, the newest technological idea.

His eyes narrow, "I wonder......"

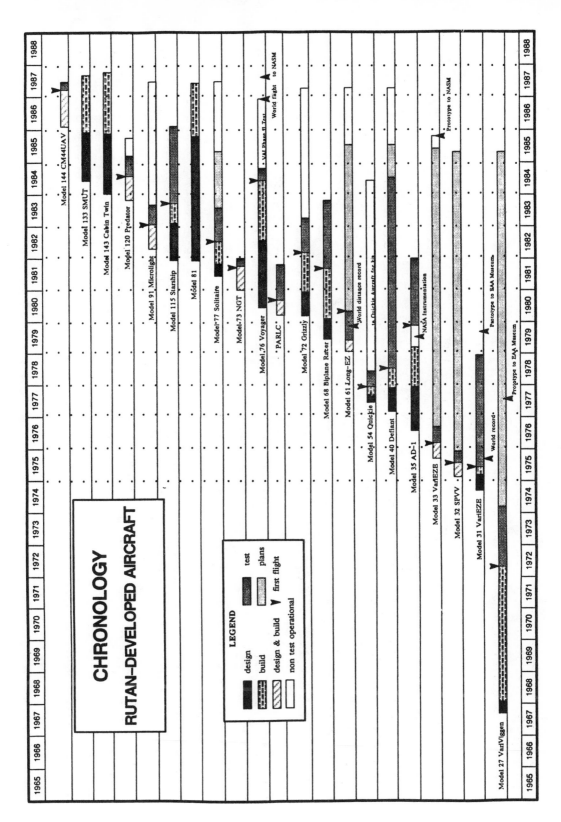

Chronology of Rutan-developed Aircraft.
Chart courtesy Burt Rutan.

BIBLIOGRAPHY

Anderson, Seth B. "Overview of Stall/Spin Characteristics of General Aviation Aircraft." *Sport Aviation*, May 1989, pp. 19-25.

AOPA Pilot, June 1988.

AOPA Pilot, February 1988, p. 21.

AOPA Pilot, September 1988, p. 28.

AOPA Pilot, September 1988, p. 21.

AOPA Pilot, August 1987, p. 73.

AOPA Pilot, August 1987, p. 72.

AOPA Pilot, June 1989, p. 69.

AOPA Pilot, January 1991, p. 34.

Aviation Week & Space Technology, June 5, 1989.

Borman, Frank and Serling, Robert J. *Countdown*. New York: William Morrow & Company, Inc., pp. 74-75.

Borman, Frank with Robert J. Serling. *Countdown*. New York: William Morrow and Company, 1988.

Bostwick, Charles F. "Winged Rocket Pegasus Rolls Out." *Valley Press*, August 11, 1989, p. A1, A5.

Canard, p. 105.

Canard Aircraft, p. 18-27.

Canard Pusher, April 1984.

Canard Pusher, January 1982.

Canard Pusher, July 1984.

Canard Pusher, January 1985.

Canard Pusher, January 1984.

Canard Pusher, October 1982.

Canard Pusher, July 1982.

Canard Pusher, January 1982.

Canard Pusher, April 1981.

Canard Pusher, January 1982.

Canard Pusher, April 1987.

Canard Pusher, April 1989.

Canard Pusher, April 1988.

Canard Pusher, October 1989, p. 4.

Canard Pusher, October 1977.

Canard Pusher, January 1988.

Canard Pusher, October 1981.

Canard Pusher, (Issue # 45), p. 2.

Canard Pusher, October 1985.

Canard Pusher, (Issue # 46), p. 5.

Canard Pusher, October 1986.

Canard Pusher, January 1986, p. 1, 2.

Canard Pusher, July 1985.

Canard Pusher, April 1987.

Canard Pusher, (Issue #15), October 1977.

Canard Pusher, April 1976.

Canard Pusher, April 1979.

Canard Pusher, October 1975.

Canard Pusher, January 1977.

Canard Pusher, April 1978.

Canard Pusher, (Issue #20), April 1979.

Canard Pusher, June 1980.

Canard Pusher, July 1981.

Canard Pusher, April 1981.

Caswell, Chris. "America's Cup News." *Yachting*, August 1988, pp. 34-35.

Collins, Richard L. "Rising Star." *AOPA Pilot*, October 1990, pp. 44-50.

Community Fact Book, Palmdale, California: Palmdale Chamber of Commerce, 1988, 1989.

Conner, Dennis with Bruce Stannard. *Comeback: My Race for the America's Cup*. New York: St. Martin's Press, 1987.

Cook, Marc E. "The Future According to Rutan." *AOPA Pilot*, October 1989, pp. 133-135.

Cook, Marc E. "Beechcraft Starship Certified." *AOPA Pilot*, 1988.

Cox, Jack. "California Quest." *Sport Aviation*, August 1989, p. 45.

Cox, Jack. "The Return of the Voyager: This is Where it all Started." *Sport Aviation*, September 1987, pp. 19-22.

Cox, Jack. "California Quest." *Sport Aviation*, August 1989, p. 43.

Cox, Jack. "Reno: The View From the Pits." *Sport Aviation*, February 1989, pp. 43-58.

Cox, Jack. "John Roncz: Aristotle of Airfoils." *Sport Aviation*, July 1985, pp. 31-36.

Downie, Don and Julia. *A Complete Guide to Rutan Aircraft*, pp. 157-166.

"EAA Oshkosh Awards." *Sport Aviation*, October 1990, p. 105.

Fialka, John J. "Rutan Has Tough Time Making Simple Idea Fly with Pentagon That Likes Things Big, Expensive." *Wall Street Journal*, May 29, 1990.

Flying, February 1989, p. 56.

Flying, April 1990.

Flying, March 1989.

Flying, February 1989.

Flying, July 1987, p 20.

Flying, February 1989, p. 57.

Flying, December 1987.

Flying, February 1989, p. 48.

Flying, January 1990, p. 82.

Flying, February 1989, pp. 56-57.

Flying, February 1990, pp. 94-95.

Flying, February 1989, p. 56.

"Future Falcon Jet." *Flying*, June 1989.

Garrison, Peter. "Once Upon a Winglet." *Flying*, August 1989, pp. 108-111.

Garrison, Peter. "Rutan's Triumph." *Flying*, August 1990, pp. 74-80.

"Gates Learjet Unveils Two New Models, the 31 and the 55C." *Flying*, December 1987, p. 93.

Leadabrand, Russ. *A Guidebook to the Mojave Desert of California*. Los Angeles: Ward Richie Press, 1966, pp. 23-29, 60-67.

Lennon, Andy. *Canard: A Revolution in Flight*, p. 105.

Markam, Beryl. *West With the Night*. San Francisco: North Point Press, 1983 Reprint of 1942 book.

Marshall, Andy. *Composite Basics*.

McClellan, J. Mac. "Lear 55C: The Delta Difference." *Flying*, March 1989, p. 64.

McClellan, J. Mac. "Avanti Certified." August 1990, p. 23.

McClellan, J. Mac. "Reporting Points." *Flying*, August 1990, p. 22.

McClellan, J. Mac. "Flying the Starship." *Flying*, October 1990, p. 28-38.

McClellan, J. Mac. "The Starship Chronicles: The Evolution of Beech's Radical Design." *Flying*, March 1989, p. 56.

Newsweek, May 25, 1987.

Norris, Jack. (Technical Director in Voyager Mission Control)

Parker, Laura. "Automated Airbus Flies into Debate on Safety of Passive Pilots." *Washington Post*, June 19, 1989.

"Pilot Briefing." *AOPA Pilot*, December 1990, p. 32.

Popular Science, February 1990, p. 61.

Prince George's Journal, March 29, 1989.

RAF Newsletter, October 1984.

"Reporting Points." *Flying*, June 1990, p. 14.

Scaled Composites, January 1988.

Schefter, Jim. "21st Century Pyramid: The Ultimate Energy Efficient House." *Popular Science*, November 1989.

Schefter, Jim. "Wild Wings Reshape the Way We Fly." *Popular Science*, February 1990, pp. 58-63, 90.

Schefter, Jim. "Stealth House." *Popular Science*.

Schefter, Jim. "Wild Wings Reshape the Way We Fly." *Popular Science*, February 1990, pp. 58-63, 90.

Schiff, Barry. "The Triumph of Technology." *AOPA Pilot*, June 1990, pp. 44-48.

Soaring, 1984.

Sport Aviation, September 1987, p. 6.

Sport Aviation, April 1990, pp. 61-98.

Sport Aviation, July 1989, p. 9.

Sport Aviation, January 1989, p. 49.

Sport Aviation, April 1987, p. 11.

Sport Aviation, July 1985.

Sport Aviation, January 1990, p. 7.

Sport Aviation, May 1990, p. 97.

Sport Aviation, April 1987, p. 11.

Sport Aviation, April 1987, p. 6.

Sport Aviation, June 1975.

Sport Aviation, December 1988.

Sport Aviation, May 1990, p. 98.

Sport Aviation, July 1988, p. 11.

Sport Aviation, July 1989, p. 5.

Sport Aviation, October 1990, p. 113.

Sport Aviation, December 1988, p. 23.

Sport Aviation, May 1974, pp. 16-17.

Sport Aviation, June 1988, p. 6.

Sport Aviation, August 1973, p. 11.

Sport Aviation, October 1987, p. 38.

Sport Aviation, January 1990, p. 59.

Sport Aviation, March 1975, p. 58.

Success, November 1988.

"The Courts and the Cup." *Washington Post*, April 19, 1990, p. D6.

The Official Log, Flight Analysis and Narrative Explanation, P.O. Box 7663, Northridge, CA 91327 (818)360-1105.

"The Cup Turneth Over." *Time*, April 10,1989, p. 42.

VariViggen News, (Issue #3).

VariViggen News, July 1975.

VariViggen News, October 1974.

VariViggen News, April 1975.

VariViggen News, (Issue #1), May 1974.

Vartabedian, Ralph. "Voyager Designer Unveils New Double-Winged Military Plane." *Los Angeles Times*, January 23, 1988, p. 1.

"Voyager Comes Home." *Sport Aviation*, October 1987, pp. 14-15.

Voyager Enterprises, March 1990.

Walsh, John Evangelist. *One Day at Kitty Hawk: The Untold Story of the Wright Brothers.* New York: Thomas Y. Crowell Co., 1975, pp. 15, 88-100, 196-197.

Washington Post, March 29, 1989.

Washington Post, April 4, 1989.

Washington Post, April 2, 1989, p. C3.

Weick, Fred E. and Hansen, James R. *From the Ground Up*, Smithsonian Institution Press, Washington, D.C., 1988.

Yeager, Jeana, and Rutan, Dick, with Patton, Phil. *Voyager*, pp. 38, 42, 45, 85, 329, 331.

INDEX